BIBLICAL PRINCIPLES OF LEADERSHIP

TIMELESS WISDOM FOR MODERN LEADERS

CALEB OCHIMANA

DISCLAIMER:

The information contained in this book is for general informational purposes only. While every effort has been made to provide accurate and up-to-date information, the author makes no representations or warranties of any kind, express or implied, about the completeness, accuracy, reliability, suitability, or availability with respect to the book or the information, products, services, or related graphics contained in the book for any purpose.

Any reliance you place on such information is strictly at your own risk. The author will not be liable for any losses or damages arising from the use of this book or the information contained herein.

The inclusion of any links does not necessarily imply a recommendation or endorse the views expressed within them. Every effort is made to keep the book up and running smoothly. However, the author takes no responsibility for, and will not be liable for, the book being temporarily unavailable due to technical issues beyond their control.

It is advisable to consult appropriate professionals for advice tailored to your specific situation.

DEDICATION

To those who lead with courage, compassion, and unwavering faith, this book is dedicated to you. May the timeless wisdom found within the pages of "Biblical Principles of Leadership: Timeless Wisdom for Modern Leaders" inspire and guide you on your journey of leadership. Your dedication to serving others and your commitment to upholding integrity and righteousness are a beacon of hope in a world yearning for true leadership.

Caleb Ochimana

CONTENTS

ACKNOWLEDGMENTS

This book, "Biblical Principles of Leadership: Timeless Wisdom for Modern Leaders," is the culmination of a collective effort and the convergence of numerous individuals' support, encouragement, and expertise. I am deeply grateful to all those who have contributed to its creation.

First and foremost, I extend my heartfelt appreciation to my wife, Helen Ochimana, whose vision, passion, and dedication have been the guiding light throughout this endeavor. Your insights into biblical principles of leadership have enriched these pages immeasurably.

I extend my sincere gratitude to the editorial team, whose professionalism, support, and commitment to excellence have been instrumental in bringing this book to fruition. Your unwavering belief in the project has been invaluable.

I am indebted to the scholars, theologians, and leaders whose work and teachings have served as the foundation for this book. Your wisdom has provided the framework upon which these principles of leadership are built.

I am deeply thankful to my family and friends for their patience, understanding, and unwavering support throughout the writing process. Your love and encouragement have been a constant source of strength and inspiration.

Finally, I express my gratitude to the readers, whose interest in exploring the intersection of biblical wisdom and contemporary leadership challenges has motivated me to share these insights.

To all who have contributed in ways seen and unseen, thank you for being a part of this journey.

With heartfelt appreciation,

Caleb Ochimana

INTRODUCTION

In the ever-evolving landscape of leadership, where trends come and go like fleeting shadows, there exists a source of wisdom that transcends the sands of time, offering enduring guidance to those who dare to lead with purpose, resilience, and authenticity. **"Biblical Principles of Leadership: Timeless Wisdom for Modern Leaders"** invites you on a transformative journey through the sacred pages of one of the world's most revered texts, where ageless narratives and profound insights converge to illuminate the path to extraordinary leadership.

In this compelling exploration, we delve into the timeless tales of visionaries, trailblazers, and influencers who shaped destinies, navigated adversity, and left an indelible mark on the tapestry of human history. Drawing from the rich tapestry of biblical stories, we uncover profound lessons that resonate with the challenges and opportunities faced by leaders in our contemporary world. From the battlefield wisdom of David to the visionary leadership of Moses, each chapter unveils a mosaic of principles that transcend cultural and temporal boundaries, providing invaluable insights for those seeking to lead with purpose, integrity, and wisdom.

As we embark on this enlightening voyage, we discover how the Bible's teachings offer not mere anecdotes, but a living blueprint for effective leadership—one that extends beyond religious boundaries to speak to the universal human experience. Whether you are a seasoned executive, an aspiring entrepreneur, or a community leader, the pages of this book serve as a compass, guiding you toward profound self-discovery and equipping you with the tools to inspire, empower, and lead with enduring impact.

Join us in uncovering the hidden gems of leadership wisdom embedded in the ancient scriptures, and witness how the ageless narratives of the Bible provide a wellspring of guidance for leaders navigating the complexities of the modern world. **"Biblical Principle of Leadership"** is not just a book; it is a roadmap to leadership excellence, an invitation to learn from the greatest leaders of antiquity, and a testament to the enduring power of wisdom that transcends generations. Get ready to embark on a transformative journey that will redefine your approach to leadership and inspire you to leave a legacy that echoes through the annals of time.

The Bible, comprising both the Old and New Testaments, is a compilation of sacred scriptures that have shaped the moral and ethical foundations of Western civilization. It narrates stories of leaders, prophets, and individuals who navigated challenges, demonstrated resilience, and exhibited exemplary leadership qualities. By examining these narratives, we can extract valuable insights that resonate across cultures and epochs.

The stories of leaders such as Moses, David, Solomon, and others offer a rich tapestry of experiences that provide lessons in decision-making, integrity, humility, and perseverance. These biblical figures faced adversity, confronted moral dilemmas, and led their communities through trials, offering a source of inspiration and guidance for leaders in any context.

The Relevance of Biblical Wisdom for Modern Leaders

The relevance of biblical wisdom for modern leaders lies in its ability to address fundamental aspects of leadership that transcend the boundaries of time and culture. Whether navigating ethical challenges, fostering teamwork, or making strategic decisions, the principles found in the Bible can offer valuable perspectives.

Biblical teachings emphasize the importance of qualities such as servant leadership, compassion, justice, and humility. Leaders today can draw inspiration from these principles to cultivate a leadership style that prioritizes the well-being of their teams and the greater good. The Bible's emphasis on ethical conduct and moral courage serves as a timeless guide for leaders facing complex and ethically challenging situations.

Furthermore, the biblical narrative encourages leaders to seek wisdom, a quality prized for its ability to discern right from wrong, make sound judgments, and foster a culture of continuous learning and improvement. By incorporating these teachings into their leadership approach, modern leaders can build resilient and ethically grounded organizations.

In conclusion, exploring leadership principles from the Bible unveils a treasury of timeless wisdom that resonates with the challenges faced by leaders in the contemporary world. As we embark on this journey through biblical narratives, we will uncover insights that transcend religious boundaries, offering a universal guide for effective and ethical leadership.

THE CALL TO LEADERSHIP

The call to leadership is a powerful and transformative summons to take on a role of responsibility, influence, and guidance. **Leadership is not merely a position or title; it is a dynamic and evolving process that requires a unique set of skills, qualities, and a deep sense of purpose.** Whether in business, politics, education, or any other field, the call to leadership is both an opportunity and a challenge. Some key aspects of the call to leadership include Vision and Purpose, Inspiration and Influence, Adaptability and Resilience, Effective Communication, Empathy and Emotional Intelligence, Courage and Risk-taking, Continuous Learning, Ethical Leadership, Servant Leadership, Team Building and Collaboration.

Leaders often have a clear vision of the future and a sense of purpose that goes beyond personal ambition. They are driven by a desire to make a positive impact on their organization, community, or society.

Effective leaders inspire others to achieve their best potential. They lead by example, motivate through their actions and words, and build a sense of trust and respect among their followers.

Leadership involves navigating through uncertainty and facing challenges. A true leader is adaptable, resilient, and able to learn from setbacks. They view obstacles as opportunities for growth and innovation.

Communication is a cornerstone of leadership. Leaders must articulate their vision, listen to the concerns of others, and foster open and transparent dialogue. Clear communication helps build trust and alignment within a team or organization.

Understanding the emotions and perspectives of others is crucial for effective leadership. Empathy fosters a positive organizational culture and helps leaders make informed decisions that consider the well-being of their team members.

Leadership often requires making tough decisions and taking calculated risks. Leaders must have the courage to step outside their comfort zones, challenge the status quo, and make decisions that serve the greater good.

Leadership is a journey of continuous learning and improvement. Leaders seek out opportunities for professional development, stay informed about industry trends, and are open to feedback.

A call to leadership includes a commitment to ethical behavior and integrity. Leaders set an ethical tone for their organizations and are responsible for creating a culture of honesty, fairness, and accountability.

Leaders recognize the value of a cohesive and collaborative team. They invest in team building, foster a sense of belonging, and promote diversity and inclusion.

The concept of servant leadership emphasizes the leader's role in serving and supporting the needs of their team. This approach builds a foundation of trust and loyalty among team members.

The call to leadership is not a one size fits all proposition. It requires self-awareness, a commitment to personal growth, and a genuine desire to contribute to something larger than oneself. It is a journey that involves both challenges and rewards, and those who answer the call can positively impact individuals, organizations, and even society.

Biblical Foundation for Call to Leadership

The theme of leadership is deeply ingrained within the narratives and teachings of the Bible, permeating both the Old and New Testaments. Throughout its pages, individuals are called upon to assume positions of leadership, whether it be in guiding their communities, leading armies, or shepherding God's people. These calls to leadership encompass a variety of qualities and responsibilities, providing a rich tapestry of examples for understanding what it means to lead in accordance with divine principles.

Old Testament Examples of Leadership Calls:

♦ **Moses:** One of the most prominent examples of a call to leadership in the Bible is found in the story of Moses. In Exodus chapters 3 and 4, Moses encounters God in the burning bush, where he is commissioned to lead the Israelites out of slavery in Egypt. Despite his initial reluctance and feelings of inadequacy, Moses accepts this divine call, demonstrating obedience, faith, and humility in his leadership journey.

♦ **Joshua:** Following the death of Moses, Joshua is appointed as his successor and tasked with leading the Israelites into the Promised Land. In Joshua 1, God assures Joshua of His presence and commands him to be strong and courageous in fulfilling his leadership responsibilities. Joshua's obedience and reliance on God serve as exemplary traits for future leaders.

♦ **David:** From his anointing by the prophet Samuel as a young shepherd boy to his eventual reign as king of Israel, David's leadership journey is marked by faith, courage, and a heart for God. Despite facing numerous challenges and temptations, David is described as a man after God's own heart, demonstrating the qualities of a humble and righteous leader.

New Testament Examples of Leadership Calls:

♦ **Jesus' Disciples:** In the Gospels, Jesus calls ordinary individuals to follow Him and become leaders in His kingdom. For example, in Matthew 4:19, Jesus tells Peter and Andrew, **"Follow me, and I will make you fishers of men."** Throughout His ministry, Jesus invests in these disciples, teaching them about servant leadership, humility, and sacrificial love.

♦ **Paul:** Saul of Tarsus, later known as the apostle Paul, undergoes a radical transformation upon encountering the risen Christ on the road to Damascus (Acts 9). Commissioned by Jesus Himself to be a witness to the Gentiles, Paul becomes a prolific missionary and church planter, exemplifying boldness, perseverance, and dedication to spreading the gospel message.

Key Themes and Lessons on Leadership:

♦ **Divine Appointment**: Many biblical leaders are chosen by God Himself, emphasizing the divine calling and sovereignty in the selection of leaders. This underscores the importance of seeking God's guidance and direction in leadership roles.

♦ **Servant Leadership**: Jesus models servant leadership by washing His disciples' feet (John 13) and instructs His followers to lead by serving others. Biblical leadership is characterized by humility, compassion, and a willingness to sacrificially serve those under one's care.

♦ **Integrity and Character**: Throughout the Bible, leaders are called to walk in righteousness and integrity, exemplifying moral uprightness and faithfulness to God's commands. The stories of leaders like David also highlight the importance of repentance and accountability in leadership.

♦ **Courage and Faith**: Many biblical leaders face daunting challenges and opposition, yet they demonstrate courage and unwavering faith in God's promises. Their examples inspire future leaders to trust in God's provision and guidance, even during uncertainty and adversity.

In conclusion, the call to leadership in the Bible encompasses a diverse array of individuals and stories, each providing valuable insights into the qualities, responsibilities, and challenges of effective leadership. Whether through the Old Testament narratives of Moses and David or the New Testament examples of Jesus' disciples and the apostle Paul, the Bible offers timeless principles for aspiring leaders to emulate as they seek to fulfill their God-given calling to lead with wisdom, humility, and love.

The Story of Moses: Answering the Call

The story of Moses is a significant narrative found in the religious texts of Judaism, Christianity, and Islam. It is a tale of faith, resilience, and leadership. The story is primarily documented in the biblical books of Exodus, Leviticus, Numbers, and Deuteronomy.

Moses was born in Egypt during a time when the Israelites, the descendants of Jacob, were enslaved by the Egyptians. Due to the Pharaoh's decree to kill all male Hebrew infants, Moses' mother placed him in a basket and set him adrift on the Nile River. He was discovered by Pharaoh's daughter and raised in the royal palace.

As Moses grew older, he became aware of his Hebrew heritage. One day, witnessing the oppression and suffering of his people, he intervened in a conflict between an Egyptian taskmaster and a Hebrew slave, resulting in the death of the Egyptian. Fearing punishment, Moses fled to the land of Midian.

While in Midian, Moses worked as a shepherd. One day, as he tended to his flock on Mount Horeb, he encountered a burning bush that was not consumed by the fire. From the midst of the bush, God spoke to Moses, commissioning him to return to Egypt and lead the Israelites out of bondage.

Moses was initially hesitant and raised several objections, citing his lack of eloquence and his uncertainty about how the Israelites would accept him. However, God assured him that He would be with him, guiding and empowering him.

Moses, accompanied by his brother Aaron, returned to Egypt, and confronted Pharaoh, demanding the release of the Israelites. This led to a series of ten plagues, including the famous plagues of blood, frogs, and the Passover, which finally convinced Pharaoh to let the Israelites go.

After their liberation, Moses led the Israelites through the wilderness toward the Promised Land. He guided them through challenges, including the crossing of the Red Sea, providing manna from heaven, and receiving the Ten Commandments on Mount Sinai.

Moses faced numerous challenges as a leader, including dealing with the people's complaints, rebellion, and instances of disobedience. His leadership was tested, and he demonstrated patience, faith, and reliance on God.

Moses' leadership played a crucial role in shaping the identity of the Israelites. He did not enter the Promised Land but was permitted to see it from a distance before his death. His legacy endured through the laws and teachings he conveyed, and he is remembered as one of the greatest prophets and leaders in religious history.

The story of Moses serves as a timeless example of answering the call of leadership, overcoming challenges, and relying on faith and divine guidance in the pursuit of a greater purpose.

Some leadership lessons that can be drawn from the experiences of Moses

♦ **Vision and Purpose:** Moses had a clear vision of liberating his people from slavery and leading them to the Promised Land. A leader should articulate a compelling vision that inspires and motivates their followers.

♦ **Resilience in the Face of Adversity:** Moses faced numerous challenges, from confrontations with Pharaoh to leading a large group of people through a harsh wilderness. Leaders must be resilient in the face of adversity and maintain their focus on the long-term goals.

♦ **Effective Communication:** Moses was known for his communication with both God and the people of Israel. Effective communication is crucial for a leader to convey the vision, instructions, and values clearly.

♦ **Empowering Others:** Moses appointed capable individuals to assist him in various tasks, distributing responsibilities and empowering others. Delegating tasks and trusting others can lead to a more effective and efficient team.

♦ **Leading by Example:** Moses exemplified the values and principles he preached. Leaders who lead by example gain the trust and respect of their followers, fostering a culture of integrity and commitment.

♦ **Adaptability: Moses** encountered unexpected challenges and had to adapt his plans accordingly. Leaders should be flexible and adaptable, ready to adjust strategies in response to changing circumstances.

♦ **Patience and Perseverance:** The journey from Egypt to the Promised Land took much longer than anticipated, and Moses faced numerous trials. Patience and perseverance are essential qualities for leaders, especially in long-term endeavors.

♦ **Conflict Resolution:** Moses dealt with internal conflicts among the Israelites. A leader should be skilled in conflict resolution, promoting unity and resolving disputes to maintain a cohesive group.

♦ **Courage and Conviction:** Moses displayed courage in challenging situations, such as confronting Pharaoh and leading the Israelites through the Red Sea. Leaders need courage to make tough decisions and stick to their convictions.

♦ **Spiritual and Ethical Leadership:** Moses' leadership was deeply rooted in his faith and adherence to ethical principles. Leaders who incorporate spirituality and ethics into their leadership style can create a sense of purpose and moral guidance for their followers.

While Moses' leadership is often studied in a religious context, the lessons drawn from his experiences can be valuable in various leadership settings, providing insights into effective and principled leadership.

The Story of Joshua: Answering the Call

Joshua, a central figure in the Bible, emerges as a quintessential leader whose story epitomizes the qualities of courage, faith, and obedience. His journey from being Moses' protege to leading the Israelites into the Promised Land displays remarkable leadership attributes that continue to inspire individuals across cultures and generations.

Joshua's narrative begins during the Exodus, where he is introduced as Moses' assistant, known for his loyalty and dedication. His first notable act of leadership occurs during the battle against the Amalekites, where he leads the Israelite army to victory through his strategic prowess and reliance on divine guidance.

As Moses' successor, Joshua witnesses firsthand the challenges of leadership during the Israelites' wilderness wanderings. Despite facing rebellion, doubt, and adversity among his people, Joshua remains steadfast in his commitment to follow God's commands and lead with integrity.

Joshua's defining moment comes when he is tasked with leading the Israelites across the Jordan River into the Promised Land. Despite the daunting prospect of facing fortified cities and formidable adversaries, Joshua displays unwavering courage and faith in God's promises. His famous declaration, **"Be strong and courageous,"** serves as a rallying cry for the Israelites and a testament to his unshakable trust in divine providence.

Throughout the conquest of Canaan, Joshua demonstrates strategic acumen and military prowess. He devises bold tactics, such as the conquest of Jericho through unconventional means, which highlight his creativity and willingness to think creatively. Joshua's ability to adapt to changing circumstances and capitalize on opportunities underscores his effectiveness as a leader.

Despite his success and authority, Joshua remains humble and obedient to God's commands. He leads by example, prioritizing obedience to divine law above personal ambition or glory. Joshua's humility fosters unity and cohesion among the Israelites, setting a precedent for servant leadership that resonates throughout biblical history.

Joshua's leadership leaves an indelible mark on the Israelite nation, paving the way for their settlement in the Promised Land. His legacy endures through the establishment of the twelve tribes of Israel and the perpetuation of monotheistic worship. Joshua's story serves as a timeless example of effective leadership rooted in faith, courage, humility, and obedience.

In conclusion, Joshua's journey from apprentice to leader exemplifies the transformative power of visionary leadership guided by faith and moral conviction. His call to leadership transcends the pages of scripture, offering invaluable lessons for individuals seeking to make a positive impact in their communities and beyond.

The Story of David: Answering the Call

David's journey in the Bible is a compelling narrative of leadership, resilience, faith, and human imperfection. From humble beginnings as a shepherd boy to becoming the celebrated King of Israel, David's story is a timeless testament to the qualities of effective leadership.

David's story begins in the book of 1 Samuel, where he is introduced as the youngest son of Jesse, a shepherd boy in Bethlehem. Despite his insignificant status, he is chosen by God through the prophet Samuel to be anointed as the future King of Israel, replacing Saul. This act underscores the biblical theme that **leadership is not determined by outward appearances but by inner qualities and divine calling.**

One of the most iconic episodes in David's life is his confrontation with the Philistine giant, Goliath. While the entire Israelite army trembles in fear, David, armed only with his faith in God and a slingshot, steps forward to face the enemy. His victory over Goliath demonstrates courage, resourcefulness, and unwavering trust in God's strength, setting a powerful example of leadership through decisive action in the face of adversity.

David's relationship with Jonathan, Saul's son, is a poignant example of loyalty and friendship. Despite being Saul's chosen successor, David, maintains a deep bond with Jonathan, even in the face of Saul's jealousy and attempts to kill him. Their friendship exemplifies the importance of trust, mutual support, and loyalty in leadership, as David navigates political intrigue and betrayal with integrity.

Despite his eventual rise to power, David's leadership is marked by moments of moral complexity and human fallibility. His affair with Bathsheba and the subsequent murder of her husband, Uriah, reveal his capacity for moral failure. However, David's response to his sin, upon being confronted by the prophet Nathan, highlights his humility, repentance, and reliance on God's mercy. His willingness to acknowledge his mistakes and seek forgiveness underscores the importance of humility and accountability in effective leadership.

As King of Israel, David exemplifies the qualities of a shepherd leader, caring for his people with compassion and justice. His establishment of Jerusalem as the capital city, his military conquests, and his efforts to unify the tribes of Israel reflect his vision and strategic leadership. Moreover, David's commitment to worship and his role as a psalmist demonstrate his spiritual leadership, guiding the nation in devotion to God.

David's reign is marked by both triumphs and tribulations, but his legacy endures as one of Israel's greatest kings. His accomplishments laid the foundation for the prosperous reign of his son, Solomon, who built the temple in Jerusalem. David's willingness to prepare the next generation for leadership reflects his wisdom and concern for the continuity of God's purposes among his people.

In conclusion, David's journey in the Bible serves as a timeless call to leadership, inspiring individuals to embrace their calling with courage, integrity, humility, and a reliance on divine guidance. **His story reminds us that effective leadership is not merely about worldly power or success but about serving others with compassion, wisdom, and faithfulness to God's purposes.**

The Story of Peter: Answering the Call

The story of Peter in the Bible is a compelling narrative of transformation, resilience, and leadership. Peter, originally known as Simon, was a fisherman by trade when he encountered Jesus Christ. His journey from an ordinary fisherman to one of the most prominent figures among Jesus' disciples offers profound insights into the qualities of leadership and the power of redemption.

Peter's journey begins with a simple encounter with Jesus by the Sea of Galilee. Jesus calls Peter and his brother Andrew to follow him, promising to make them **"fishers of men"** (Matthew 4:18-20). This initial call sets the stage for Peter's transformation from a fisherman to a leader in the early Christian movement.

Throughout the Gospels, Peter is portrayed as impulsive and passionate. He often speaks and acts without hesitation, demonstrating a boldness that sets him apart from the other disciples. One of the most famous examples of Peter's boldness is his declaration of Jesus as the Messiah (Matthew 16:16). Despite his flaws and doubts, Peter's zeal for Jesus never wavers.

Peter's journey is also marked by moments of profound faith, doubt, and fear. The most well-known instance of Peter's doubt is his denial of Jesus during the events leading up to the crucifixion. Despite his earlier assertion that he would never deny Jesus, Peter succumbs to fear and denies him three times (Matthew 26:69-75). However, even in his moment of failure, Peter finds redemption and restoration through Jesus' forgiveness.

Despite his shortcomings, Peter emerges as a central figure among the disciples and plays a key leadership role in the early Christian community. After Jesus' resurrection, Peter becomes a prominent spokesperson for the fledgling Christian movement. He preaches boldly on the day of Pentecost, leading thousands to convert to Christianity (Acts 2). Peter's leadership is characterized by his unwavering commitment to spreading the message of Jesus Christ, despite facing opposition and persecution.

Peter's leadership journey is also marked by humility and growth. He learns from his mistakes and experiences personal transformation through his encounters with Jesus. One of the most poignant moments of Peter's growth is his reconciliation with Jesus after the resurrection. Jesus not only forgives Peter for his denial but also reaffirms his faith and entrusts him with the responsibility of shepherding his followers (John 21:15-19).

Peter's leadership legacy extends far beyond his own lifetime. He plays a pivotal role in shaping the early Christian church and is regarded as one of its foundational figures. His letters, preserved in the New Testament, continue to inspire, and guide Christians around the world. Peter's leadership journey serves as a testament to the transformative power of faith, forgiveness, and unwavering commitment to a higher purpose.

In conclusion, the story of Peter in the Bible offers valuable lessons on leadership, resilience, and the redemptive power of faith. Despite his flaws and shortcomings, Peter's journey from an ordinary fisherman to a bold and influential leader demonstrates the transformative impact of encountering Jesus Christ. His example continues to inspire Christians to embrace their call to leadership with humility, faith, and unwavering commitment to the message of Christ.

The Story of Paul: Answering the Call

Paul, also known as Saul of Tarsus, stands as one of the most prominent figures in the Bible, particularly in the New Testament. His journey from persecutor of Christians to one of the most fervent proponents of Christianity is a testament to the transformative power of faith and divine intervention. Paul's call to leadership is a pivotal aspect of his narrative, marked by profound experiences and unwavering dedication to spreading the teachings of Jesus Christ.

Paul was born in Tarsus, a city in the Roman province of Cilicia (**modern-day Turkey**), to Jewish parents of the tribe of Benjamin. He was a Pharisee, trained under the esteemed Rabbi Gamaliel in Jerusalem, which equipped him with a deep understanding of Jewish law and tradition. Initially, Paul zealously persecuted early Christians, viewing them as heretics threatening the sanctity of Judaism. His persecution included approving the stoning of Stephen, one of the earliest Christian martyrs.

Paul's transformation from a persecutor to a proclaimer of Christianity is famously depicted in his encounter with the risen Jesus on the road to Damascus. As he journeyed to Damascus with intent to arrest Christians, a blinding light from heaven surrounded him, and he heard a voice saying, "Saul, Saul, why are you persecuting me?" This divine encounter left Paul blinded and shaken. He was led into Damascus, where he spent three days in blindness, fasting and praying.

During these days, Paul experienced a profound spiritual transformation. Ananias, a disciple of Jesus, was sent by the Lord to restore Paul's sight and baptize him. From that moment, Paul's life was forever changed. He became a devoted follower of Jesus Christ, embracing the faith he once sought to destroy. This conversion marked the beginning of his journey as a leader in the early Christian movement.

Paul's leadership in the early Christian community was characterized by his tireless efforts to spread the gospel message throughout the Roman Empire. He embarked on several missionary journeys, traveling extensively to preach and establish churches in various cities. Despite facing numerous challenges, including persecution, imprisonment, and opposition from both Jews and Gentiles, Paul remained steadfast in his commitment to his calling.

Paul's leadership extended beyond physical presence; it was manifested in his teachings and epistles. His letters, found in the New Testament, are foundational to Christian theology and ethics. In his epistles, Paul addressed theological issues, provided pastoral guidance to early Christian communities, and emphasized the importance of love, faith, and unity among believers. His writings continue to inspire and guide Christians worldwide.

Paul's legacy as a leader in the early Christian church is undeniable. His missionary endeavors laid the groundwork for the global spread of Christianity, and his theological insights shaped Christian doctrine for centuries to come. Despite his past as a persecutor, Paul's humility, perseverance, and unwavering faith in Christ propelled him to become one of the most influential figures in Christian history.

In conclusion, Paul's call to leadership exemplifies the transformative power of God's grace and the potential for redemption in the most unlikely of individuals. From persecutor to apostle, Paul's journey is a testament to the transformative power of faith and the profound impact one person can have on history.

Discovering your purpose and mission as a leader

Discovering your purpose and mission as a leader is a deeply introspective and transformative journey that involves understanding yourself, your values, and your aspirations in the context of leading others towards a common goal. It is about aligning your personal and professional values with a larger vision and leveraging your strengths to make a positive impact on the world around you.

How to Discover your Purpose as a Leader

Self-Reflection

♦ **Understanding Your Core Values**: Reflect on what matters most to you in life. These could be integrity, compassion, creativity, justice, or any other principles that resonate with you deeply.

♦ **Identifying Strengths and Weaknesses**: Assess your skills, talents, and areas for growth. Understanding what you excel at and where you need improvement is crucial for effective leadership.

♦ **Examining Passions and Interests**: Consider the activities or causes that ignite your enthusiasm. Your purpose often aligns with what you are truly passionate about.

♦ **Reflecting on Past Experiences**: Analyze your past successes, failures, and pivotal moments. They can provide valuable insights into your strengths, values, and areas where you have made the most impact.

Clarifying Your Vision

♦ **Defining Success on Your Own Terms**: Resist the temptation to conform to societal expectations of success. Instead, define what success means to you personally and professionally.

♦ **Articulating Your Vision**: Envision the kind of leader you aspire to be and the impact you want to have on your team, organization, or community. Your vision should be inspiring, ambitious, and aligned with your values.

♦ **Setting Long-Term Goals**: Establish concrete goals that align with your vision. These goals should be challenging yet achievable, and they should serve as milestones on your leadership journey.

♦ **Creating a Personal Mission Statement**: Distill your purpose, values, and vision into a concise mission statement that encapsulates what you stand for as a leader. This statement will guide your actions and decisions, serving as a northern star in times of uncertainty.

Seeking Feedback and Perspective

♦ **Engaging in Dialogue**: Have open and honest conversations with mentors, colleagues, and trusted friends about your leadership style, strengths, and areas for improvement.

♦ **Seeking Feedback**: Actively seek feedback from those you lead and serve. Their perspectives can offer valuable insights into your leadership effectiveness and areas where you can grow.

♦ **Embracing Continuous Learning**: Stay curious and open-minded, seeking out opportunities for personal and professional development. Leadership is a journey of growth and self-discovery, and there is always more to learn.

In conclusion, discovering your purpose and mission as a leader is an ongoing process of self-reflection, visioning, feedback, action, and resilience. By aligning your personal values with a larger vision, empowering others, and embracing challenges with authenticity and resilience, you can make a meaningful and lasting impact as a leader in your organization and beyond.

30 Days Call to Leadership Meditation

1. "And I sought for a man among them who should build up the wall and stand in the breach before me for the land, that I should not destroy it, but I found none." - Ezekiel 22:30

2. "But you are a chosen race, a royal priesthood, a holy nation, a people for his own possession, that you may proclaim the excellencies of him who called you out of darkness into his marvelous light." - 1 Peter 2:9

3. "And he said to them, 'Follow me, and I will make you fishers of men.'" - Matthew 4:19

4. "But whoever would be great among you must be your servant." - Matthew 20:26

5. "Let no one despise you for your youth, but set the believers an example in speech, in conduct, in love, in faith, in purity." - 1 Timothy 4:12

6. "And he gave the apostles, the prophets, the evangelists, the shepherds and teachers, to equip

the saints for the work of ministry, for building up the body of Christ." - Ephesians 4:11-12

7. "For even the Son of Man came not to be served but to serve, and to give his life as a ransom for many." - Mark 10:45

8. "Keep your conduct among the Gentiles honorable, so that when they speak against you as evildoers, they may see your good deeds and glorify God on the day of visitation." - 1 Peter 2:12

9. "Shepherd the flock of God that is among you, exercising oversight, not under compulsion, but willingly, as God would have you; not for shameful gain, but eagerly." - 1 Peter 5:2

10. "But be doers of the word, and not hearers only, deceiving yourselves." - James 1:22

11. "Do your best to present yourself to God as one approved, a worker who has no need to be ashamed, rightly handling the word of truth." - 2 Timothy 2:15

12. "But I do not account my life of any value nor as precious to myself, if only I may finish my course and the ministry that I received from the Lord Jesus, to testify to the gospel of the grace of God." - Acts 20:24

13. "Do nothing from selfish ambition or conceit, but in humility count others more significant than yourselves." - Philippians 2:3

14. "For God gave us a spirit not of fear but of power and love and self-control." - 2 Timothy 1:7

15. "And we know that for those who love God all things work together for good, for those who are called according to his purpose." - Romans 8:28

16. "As each has received a gift, use it to serve one another, as good stewards of God's varied grace." - 1 Peter 4:10

17. "So, you also must be ready, for the Son of Man is coming at an hour you do not expect." - Matthew 24:44

18. "But seek first the kingdom of God and his righteousness, and all these things will be added to you." - Matthew 6:33

19. "For we are his workmanship, created in Christ Jesus for good works, which God prepared beforehand, that we should walk in them." - Ephesians 2:10

20. "Commit your work to the Lord, and your plans will be established." - Proverbs 16:3

21. "And whatever you do, in word or deed, do everything in the name of the Lord Jesus, giving thanks to God the Father through him." - Colossians 3:17

22. "Do not be conformed to this world, but be transformed by the renewal of your mind, that by testing you may discern what is the will of God, what is good and acceptable and perfect." - Romans 12:2

23. "Let your light shine before others, so that they may see your good works and give glory to your Father who is in heaven." - Matthew 5:16

24. "For the Lord your God is he who goes with you to fight for you against your enemies, to give you the victory." - Deuteronomy 20:4

25. "But the fruit of the Spirit is love, joy, peace, patience, kindness, goodness, faithfulness, gentleness, self-control; against such things there is no law." - Galatians 5:22-23

26. "But thanks be to God, who in Christ always leads us in triumphal procession, and through us spreads the fragrance of the knowledge of him everywhere." - 2 Corinthians 2:14

27. "I can do all things through him who strengthens me." - Philippians 4:13

28. "And let us not grow weary of doing good, for in due season we will reap, if we do not give up." - Galatians 6:9

29. "For God is not unjust so as to overlook your work and the love that you have shown for his name in serving the saints, as you still do." - Hebrews 6:10

30. "Finally, be strong in the Lord and in the strength of his might." - Ephesians 6:10

VISION AND STRATEGY

Vision and strategy are two essential components of effective leadership. They work together to guide an organization toward its goals and provide a framework for decision-making. Let us explore each concept individually and their interconnectedness:

Vision

Vision is a clear, inspiring, and aspirational picture of the future that a leader communicates to the organization. It answers the question, **"Where are we headed?"** A compelling vision motivates and aligns team members, fostering a sense of purpose and direction. It helps create a shared understanding of the organization's purpose, values, and long-term objectives.

Characteristics of a Strong Vision:

♦ **Inspiring:** A vision should inspire and challenge individuals to achieve something meaningful.

- **Clear:** The vision must be easily understood and communicated throughout the organization.
- **Future-Oriented:** It focuses on the future and describes an ideal state.

Strategy

Strategy is a plan of action designed to achieve vision. It outlines how an organization will allocate its resources, make decisions, and gain a competitive advantage to fulfill its long-term objectives.

Strategy provides the roadmap for turning the vision into reality. It involves setting goals, making choices about resource allocation, and defining the steps needed to move the organization forward.

Components of a Strong Strategy:

- **Clear Objectives:** Specific, measurable, achievable, relevant, and time-bound (SMART) objectives provide clarity.
- **Resource Allocation:** Effective strategy involves allocating resources (financial, human, and others) strategically.
- **Adaptability:** A good strategy is adaptable to changing circumstances and can be revised as needed.

A vision without a strategy may remain a lofty ideal without a practical plan for implementation. Conversely, a strategy without a clear vision may lack direction and fail to inspire.

The **vision** provides the **"why"** and the **strategy** provides the **"how."** They complement each other to create a comprehensive framework for organizational success.

Effective leaders continually assess and adjust both vision and strategy in response to internal and external changes.

Leaders must effectively communicate the vision and strategy to all members of the organization. This involves regular and transparent communication to ensure everyone understands their role in achieving the shared vision.

In summary, visionary leaders articulate a compelling vision that serves as the North Star for the organization, and strategic leaders develop and execute plans to bring that vision to fruition. The successful integration of vision and strategy is crucial for guiding an organization toward sustained success and relevance in a dynamic environment.

Crafting a vision and strategic planning are crucial components of effective leadership. These elements help guide an organization toward its goals, foster alignment among team members, and provide a framework for decision-making. Here are steps you can take to develop a vision and engage in strategic planning:

Crafting a Vision:

- **Define Your Values:** Identify the core values that will underpin your organization's culture and decision-making.

- **Understand the Current State:** Assess the current state of the organization, considering strengths, weaknesses, opportunities, and threats (SWOT analysis).

- **Envision the Future:** Clearly articulate your vision for the organization's future. This should be a compelling and inspiring description of what success looks like.

- **Involve Stakeholders:** Engage key stakeholders, including employees, customers, and partners, in the visioning process. Gather their insights and feedback.

- **Communicate Effectively:** Clearly and consistently communicate the vision throughout the organization. Use various channels and platforms to ensure that everyone understands and aligns with the vision.

Strategic Planning:

◆ **Set SMART Goals:** Establish Specific, Measurable, Achievable, Relevant, and Time-bound goals that align with the vision. These goals provide a roadmap for your strategic plan.

◆ **SWOT Analysis: Conduct a comprehensive SWOT analysis to identify internal strengths and weaknesses, and external opportunities and threats.**

◆ **Prioritize Initiatives:** Determine the most critical initiatives that will contribute to achieving your goals. Prioritize them based on impact and feasibility.

◆ **Allocate Resources:** Identify the resources (financial, human, technological) required to execute the strategic plan. Allocate resources effectively to support the prioritized initiatives.

◆ **Build Action Plans:** Develop detailed action plans for each initiative. Specify tasks, responsibilities, timelines, and key performance indicators (KPIs).

◆ **Monitor and Adjust:** Regularly monitor progress against the plan. Be prepared to adjust strategies based on changing internal and external factors.

♦ **Foster a Culture of Adaptability:** Encourage a culture that embraces change and adapts to current information. This will help the organization stay agile in a dynamic environment.

♦ **Feedback Loops:** Establish feedback mechanisms to gather input from employees and stakeholders. Use this feedback to refine and improve the strategic plan continuously.

♦ **Celebrate Milestones:** Celebrate achievements and milestones to boost morale and reinforce the organization's commitment to the vision.

Remember, crafting a vision and strategic planning is an ongoing process. As a leader, it is important to stay engaged, communicate effectively, and be willing to adapt as needed to ensure the organization's success.

Biblical Foundation for Vision and Strategy

Vision and strategy are fundamental themes throughout the Bible, interwoven within its narratives, teachings, and prophetic messages. While the terminology may not always directly mirror modern business language, the principles of vision and strategy are unmistakably present in the overarching narrative of God's interaction with humanity, the establishment of His kingdom, and the guidance provided for His people.

Vision in the Bible

Divine Vision:

The Bible opens with the grand narrative of creation, presenting God's vision for the world and humanity. In Genesis 1:26-28, God articulates His vision for humanity to be fruitful, multiply, and have dominion over the earth.

Throughout the Old Testament, various prophets receive visions from God concerning the future of Israel, neighboring nations, and the establishment of God's kingdom on earth. Examples include Isaiah's vision of the Lord in Isaiah 6 and Ezekiel's vision of the valley of dry bones in Ezekiel 37.

Messianic Vision:

A central theme in both the Old and New Testaments is the vision of a coming Messiah who would redeem humanity. This vision is articulated through prophecies such as Isaiah 9:6-7 and Micah 5:2 in the Old Testament, which foretell the birth of a Savior.

In the New Testament, Jesus Himself outlines His vision and mission in Luke 4:18-19 when He declares that He has come to proclaim good news to the poor, freedom for the prisoners, recovery of sight for the blind, and to set the oppressed free.

Kingdom Vision:

Jesus frequently spoke about the "kingdom of God" or the "kingdom of heaven" in His teachings, presenting a vision of a new order where God reigns supreme. He used parables such as mustard seed and yeast to illustrate the growth and impact of this kingdom (Matthew 13:31-33).

The book of Revelation provides a vision of the culmination of history, where God's kingdom is fully established, and there is a new heaven and a new earth (Revelation 21:1-4).

Strategy in the Bible:

Covenantal Strategy:

God establishes covenants with individuals like Abraham (Genesis 12:1-3), Noah (Genesis 9:8-17), and David (2 Samuel 7:12-16) as part of His strategic plan to fulfill His overarching vision.

These covenants serve as strategic agreements through which God promises blessings, protection, and a future for His people in exchange for their loyalty and obedience.

Redemptive Strategy:

The central strategy of God's plan for humanity is redemption. This is most fully realized through the sacrificial death and resurrection of Jesus Christ, which serves as the ultimate solution to humanity's sin problem.

Jesus' ministry on earth, including His teachings, miracles, and His death and resurrection, is part of God's strategic plan to reconcile humanity to Himself.

Missional Strategy:

God's strategy for spreading His kingdom involves commissioning His followers to be ambassadors and witnesses. In the Great Commission (Matthew 28:18-20), Jesus instructs His disciples to make disciples of all nations, baptizing them and teaching them to obey His commands.

The early church in the book of Acts provides a model of strategic expansion as they spread the message of Jesus from Jerusalem to the ends of the known world.

Integration of Vision and Strategy:

Alignment with God's Will:

A recurring theme in the Bible is the importance of aligning human vision and strategy with God's will. Proverbs 19:21 states, **"Many are the plans in a person's heart, but it is the LORD's purpose that prevails."**

Biblical figures such as Moses, David, and Paul exemplify the importance of seeking God's guidance and following His strategic direction.

Faith and Obedience:

The Bible teaches that faithfulness and obedience to God are essential components of executing His vision and strategy. Hebrews 11 provides a catalog of heroes of faith who trusted in God's promises and followed His guidance, often in the face of great adversity.

Flexibility and Adaptation:

While God's overarching vision remains constant, the strategies employed to fulfill that vision may vary depending on the context and circumstances. Biblical characters frequently demonstrate adaptability and flexibility in response to God's leading.

The Bible presents a rich tapestry of vision and strategy, rooted in God's eternal purposes for humanity. From the divine vision of creation and redemption to the strategic implementation of covenants, missions, and redemptive acts, the Bible provides timeless wisdom for individuals, communities, and organizations seeking to discern and fulfill their God-given purposes.

Examples of Vision and Strategy

The Bible offers numerous examples of vision and strategy, often demonstrated through the lives of various biblical figures and the overarching narrative of God's plan for humanity. Here are a few examples:

Vision of Noah:

In the story of Noah and the ark (Genesis 6-9), Noah receives a vision from God instructing him to build an ark to save his family and pairs of animals from a coming flood. Noah follows this vision meticulously, constructing the ark according to God's specifications and thereby executing a strategy for survival amidst the impending catastrophe.

Joseph's Strategic Leadership:

Joseph, the son of Jacob, demonstrates strategic leadership throughout his life, particularly during his time in

Egypt. He interprets Pharaoh's dreams, forecasting seven years of plenty followed by seven years of famine. Joseph develops a strategy to store grain during the years of plenty, ensuring Egypt's survival during the famine and saving countless lives, including those of his own family (Genesis 41-45).

Vision of the Promised Land:

Throughout the Old Testament, God communicates a vision of the Promised Land to various leaders of the Israelites, including Abraham, Moses, and Joshua. This vision serves as a driving force for the Israelites' journey and eventual conquest of the land, guiding their strategy for settlement and establishing a homeland for the descendants of Abraham.

Strategic Warfare of Joshua:

In the book of Joshua, we see strategic military tactics employed under Joshua's leadership as the Israelites conquer the Promised Land. Tactics such as reconnaissance, surprise attacks (like the taking of Jericho), and coordinated campaigns demonstrate a strategic approach to fulfilling God's vision for the Israelites.

Jesus' Vision and Strategy for Ministry:

Jesus Christ exemplifies vision and strategy in his ministry on earth. He articulates a clear vision of the Kingdom of God, preaching repentance, forgiveness, and reconciliation. Jesus strategically selects and trains disciples, employs various teaching methods (parables, miracles, personal interactions), and navigates political and religious challenges to advance his mission.

Paul's Missionary Strategy:

The apostle Paul demonstrates vision and strategy in spreading the Gospel throughout the Roman Empire. He formulates a strategic plan to reach key cities and regions, establishes networks of churches, and adapts his approach to diverse cultural contexts, all with the overarching vision of making Christ known to both Jews and Gentiles.

These examples from the Bible illustrate how vision and strategy are integral to accomplishing God's purposes and fulfilling one is calling or mission. They emphasize the importance of discerning God's vision, developing strategic plans aligned with that vision, and faithfully executing those plans with wisdom and perseverance.

Noah

The story of Noah in the Bible is a powerful narrative that holds profound lessons on vision and strategy, illustrating themes of faith, perseverance, and divine guidance. Noah's story, found primarily in the book of Genesis chapters 6 to 9, provides insights into the importance of having a clear vision, developing a strategy to achieve it, and remaining steadfast in the face of challenges.

Noah's story begins with God's observation of the wickedness prevailing on Earth and His decision to bring about a flood to cleanse it. In Genesis 6:13, God says to Noah, "I am going to put an end to all people, for the earth is filled with violence because of them. I am surely going to destroy both them and the earth." However, God also sees something unique in Noah: his righteousness and faithfulness. In verse 8, it is written, "But Noah found favor in the eyes of the Lord."

Noah receives a divine vision from God instructing him to build an ark to save himself, his family, and a remnant of the animal kingdom. This vision is not only about physical salvation from the impending flood but also about preserving life and the divine order on Earth. Noah's vision is to obey God's command faithfully, believing in the promise of salvation amidst impending destruction.

Upon receiving the vision, Noah faces the monumental task of building the ark. This task requires meticulous planning, resource management, and unwavering commitment. Noah follows a strategic plan laid out by God, which includes specific instructions regarding the dimensions, materials, and purpose of the ark (Genesis 6:14-16).

Noah demonstrates strategic foresight by following God's guidance meticulously, despite the incredulity and ridicule he faces from others. He gathers the necessary resources, engages in the laborious process of constructing the ark, and prepares for the flood according to the timeline revealed by God.

Noah's journey is fraught with challenges and obstacles, both logistical and emotional. Building an ark, of such magnitude would have required significant time, effort, and resources. Moreover, Noah and his family endured skepticism and mockery from their peers as they worked tirelessly on the ark, steadfast in their belief in God's vision.

Despite the daunting nature of the task and the prolonged period of waiting for the flood, Noah remains faithful and obedient to God's plan. His perseverance in the face of adversity is a testament to his unwavering commitment to his vision and his trust in God's promise of deliverance.

Throughout the story, God's guidance is evident as He provides Noah with the wisdom, strength, and protection necessary to fulfill his vision. When the flood finally arrives,

Noah and his family, along with the animals, are safely sheltered within the ark, fulfilling God's plan for their preservation.

After the floodwaters recede, God establishes a covenant with Noah, symbolized by the rainbow, promising never again to destroy the earth with a flood. This covenant not only reaffirms God's faithfulness to His creation but also serves as a testament to Noah's faith and obedience.

Lessons Learned:

The story of Noah encapsulates timeless lessons on vision and strategy:

♦ **Faith and Obedience:** Noah's unwavering faith in God's vision and his obedience to divine instructions serve as a model for believers to trust in God's plan, even when it seems implausible.

♦ **Strategic Planning:** Noah's strategic approach to building the ark underscores the importance of careful planning, resource management, and perseverance in achieving long-term goals.

♦ **Perseverance in Adversity:** Noah's resilience in the face of skepticism, ridicule, and the arduous task of building the ark teaches us the value of perseverance and steadfastness in pursuing our vision, despite challenges.

♦ **Divine Guidance:** The story highlights the significance of seeking and heeding divine guidance in navigating life's challenges and fulfilling one's purpose.

In conclusion, the narrative of Noah in the Bible offers a profound portrayal of vision and strategy, emphasizing the importance of faith, perseverance, and divine guidance in the pursuit of God's purpose. Through Noah's example, believers are encouraged to trust in God's vision, develop strategic plans aligned with His will, and remain steadfast in their commitment to fulfilling His purpose, regardless of the obstacles they may face.

Joseph

Joseph in the Bible is a significant figure whose story exemplifies the power of vision and strategic thinking. His narrative, chronicled primarily in the Book of Genesis, spans from his youth to his rise to power in Egypt. Through various trials and triumphs, Joseph demonstrates key principles of vision and strategy that are timeless and applicable even in contemporary contexts.

Joseph's story begins with his dreams, which serve as the foundation of his vision. In these dreams, he sees himself in positions of authority, symbolized by sheaves of grain bowing down to him and celestial bodies paying homage to him. Despite facing ridicule and animosity from his brothers for sharing these dreams, Joseph remains steadfast in his belief in their significance.

Joseph's visions provide him with a clear sense of purpose and destiny. They fuel his determination to pursue his dreams despite the obstacles he encounters along the way.

Joseph's vision extends beyond immediate circumstances. He understands that his dreams signify future events and maintains faith in their fulfillment, even during periods of adversity.

Joseph's journey involves strategic decision-making and actions that enable him to realize his vision. His strategic prowess is evident in various aspects of his life, from managing his family affairs to navigating the complexities of Egyptian politics.

When Joseph is sold into slavery by his jealous brothers, he does not succumb to despair. Instead, he adapts to his new circumstances, quickly earning the trust of his master, Potiphar, and excelling in his service.

Whether as a slave, a prisoner, or later as a ruler, Joseph demonstrates excellence in every task entrusted to him. His diligence and competence earned him favor and advancement, highlighting the importance of consistently delivering high-quality work.

Throughout his life, Joseph forges strategic relationships that contribute to his success. From interpreting dreams for fellow prisoners to interpreting Pharaoh's dreams, Joseph leverages these connections to position himself favorably and advance his objectives.

Joseph's ability to interpret dreams proves pivotal during times of crisis. His interpretation of Pharaoh's dreams not only saves Egypt from famine but also elevates Joseph to a position of unparalleled authority, enabling him to fulfill his vision of leadership.

Lessons Learned:

Joseph's story offers several valuable lessons on vision and strategy:

♦ **Faith in Vision:** Despite adversity and setbacks, maintaining faith in one's vision is crucial for its realization.

♦ **Strategic Adaptability:** Flexibility and adaptability are essential when circumstances change unexpectedly.

♦ **Excellence and Integrity:** Consistently delivering excellence and maintaining integrity contribute to long-term success.

♦ **Strategic Networking:** Building and leveraging strategic relationships can open doors and create opportunities.

♦ **Crisis as Opportunity:** Viewing crises as opportunities for growth and advancement can lead to innovative solutions and breakthroughs.

Joseph's journey underscores the transformative power of vision and strategic thinking, illustrating how these principles can guide individuals through challenges and toward the fulfillment of their aspirations.

Joshua

In the context of the Bible, the story of Joshua provides profound insights into leadership, vision, and strategy. Joshua, who succeeded Moses as the leader of the Israelites, faced immense challenges as he led the Israelites into the Promised Land. His journey is marked by unwavering faith, strategic thinking, and a clear vision guided by divine direction.

Joshua's vision was deeply rooted in his faith and his belief in the promises of God. Before embarking on the conquest of Canaan, Joshua received divine guidance and assurance from God Himself. In Joshua 1:2-9, God speaks directly to Joshua, reassuring him of His presence and promising success if Joshua remained faithful and courageous. This divine encounter laid the foundation for Joshua's vision, instilling in him the confidence and determination needed to lead the Israelites.

Joshua's vision was clear: to lead the Israelites into the land that God had promised to their ancestors. He understood the significance of this mission, not just for the present generation but for generations to come. This clarity of purpose provided Joshua with a guiding light amid the uncertainties and challenges he faced.

Joshua was not merely a visionary but also a strategic planner. He understood the importance of preparation and planning for the battles ahead. Before crossing the Jordan River, Joshua sent spies to gather intelligence about the land and its inhabitants (Joshua 2). He meticulously planned the conquest of Jericho, employing unconventional tactics guided by divine instruction (Joshua 6).

Joshua's vision would have amounted to nothing without the courage to pursue it relentlessly. Throughout his leadership, Joshua demonstrated unwavering courage in the face of formidable obstacles. Whether facing the daunting walls of Jericho or the alliance of Canaanite kings, Joshua stood firm, trusting in God's promises, and leading his people with unwavering resolve.

Despite having a sharp vision, Joshua remained adaptable and flexible in his approach. He understood that circumstances could change, requiring adjustments to the strategy. When the Gibeonites deceived the Israelites into making a treaty with them, Joshua did not let this setback deter him. Instead, he adapted his plans, incorporating the Gibeonites into the fold while still pursuing the broader vision of conquering the land (Joshua 9).

Joshua recognized the importance of unity among the Israelites in realizing his vision. He ensured that all the tribes were represented and involved in the conquest of Canaan, fostering a sense of unity and solidarity among the people. By valuing inclusivity, Joshua strengthened the cohesion of the Israelite community, enabling them to overcome internal divisions and external threats.

Joshua's vision was not just about conceptualization but about execution. He led by example, demonstrating faithfulness to God's commands and inspiring others to do the same. Under his leadership, the Israelites remained committed to their mission, pressing forward with determination until they had possessed the land that God had promised them.

In summary, Joshua's leadership exemplifies the importance of vision, strategy, and faith in accomplishing monumental tasks. His story serves as a timeless testament to the power of divine guidance, strategic planning, courage, and unwavering faith in realizing a vision against all odds.

Nehemiah

The story of Nehemiah in the Bible provides a compelling narrative of visionary leadership and strategic planning. Nehemiah was a Jewish leader living in exile during the Babylonian captivity of the Israelites. He served as the cupbearer to King Artaxerxes I of Persia, a position of considerable influence and trust. The narrative unfolds in the book of Nehemiah in the Old Testament, primarily focusing on Nehemiah's efforts to rebuild the walls of Jerusalem, which had been destroyed by the Babylonians.

Vision:

♦ **Awareness of the Problem**: Nehemiah receives a report about the dire state of Jerusalem's walls, which were crucial for the city's security and identity. This awareness ignites his vision to restore and rebuild the walls.

♦ **Emotional Connection**: Nehemiah's vision is deeply personal and tied to his identity as an Israelite. He is moved to tears upon hearing the news and expresses a profound desire to see Jerusalem restored.

♦ **Divine Guidance**: Nehemiah's vision is not merely driven by personal ambition but is grounded in his faith and belief in God's promises to his people. He sees himself as an instrument of God's will in restoring Jerusalem.

Strategy:

♦ **Planning and Preparation**: Before presenting his vision to King Artaxerxes, Nehemiah spends time planning and praying. He formulates a detailed strategy for the project, considering factors such as resources, manpower, and logistics.

♦ **Gaining Support**: Nehemiah understands the importance of gaining support for his vision. He approaches King Artaxerxes to seek permission, support, and resources for the rebuilding project. Nehemiah's humility, reverence, and strategic presentation persuaded the king to grant his requests.

♦ **Assessment and Evaluation**: Upon arriving in Jerusalem, Nehemiah conducts a thorough assessment of the situation, inspecting the damage to the walls and rallying support from the people. He carefully evaluates the resources available and the challenges that lie ahead.

♦ **Mobilization and Organization**: Nehemiah mobilizes the people of Jerusalem, organizing them into teams to work on different sections of the wall.

He assigns specific tasks, coordinates efforts, and instills a sense of unity and purpose among the workers.

◆ **Dealing with Opposition**: Nehemiah faces opposition from various quarters, including neighboring governors and detractors within Jerusalem itself. He employs both strategic diplomacy and firm leadership to address challenges and maintain focus on the vision.

◆ **Adaptability and Problem-solving**: Throughout the project, Nehemiah demonstrates flexibility and adaptability in response to changing circumstances and unexpected challenges. He devises creative solutions to overcome obstacles and keep the project on track.

◆ **Celebrating Success and Legacy**: Upon completing the walls, Nehemiah leads the people in a celebration of their achievement. He also establishes measures to ensure the ongoing maintenance and security of the city, leaving behind a legacy of leadership and vision.

In summary, Nehemiah's story in the Bible illustrates the power of vision and strategic leadership in achieving ambitious goals. His example serves as a timeless inspiration for leaders across generations, emphasizing the importance of faith, planning, perseverance, and collaboration in realizing a shared vision for a better future.

Jesus

The vision and strategy of Jesus in the Bible encompass profound teachings, parables, and actions aimed at bringing about spiritual transformation, social justice, and the establishment of the Kingdom of God on Earth. While there is no explicit business or organizational strategy outlined in the Bible, Jesus' teachings and actions can be examined through the lens of leadership, vision, and strategy in a broader sense.

Vision

Jesus' vision, as portrayed in the Bible, is multifaceted and deeply spiritual. At its core is the concept of the Kingdom of God, which he frequently spoke about through parables and teachings. This Kingdom is not a geopolitical entity but rather a realm where God's will be fully realized, characterized by love, justice, mercy, and reconciliation. Jesus envisioned a world where people would live in harmony with God, one another, and creation.

His vision extended beyond the immediate circumstances of his time, encompassing eternity and the salvation of humanity. He proclaimed a message of repentance, forgiveness, and redemption, inviting people to turn away from sin and embrace a new way of life characterized by faith and righteousness.

Strategy

♦ **Teaching through Parables**: Jesus often used parables—short, fictional stories with moral lessons—to convey profound truths about the Kingdom of God. This storytelling strategy allowed him to communicate complex spiritual concepts in a way that was relatable and easily understood by his audience.

♦ **Leading by Example**: Jesus did not just preach; he lived out his teachings in his daily interactions. His actions, such as healing the sick, feeding the hungry, and showing compassion to the marginalized, demonstrated the values of love, mercy, and justice that he espoused. This approach inspired his followers to emulate his behavior and become agents of positive change in their communities.

♦ **Building Relationships**: Central to Jesus' strategy was the cultivation of personal relationships. He invested time in building rapport with his disciples and others he encountered, engaging in meaningful conversations, and addressing their spiritual needs. This relational approach formed the foundation of his ministry and empowered his followers to carry on his mission after his death.

♦ **Empowering Others**: Jesus empowered his disciples to continue his work by imparting to them his teachings, authority, and commission. He equipped them with the necessary tools and guidance to spread the message of the Kingdom of God and make disciples of all nations.

♦ **Challenge to the Status Quo**: Jesus' ministry was often characterized by a challenge to the prevailing religious and social norms of his time. He confronted religious hypocrisy, denounced oppression, and injustice, and advocated for the marginalized and downtrodden. This confrontational aspect of his strategy aimed to provoke introspection and societal transformation.

♦ **Sacrificial Leadership**: Ultimately, Jesus' strategy culminated in his sacrificial death on the cross. By willingly laying down his life, he demonstrated the depth of his love and commitment to humanity and provided the ultimate example of servant leadership.

In summary, Jesus' vision, and strategy, as depicted in the Bible, revolve around the establishment of God's Kingdom through transformative teachings, exemplary leadership, relational engagement, empowerment of others, challenge to the status quo, and sacrificial love. While not formulated in the language of contemporary business strategies, his approach remains profoundly influential and continues to inspire individuals and communities worldwide.

Paul

In the Bible, the apostle Paul emerges as a central figure, not only in spreading the message of Christianity but also in articulating a profound vision and strategy for the growth and organization of the early Christian communities. Paul's vision and strategy were instrumental in shaping the trajectory of early Christianity and continue to influence Christian thought and practice today.

Paul's Vision:

Paul's vision was expansive, emphasizing the universality of salvation through Jesus Christ. He preached that salvation was available to all humanity, irrespective of ethnicity, nationality, or social status. This inclusive vision challenged prevailing notions of exclusivity and tribalism.

Central to Paul's vision was the concept of grace – the idea that salvation comes not through adherence to religious laws or rituals but through faith in Jesus Christ and the grace of God. This emphasis on grace was a radical departure from legalistic interpretations of religion prevalent in his time.

Paul envisioned the Christian community as a cohesive and interconnected body, with each member playing a unique role. He used the metaphor of the body to emphasize the importance of unity, diversity, and mutual dependence among believers.

Paul's vision included the idea of believers being transformed into a new creation through their relationship with Christ. This transformation was not merely individual but had implications for society and the world at large, ushering in a new era of reconciliation and restoration.

Paul's Strategy:

♦ **Missionary Journeys:** Paul embarked on several missionary journeys, traveling extensively throughout the Mediterranean world to proclaim the message of Christ. These journeys were strategic, targeting key urban centers and regions where his message could reach diverse audiences and spread rapidly.

♦ **Strategic Partnerships:** Paul forged strategic partnerships with fellow believers, churches, and community leaders to support his missionary endeavors. He collaborated with individuals like Barnabas, Silas, Timothy, and Titus, leveraging their unique gifts and resources to advance the gospel.

♦ **Adaptability and Contextualization:** Paul demonstrated adaptability in his approach, contextualizing the message of Christ to diverse cultural contexts and audiences. He employed various rhetorical strategies, using familiar language and symbols to communicate the gospel effectively to both Jews and Gentiles.

♦ **Establishment of Churches:** A key aspect of Paul's strategy was the establishment and nurturing of Christian communities (churches) in the places he visited. These communities served as centers for worship, instruction, fellowship, and mutual support, embodying the values of the kingdom of God.

♦ **Epistolary Communication:** Paul's letters, preserved in the New Testament, served as a vital component of his strategy for nurturing and guiding the early Christian communities. Through his letters, he addressed theological questions, provided pastoral guidance, and offered encouragement to believers.

♦ **Legacy:** Paul's vision and strategy left a legacy that continues to shape Christian theology, ecclesiology, and mission today. His emphasis on grace, universal salvation, and the unity of believers remains foundational to Christian thought. Moreover, his missionary zeal and strategic approach to spreading the gospel laid the groundwork for the global expansion of Christianity. Paul's writings continue to inspire and challenge Christians to live out their faith with boldness, compassion, and integrity, contributing to the ongoing growth and transformation of the church and the world.

30 Days Vision and Strategy Meditation

1. Proverbs 29:18 (NIV): "Where there is no revelation, people cast off restraint; but blessed is the one who heeds wisdom's instruction."

2. Habakkuk 2:2-3 (NIV): "Then the Lord replied: 'Write down the revelation and make it plain on tablets so that a herald may run with it. For the revelation awaits an appointed time; it speaks of the end and will not prove false. Though it lingers, wait for it; it will certainly come and will not delay.'"

3. Proverbs 16:3 (NIV): "Commit to the Lord whatever you do, and he will establish your plans."

4. Psalm 20:4 (NIV): "May he give you the desire of your heart and make all your plans succeed."

5. Proverbs 19:21 (NIV): "Many are the plans in a person's heart, but it is the Lord's purpose that prevails."

6. Proverbs 15:22 (NIV): "Plans fail for lack of counsel, but with many advisers they succeed."

7. James 4:13-15 (NIV): "Now listen, you who say, 'Today or tomorrow we will go to this or that city, spend a year there, carry on business and make money.' Why, you do not even know what will happen tomorrow. What is your life? You are a

mist that appears for a little while and then vanishes. Instead, you ought to say, 'If it is the Lord's will, we will live and do this or that.'"

8. Proverbs 24:27 (NIV): "Put your outdoor work in order and get your fields ready; after that, build your house."

9. Proverbs 21:5 (NIV): "The plans of the diligent lead to profit as surely as haste leads to poverty."

10. Ecclesiastes 3:1 (NIV): "There is a time for everything, and a season for every activity under the heavens."

11. Luke 14:28 (NIV): "Suppose one of you wants to build a tower. Won't you first sit down and estimate the cost to see if you have enough money to complete it?"

12. Proverbs 16:9 (NIV): "In their hearts humans plan their course, but the Lord establishes their steps."

13. Proverbs 20:18 (NIV): "Plans are established by seeking advice; so, if you wage war, obtain guidance."

14. Proverbs 21:30 (NIV): "There is no wisdom, no insight, no plan that can succeed against the Lord."

15. Isaiah 32:8 (NIV): "But the noble makes noble plans, and by noble deeds they stand."

16. Proverbs 24:3-4 (NIV): "By wisdom a house is built, and through understanding it is

established; through knowledge its rooms are filled with rare and beautiful treasures."

17. Proverbs 3:5-6 (NIV): "Trust in the Lord with all your heart and lean not on your own understanding; in all your ways submit to him, and he will make your paths straight."

18. Philippians 4:13 (NIV): "I can do all this through him who gives me strength."

19. Proverbs 16:1 (NIV): "To humans belong the plans of the heart, but from the Lord comes the proper answer of the tongue."

20. Jeremiah 29:11 (NIV): "For I know the plans I have for you," declares the Lord, "plans to prosper you and not to harm you, plans to give you hope and a future."

21. Psalm 90:12 (NIV): "Teach us to number our days, that we may gain a heart of wisdom."

22. Proverbs 14:15 (NIV): "The simple believe anything, but the prudent give thought to their steps."

23. Proverbs 11:14 (NIV): "For lack of guidance a nation falls, but victory is won through many advisers."

24. Proverbs 27:12 (NIV): "The prudent see danger and take refuge, but the simple keep going and pay the penalty."

25. Proverbs 4:25-27 (NIV): "Let your eyes look straight ahead; fix your gaze directly before you. Give careful thought to the paths for your feet and

be steadfast in all your ways. Do not turn to the right or the left; keep your foot from evil."

26. Proverbs 2:6 (NIV): "For the Lord gives wisdom; from his mouth comes knowledge and understanding."

27. Proverbs 12:15 (NIV): "The way of fools seems right to them, but the wise listen to advice."

28. Proverbs 15:31 (NIV): "Whoever heeds life-giving correction will be at home among the wise."

29. Proverbs 19:8 (NIV): "The one who gets wisdom loves life; the one who cherishes understanding will soon prosper."

30. Ecclesiastes 11:4 (NIV): "Whoever watches the wind will not plant; whoever looks at the clouds will not reap."

These verses offer guidance on seeking wisdom, planning diligently, trusting in God's providence, and seeking counsel from others in our endeavors.

LEADING BY EXAMPLE

"Leading by example" is a leadership philosophy that emphasizes the importance of setting a positive and influential precedent through one's own actions and behavior. This approach involves demonstrating the values, work ethic, and standards that you expect from others. Some key aspects of leading by example: Integrity, Work Ethic, Accountability, Positive Attitude, Communication, Continuous Learning, Empathy, Adaptability, Resilience, and Recognition.

Leaders should uphold high ethical standards and demonstrate honesty and transparency in their actions. This builds trust and encourages others to follow suit. Leaders who work hard and are committed to their tasks inspire their team members to do the same. Leading by example in terms of dedication and diligence can create a positive work culture.

Accepting responsibility for one's actions, whether they are successes or failures, is crucial. When leaders demonstrate accountability, it sets an expectation for others to do the same. Maintaining a positive and optimistic outlook, even in challenging situations, can be contagious. Leaders who approach difficulties with a problem-solving mindset inspire their team to do the same.

Effective communication is essential for leadership. Leaders who lead by example communicate clearly, actively listen, and foster an open and honest dialogue within the team. Leaders should show a commitment to personal and professional growth. This can inspire team members to embrace a learning mindset and seek opportunities for improvement.

Demonstrating empathy and understanding toward others fosters a supportive and inclusive work environment. Leaders who show care and consideration set the tone for a compassionate workplace. In a rapidly changing world, leaders need to be adaptable. Showing a willingness to embrace change and adapt to new circumstances encourages the team to be flexible and open-minded.

Leaders face challenges, setbacks, and failures. By demonstrating resilience and perseverance, leaders inspire their team to overcome obstacles and keep moving forward.

Acknowledging and appreciating the efforts and achievements of team members is important. Leaders who recognize and celebrate successes create a positive and motivated work environment.

Leading by example is a powerful leadership strategy because it aligns words with actions, creating a consistent and authentic leadership style. It can foster a positive organizational culture and contribute to the overall success and well-being of the team.

Modelling ethical and moral behavior for your team

Modelling ethical and moral behavior for your team is essential for creating a positive and productive work environment. Some strategies and principles you can adopt to effectively demonstrate ethical and moral behavior are:

♦ **Lead by Example:** Demonstrate the values and behaviors you expect from your team members. Be a role model by consistently adhering to ethical and moral standards in your actions and decisions.

♦ **Communicate Clearly:** Clearly communicate your expectations regarding ethical conduct. Make sure your team understands the company's values, mission, and any specific ethical guidelines relevant to your industry.

♦ **Encourage Open Communication:** Foster an environment where team members feel comfortable expressing their concerns about ethical issues without fear of reprisal. Encourage open dialogue and be receptive to feedback.

♦ **Set Clear Expectations:** Establish clear guidelines for ethical behaviors within the organization. Clearly outline the consequences for unethical conduct and ensure that everyone is aware of these expectations.

♦ **Provide Training:** Offer training sessions on ethics and morality in the workplace. This can help employees understand the importance of ethical behavior and provide them with tools to navigate ethical dilemmas.

♦ **Promote a Positive Culture:** Create a positive and inclusive organizational culture that values diversity, respect, and integrity. A positive culture can help reinforce ethical behavior and make it more likely that team members will uphold these values.

♦ **Recognize and Reward Ethical Behavior:** Acknowledge and reward individuals or teams that demonstrate exemplary ethical behavior. This reinforces the importance of ethical conduct and encourages others to follow suit.

♦ **Address Ethical Issues Promptly:** If ethical issues arise, address them promptly and transparently. Show that you take ethical concerns seriously and are committed to resolving them in a fair and just manner.

♦ **Be Transparent:** Practice transparency in your decision-making processes. When appropriate, share information with your team, and explain the rationale behind your decisions to build trust.

♦ **Seek Continuous Improvement:** Regularly assess and refine your organization's ethical standards and policies. Solicit feedback from your team and be willing to adapt and improve based on evolving ethical challenges.

♦ **Encourage Personal Development:** Support your team members' personal and professional development. This can include providing resources for ethical decision-making, offering mentorship, and promoting a growth mindset.

Remember that ethical leadership is an ongoing process that requires commitment, consistency, and a genuine dedication to fostering a culture of integrity within your team and organization.

The Servant Leadership of Jesus

Servant leadership is a leadership philosophy that emphasizes serving and empowering others, prioritizing their needs and development over the leader's own interests. Many people associate the concept of servant leadership with the teachings and example of Jesus Christ. Some key aspects of the servant leadership of Jesus: Humility, Putting Others First, Empowering and Developing Others, Compassion and Love, Leading by Example, Service as a Core Principle, Forgiveness and Grace.

♦ **Humility** Jesus exhibited profound humility throughout his life. One notable example is when he washed the feet of his disciples, a task typically reserved for servants. This act symbolized his willingness to serve others in even the most humble and menial ways.

♦ **Putting Others First:** Jesus consistently put the needs of others ahead of his own. He prioritized healing the sick, feeding the hungry, and comforting the oppressed. His actions reflected a selfless dedication to the well-being of those he served.

♦ **Empowering and Developing Others:** Jesus focused on empowering and developing his disciples. He invested time in teaching and mentoring them, equipping them with the knowledge and skills they needed to continue his work after he was gone. He entrusted them with responsibilities and provided guidance to help them grow.

♦ **Compassion and Love:** Jesus' leadership was characterized by compassion and love. He showed empathy towards those who were suffering, and his teachings emphasized the importance of love for one another. His ultimate act of love was sacrificing himself for the redemption of humanity.

♦ **Leading by Example:** Jesus did not simply preach; he led by example. His actions aligned with his words, reinforcing the values and principles he taught. This consistency contributed to the credibility and impact of his leadership. John 13:14-15 (New International Version): **"Now that I, your Lord and Teacher, have washed your feet, you also should wash one another's feet. I have set you an example that you should do as I have done for you."**

♦ **Service as a Core Principle:** Central to the concept of servant leadership is the idea of service. Jesus emphasized that leadership is about serving others, stating**, "For even the Son of Man did not come to be served, but to serve, and to give his life as a ransom for many"** (Mark 10:45, NIV).

♦ **Forgiveness and Grace:** Jesus exemplified forgiveness and grace in his interactions with others. He forgave those who betrayed and crucified him, demonstrating a willingness to extend mercy and grace even in the face of immense personal suffering.

The servant leadership of Jesus serves as a powerful model for leaders in various contexts, emphasizing the importance of humility, selflessness, compassion, and a commitment to the well-being and development of others. Many leadership theories and practices incorporate these principles inspired by Jesus' leadership example.

30 Daily Meditation on Leading by Example

1. Matthew 5:16 - "In the same way, let your light shine before others, that they may see your good deeds and glorify your Father in heaven."

2. Philippians 2:3-4 - "Do nothing out of selfish ambition or vain conceit. Rather, in humility value others above yourselves, not looking to your own interests but each of you to the interests of the others."

3. 1 Timothy 4:12 - "Don't let anyone look down on you because you are young, but set an example for the believers in speech, in conduct, in love, in faith and in purity."

4. 1 Corinthians 11:1 - "Follow my example, as I follow the example of Christ."

5. Titus 2:7-8 - "In everything set them an example by doing what is good. In your teaching show integrity, seriousness and soundness of speech that cannot be condemned, so that those who oppose you may be ashamed because they have nothing bad to say about us."

6. Hebrews 13:7 - "Remember your leaders, who spoke the word of God to you. Consider the outcome of their way of life and imitate their faith."

7. 1 Peter 5:3 - "Not lording it over those entrusted to you but being examples to the flock."

8. Ephesians 5:1-2 - "Follow God's example, therefore, as dearly loved children and walk in the way of love, just as Christ loved us and gave

himself up for us as a fragrant offering and sacrifice to God."

9. 1 Thessalonians 1:7 - "And so you became a model to all the believers in Macedonia and Achaia."

10. 1 Peter 2:21 - "To this you were called, because Christ suffered for you, leaving you an example, that you should follow in his steps."

11. James 1:22 - "Do not merely listen to the word, and so deceive yourselves. Do what it says."

12. Galatians 6:9-10 - "Let us not become weary in doing good, for at the proper time we will reap a harvest if we do not give up. Therefore, as we have opportunity, let us do good to all people, especially to those who belong to the family of believers."

13. Colossians 3:17 - "And whatever you do, whether in word or deed, do it all in the name of the Lord Jesus, giving thanks to God the Father through him."

14. Romans 12:17 - "Do not repay anyone evil for evil. Be careful to do what is right in the eyes of everyone."

15. Proverbs 27:17 - "As iron sharpens iron, so one person sharpens another."

16. Matthew 20:26-28 - "Not so with you. Instead, whoever wants to become great among you must be your servant, and whoever wants to be first must be your slave— just as the Son of Man did

not come to be served, but to serve, and to give his life as a ransom for many."

17. Luke 6:31 - "Do to others as you would have them do to you."

18. 1 Corinthians 10:31 - "So whether you eat or drink or whatever you do, do it all for the glory of God."

19. Ephesians 4:22-24 - "You were taught, with regard to your former way of life, to put off your old self, which is being corrupted by its deceitful desires; to be made new in the attitude of your minds; and to put on the new self, created to be like God in true righteousness and holiness."

20. Matthew 23:11-12 - "The greatest among you will be your servant. For those who exalt themselves will be humbled, and those who humble themselves will be exalted."

21. Philippians 4:9 - "Whatever you have learned or received or heard from me or seen in me—put it into practice. And the God of peace will be with you."

22. Colossians 3:23-24 - "Whatever you do, work at it with all your heart, as working for the Lord, not for human masters, since you know that you will receive an inheritance from the Lord as a reward. It is the Lord Christ you are serving."

23. 2 Thessalonians 3:9 - "We did this, not because we do not have the right to such help, but in order to offer ourselves as a model for you to imitate."

24. 1 John 3:18 - "Dear children, let us not love with words or speech but with actions and in truth."

25. James 2:14-17 - "What good is it, my brothers and sisters, if someone claims to have faith but has no deeds? Can such faith save them? Suppose a brother or a sister is without clothes and daily food. If one of you says to them, 'Go in peace; keep warm and well fed,' but does nothing about their physical needs, what good is it? In the same way, faith by itself, if it is not accompanied by action, is dead."

26. Galatians 5:13 - "You, my brothers and sisters, were called to be free. But do not use your freedom to indulge the flesh; rather, serve one another humbly in love."

27. 1 Corinthians 16:14 - "Do everything in love."

28. 1 John 2:6 - "Whoever claims to live in him must live as Jesus did."

29. Proverbs 22:6 - "Start children off on the way they should go, and even when they are old, they will not turn from it."

Matthew 7:12 - "So in everything, do to others what you would have them do to you, for this sums up the Law and the Prophets."

COMMUNICATION AND INFLUENCE

Effective communication is crucial for leadership success. Leaders need to convey their vision, goals, and expectations clearly to inspire and guide their team. Some key principles for effective communication in leadership are:

♦ **Clarity and Conciseness:** Clearly articulate your message to avoid misunderstandings. Be concise and to the point to maintain focus and interest.

♦ **Active Listening:** Listen attentively to others. Show that you value their input by asking questions and seeking clarification.

♦ **Empathy:** Understand and consider the feelings and perspectives of others. Connect with your team on a personal level to build trust.

♦ **Openness and Transparency:** Be transparent about your decisions and share information openly. Foster an environment where team members feel comfortable expressing their thoughts.

- **Consistency:** Maintain consistency in your communication style and messaging. Ensure that your actions align with your words to build trust.

- **Adaptability:** Adjust your communication style based on the situation and the individuals involved. Be open to feedback and willing to modify your approach when necessary.

- **Positive and Encouragement:** Use positive language to motivate and inspire your team. Acknowledge and celebrate achievements to boost morale.

- **Feedback:** Provide constructive feedback in a timely and respectful manner. Encourage a culture of feedback within the team.

- **Use of Technology:** Leverage communication tools effectively, considering the preferences of your team. Balance face-to-face communication with digital channels to maintain a personal connection.

- **Visionary Communication:** Clearly articulate the vision and mission of the organization. Inspire and motivate your team by connecting their work to the organization's broader goals.

- **Conflict Resolution:** Address conflicts promptly and diplomatically. Encourage open dialogue to find mutually beneficial solutions.

- **Non-Verbal Communication:** Pay attention to your body language, gestures, and facial expressions. Be aware of how non-verbal cues may impact the message you are conveying.

- **Cultural Sensitivity:** Understand and respect cultural differences in communication styles. Adapt your approach to be inclusive and considerate of diverse perspectives.

♦ **Time Management:** Respect the time of your team members by being punctual and efficient in your communication. Prioritize key messages to avoid overwhelming your team with information.

Effective communication is an ongoing process that requires self-awareness, adaptability, and a commitment to continuous improvement. By mastering these principles, leaders can foster a positive and productive work environment.

Biblical Foundation of Communication and Influence

The Biblical foundation of communication and influence as a leadership principle finds its roots in numerous passages throughout the Bible, emphasizing the importance of effective communication and the responsible use of influence in leadership roles. From the Old Testament to the New Testament, there are teachings, examples, and principles that provide timeless wisdom for leaders seeking to communicate effectively and wield influence in a manner that aligns with moral and ethical standards.

♦ **Effective Communication:**

Proverbs 18:21 states, **"The tongue has the power of life and death, and those who love it will eat its fruit."** This verse underscores the significance of words and communication, highlighting their potential to bring either positive or negative outcomes. Leaders are called to communicate with wisdom, clarity, and intentionality, recognizing the impact their words can have on others.

Proverbs 15:1 advises, **"A gentle answer turns away wrath, but a harsh word stirs up anger."** This verse emphasizes the importance of tone and demeanor in communication. Effective leaders understand the value of diplomacy, empathy, and humility in their interactions, seeking to build bridges rather than walls through their words.

♦ **Influence and Servant Leadership:**

Jesus Christ serves as the ultimate example of servant leadership, emphasizing humility, compassion, and selflessness in leading others. In Mark 10:45, Jesus states, **"For even the Son of Man did not come to be served, but to serve, and to give his life as a ransom for many."** This foundational principle highlights that true leadership is about serving others and using one's influence for the betterment of those under one's care.

In Matthew 5:13-16, Jesus uses the metaphors of salt and light to describe the influence of his followers in the world. He encourages them to let their light shine before others so that they may see their good deeds and glorify God. This passage underscores the responsibility of leaders to be positive influences in their communities, inspiring others through their actions and character.

♦ **Wisdom and Discernment:**

Proverbs 4:7 instructs, **"The beginning of wisdom is this: Get wisdom. Though it cost all you have, get understanding."** Effective leadership requires wisdom and discernment, which are cultivated through seeking knowledge, understanding, and God's guidance. Leaders are called to make decisions with prudence and foresight, considering the long-term consequences of their actions on those they lead.

James 1:5 encourages believers to ask God for wisdom, promising that He will generously give it to those who ask without finding fault. This verse reminds leaders of the importance of relying on divine wisdom rather than their own understanding alone, recognizing that true wisdom comes from God.

♦ **Integrity and Truthfulness:**

Ephesians 4:15 exhorts believers to speak the truth in love, emphasizing the importance of honesty and integrity in communication. Leaders are called to uphold truthfulness and transparency in their interactions, fostering trust and credibility among their followers.

Proverbs 11:3 declares, **"The integrity of the upright guides them, but the unfaithful are destroyed by their duplicity."** This verse underscores the foundational role of integrity in leadership, highlighting that leaders who maintain honesty and consistency in their words and actions will be guided and upheld.

In summary, the Biblical foundation of communication and influence as a leadership principle emphasizes the importance of effective communication, servant leadership, wisdom, integrity, and truthfulness. Leaders who embrace these principles are better equipped to inspire, motivate, and positively impact those under their guidance, fulfilling their God-given calling to lead with humility, compassion, and excellence.

The Persuasive Power of King Solomon

Solomon, known for his wisdom and often considered one of the greatest biblical orators, is primarily associated with the Old Testament. His persuasive power is attributed to several factors:

♦ **Wisdom and Knowledge:** Solomon is renowned for his wisdom, which he famously requested from God in the biblical narrative. His deep understanding of human nature, justice, and the world allowed him to speak with authority and insight, making his orations compelling.

♦ **Rhetorical Skills:** Solomon's ability to articulate his thoughts and convey complex ideas in a clear and eloquent manner contributed to his persuasive power. His speeches were well-structured, employing effective rhetorical devices to engage and convince his audience.

♦ **Divine Authority:** Solomon's wisdom was believed to be a gift from God, giving his words a divine authority. This divine connection added weight to his speeches, as people were more inclined to accept and follow his guidance, considering it to be inspired by the divine.

♦ **Ethical and Moral Guidance:** Solomon's orations often contained ethical and moral teachings, drawing on principles found in the wisdom literature of the Old Testament, such as Proverbs and Ecclesiastes. His emphasis on virtue, justice, and righteousness resonated with the moral values of the audience, making his messages persuasive.

♦ **Cultural and Historical Context:** Understanding the cultural and historical context in which Solomon lived is crucial to appreciating the impact of his orations. In an era where oral communication played a significant role, the power of a skilled orator like Solomon would have been particularly influential.

♦ **Symbolic and Poetic Language:** Solomon frequently used symbolic language and poetry in his writings, making his messages more memorable and emotionally resonant. The use of metaphors, similes, and allegories added depth to his orations, making them not only intellectually compelling but also emotionally impactful.

♦ **Leadership Position:** Solomon's role as a king added to his persuasive authority. As a political and religious leader, his words carried weight not only because of their intrinsic wisdom but also because of his position of influence.

Biblical orators, such as Solomon, are known for their profound wisdom and persuasive communication skills. Solomon is often associated with wisdom and eloquence. His biblical writings, especially in the Book of Proverbs and the Song of Solomon, contain many verses that are considered to carry persuasive power. Here are a few examples:

♦ **Proverbs 16:24 (NIV): "Gracious words are a honeycomb, sweet to the soul and healing to the bones."**

This verse emphasizes the positive impact of kind and gracious words, suggesting that they have the power to bring healing and sweetness to one's soul.

♦ **Proverbs 15:1 (NIV): "A gentle answer turns away wrath, but a harsh word stirs up anger."**

Solomon here advocates for the power of gentle and wise words in defusing conflicts, showing the persuasive force of choosing one's words carefully.

♦ **Proverbs 25:15 (NIV): "Through patience a ruler can be persuaded, and a gentle tongue can break a bone."**

This verse highlights the effectiveness of patience and gentle communication in influencing even those in positions of authority.

♦ **Ecclesiastes 3:1 (NIV): "There is a time for everything, and a season for every activity under the heavens."**

This verse speaks to the wisdom of understanding the right timing for actions and decisions, emphasizing the importance of discernment in persuasive communication.

♦ **Song of Solomon 4:7 (NIV): "You are altogether beautiful, my darling; there is no flaw in you."**

While the Song of Solomon is a love poem, this verse illustrates the power of positive affirmation and how it can be used persuasively to uplift and encourage.

It is important to note that the persuasive power of these verses is often rooted in their universal themes of wisdom, kindness, patience, and understanding. When applied to various aspects of life, these principles can be compelling and influential in shaping attitudes and behaviors.

The persuasive power of Apostle Paul

The persuasive power of the Apostle Paul, as demonstrated in the New Testament of the Bible, is a subject that has been studied and admired for centuries. Paul, also known as Saint Paul, was an influential figure in early Christianity and played a crucial role in spreading the teachings of Jesus Christ. His letters, or epistles, form a significant portion of the New Testament, and they reflect his rhetorical skills and persuasive techniques. Some aspects of Paul's persuasive power are:

♦ Cultural Adaptability

Paul was highly skilled at adapting his message to different audiences. He was not confined to a single cultural or religious context and was able to communicate with Jews, Gentiles, and various cultural groups. This adaptability allowed him to connect with diverse audiences.

♦ Logical Argumentation

Paul often used logical reasoning and persuasive argumentation to support his points. In his epistles, he crafted well-reasoned arguments to address theological issues, ethical concerns, and practical matters within the Christian communities he was addressing.

Romans 1:16-17 (NIV):
"For I am not ashamed of the gospel, because it is the power of God that brings salvation to everyone who believes: first to the Jew, then to the Gentile. For in the gospel the righteousness of God is revealed—a righteousness that is by faith from first to last, just as it is written: 'The righteous will live by faith.'"

◆ Emotional Appeal

While Paul was logical and theological in his writings, he also appealed to the emotions of his audience. He expressed deep passion and empathy, creating a sense of shared experience and emotional connection with his readers.

Philippians 4:4-7 (NIV)
"Rejoice in the Lord always. I will say it again: Rejoice! Let your gentleness be evident to all. The Lord is near. Do not be anxious about anything, but in every situation, by prayer and petition, with thanksgiving, present your requests to God. And the peace of God, which transcends all understanding, will guard your hearts and your minds in Christ Jesus."

◆ Rhetorical Devices

Paul employed various rhetorical devices, such as repetition, parallelism, and vivid imagery, to make his messages memorable and impactful. His use of rhetorical techniques helped to emphasize key points and engage his audience.

Galatians 5:22-23 (NIV):
"But the fruit of the Spirit is love, joy, peace, forbearance, kindness, goodness, faithfulness, gentleness and self-control. Against such things there is no law."

Here, Paul uses a list of virtues, employing rhetorical repetition to emphasize the qualities that should characterize the lives of believers empowered by the Holy Spirit.

◆ Credibility and Authority

Paul established his credibility by emphasizing his own conversion experience and his direct encounter with the risen Christ. This gave him authority among the early Christian communities, making his message more persuasive.

Galatians 1:11-12 (NIV):

"I want you to know, brothers and sisters, that the gospel I preached is not of human origin. I did not receive it from any man, nor was I taught it; rather, I received it by revelation from Jesus Christ."

Paul establishes his credibility by asserting that his message is not based on human wisdom but comes directly from a revelation from Jesus Christ, reinforcing his authority as an apostle.

◆ Appeal to Shared Values

Paul often appealed to shared values and beliefs within the cultural context of his audience. By finding common ground, he was able to build bridges between diverse groups and convey his message effectively.

◆ Practical Guidance

In addition to theological teachings, Paul provided practical guidance for the challenges faced by early Christian communities. This pragmatic approach made his letters relevant to the daily lives of his readers, enhancing their persuasive impact.

◆ Ephesians 4:1-3 (NIV):

"As a prisoner for the Lord, then, I urge you to live a life worthy of the calling you have received. Be completely humble and gentle; be patient, bearing with

one another in love. Make every effort to keep the unity of the Spirit through the bond of peace."

Paul provides practical guidance on Christian living in these verses from Ephesians, urging believers to exhibit humility, gentleness, patience, and love to maintain unity within the community.

◆ Focus on Love and Unity

Throughout his writings, Paul emphasized the importance of love and unity within the Christian community. His emphasis on love as a guiding principle contributed to the persuasive power of his message, promoting a positive and inclusive ethos.

Overall, the persuasive power of Apostle Paul can be attributed to his ability to communicate effectively across diverse audiences, his logical and emotional appeal, his use of rhetorical devices, and his focus on shared values and practical guidance. These qualities continue to be studied and appreciated in the fields of theology, rhetoric, and communication.

30 Daily Meditation on communication and influence

1. Proverbs 16:24 - "Gracious words are like a honeycomb, sweetness to the soul and health to the body."
2. Proverbs 15:1 - "A gentle answer turns away wrath, but a harsh word stirs up anger."
3. Ephesians 4:29 - "Do not let any unwholesome talk come out of your mouths, but only what is helpful for building others up according to their needs, that it may benefit those who listen."

4. Proverbs 18:21 - "The tongue has the power of life and death, and those who love it will eat its fruit."

5. James 1:19 - "My dear brothers and sisters, take note of this: Everyone should be quick to listen, slow to speak and slow to become angry."

6. Proverbs 25:11 - "A word fitly spoken is like apples of gold in settings of silver."

7. Colossians 4:6 - "Let your conversation be always full of grace, seasoned with salt, so that you may know how to answer everyone."

8. Proverbs 12:18 - "The words of the reckless pierce like swords, but the tongue of the wise brings healing."

9. Proverbs 13:3 - "Those who guard their lips preserve their lives, but those who speak rashly will come to ruin."

10. Proverbs 17:27-28 - "The one who has knowledge uses words with restraint, and whoever has understanding is even-tempered. Even fools are thought wise if they keep silent, and discerning if they hold their tongues."

11. Matthew 5:37 - "Let your 'Yes' be 'Yes,' and your 'No,' 'No.' For whatever is more than these is from the evil one."

12. Proverbs 15:4 - "Gentle words are a tree of life; a deceitful tongue crushes the spirit."

13. Ephesians 4:15 - "Instead, speaking the truth in love, we will grow to become in every respect the mature body of him who is the head, that is, Christ."

14. Proverbs 21:23 - "Whoever keeps his mouth, and his tongue keeps himself out of trouble."

15. Matthew 12:36-37 - "But I tell you that everyone will have to give an account on the day of

judgment for every empty word they have spoken. For by your words, you will be acquitted, and by your words you will be condemned."

16. Psalm 19:14 - "May these words of my mouth and this meditation of my heart be pleasing in your sight, Lord, my Rock and my Redeemer."

17. Proverbs 16:23 - "The hearts of the wise make their mouths prudent, and their lips promote instruction."

18. Proverbs 20:15 - "Gold there is, and rubies in abundance, but lips that speak knowledge are a rare jewel."

19. James 3:1-12 - (A passage on the power and responsibility of the tongue)

20. Matthew 15:11 - "What goes into someone's mouth does not defile them, but what comes out of their mouth, that is what defiles them."

21. Proverbs 15:28 - "The heart of the righteous weighs its answers, but the mouth of the wicked gushes evil."

22. Ephesians 5:4 - "Nor should there be obscenity, foolish talk or coarse joking, which are out of place, but rather thanksgiving."

23. Proverbs 18:20 - "From the fruit of their mouth a person's stomach is filled; with the harvest of their lips, they are satisfied."

24. Proverbs 25:15 - "Through patience a ruler can be persuaded, and a gentle tongue can break a bone."

25. Proverbs 29:11 - "Fools give full vent to their rage, but the wise bring calm in the end."

26. Proverbs 31:26 - "She speaks with wisdom, and faithful instruction is on her tongue."

27. Proverbs 10:19 - "Sin is not ended by multiplying words, but the prudent hold their tongues."
28. Proverbs 15:2 - "The tongue of the wise adorns knowledge, but the mouth of the fool gushes folly."
29. 1 Peter 3:10 - "For, whoever would love life and see good days must keep their tongue from evil and their lips from deceitful speech."
30. Colossians 3:8 - "But now you must also rid yourselves of all such things as these: anger, rage, malice, slander, and filthy language from your lips."

These verses offer guidance on the power of words, the importance of wise communication, and the impact our speech can have on others.

RESILIENCE AND PERSEVERANCE

Resilience and perseverance are crucial qualities in effective leadership. Leaders who possess these attributes can navigate challenges, inspire their teams, and drive success even in the face of adversity. Here is an exploration of how resilience and perseverance contribute to effective leadership:

♦ **Navigating Challenges:**

Resilient leaders can bounce back from setbacks and adapt to changing circumstances. They maintain a positive outlook and focus on solutions rather than dwelling on problems. This ability is crucial when facing unexpected challenges or setbacks. Perseverant leaders show determination and persistence in overcoming obstacles. They do not give up easily, and their commitment to achieving goals can inspire and motivate their team to do the same.

♦ **Adaptability:**

Resilient leaders are adaptable and open to change. They can adjust their strategies and plans as needed, ensuring that the organization remains flexible in the face of unforeseen circumstances.

Perseverant leaders stay committed to long-term goals even when facing short-term difficulties. This commitment provides stability and direction, helping the team stay focused on the bigger picture.

♦ **Team Motivation:**

Resilient leaders set an example for their team by remaining composed under pressure. Their ability to stay calm and collected can reassure team members and boost morale during challenging times. Perseverant leaders inspire their teams by demonstrating unwavering commitment to shared goals. This dedication can instill a sense of purpose and determination among team members.

♦ **Learning from Failures:**

Resilient leaders view failures as opportunities for growth. They encourage a culture of learning from mistakes and adapting strategies to avoid similar pitfalls in the future. Perseverant leaders understand that setbacks are part of the journey. Instead of being discouraged by failures, they use them as steppingstones toward success, learning valuable lessons along the way.

♦ **Building Trust:**

Resilient leaders build trust by maintaining transparency and honesty, especially during challenging times. Team members appreciate leaders who communicate openly and authentically about the situation. Perseverant leaders build trust through consistency and reliability. When team members see that their leader is committed to long-term success and is willing to overcome obstacles, trust in their leadership grows.

In conclusion, resilience and perseverance complement each other in leadership. Resilience helps leaders navigate difficulties, while perseverance ensures a steadfast commitment to goals. Together, these qualities contribute to effective leadership in the face of adversity.

Building Resilience and Perseverance through challenges

Building resilience and persevering through challenges are essential skills for navigating life's ups and downs. Here are some strategies to help you develop resilience and persevere in the face of difficulties:

♦ **Develop a Growth Mindset:**
  ♦ Embrace challenges as opportunities for growth.
  ♦ View failures as learning experiences rather than setbacks.
  ♦ Believe in your ability to improve and develop new skills.
♦ **Set Realistic Goals:**
  ♦ Break down larger goals into smaller, more manageable tasks.
  ♦ Celebrate small victories along the way to stay motivated.
  ♦ Adjust your goals as needed and be flexible in your approach.
♦ **Cultivate Self-Awareness:**
  ♦ Understand your strengths and weaknesses.
  ♦ Recognize and manage your emotions effectively.

- ◆ Practice mindfulness to stay present and focused.
- ◆ **Build a Support System:**
  - ◆ Surround yourself with positive and supportive individuals.
  - ◆ Seek guidance and encouragement from friends, family, or mentors.
  - ◆ Share your challenges with others and do not be afraid to ask for help.
- ◆ **Learn from Adversity:**
  - ◆ Reflect on past challenges and identify lessons learned.
  - ◆ Develop problem-solving skills by analyzing situations objectively.
  - ◆ Use setbacks as opportunities to build resilience and adaptability.
- ◆ **Maintain a Positive Outlook:**
  - ◆ Focus on the aspects of a situation that you can control.
  - ◆ Challenge negative thoughts and reframe them in a more positive light.
  - ◆ Cultivate gratitude by acknowledging and appreciating the positive aspects of your life.
- ◆ **Take Care of Your Well-Being:**
  - ◆ Prioritize self-care, including proper nutrition, exercise, and sleep.
  - ◆ Engage in activities that bring you joy and relaxation.
  - ◆ Manage stress through techniques like deep breathing, meditation, or yoga.
- ◆ **Develop Problem-Solving Skills:**
  - ◆ Break down problems into smaller components.

- Identify potential solutions and weigh their pros and cons.
- Take decisive action and adjust your approach as needed.

♦ **Maintain a Long-Term Perspective:**
  - Recognize that challenges are often temporary.
  - Focus on the bigger picture and your long-term goals.
  - Remember past successes and how you overcame challenges.

♦ **Seek Professional Help if Needed:**
  - If you are facing significant challenges, consider seeking support from a therapist or counselor.
  - Professional guidance can provide additional tools and perspectives to help you cope.

Remember, building resilience is a continuous process, and it is okay to seek support when needed. Life is filled with challenges, but by developing resilience, you can navigate them more effectively and emerge stronger on the other side.

Biblical Foundation of Resilience and Perseverance

The Biblical foundation for resilience and perseverance as leadership principles is deeply rooted in the teachings and narratives found within the Bible, particularly in the Old and New Testaments. These principles offer valuable insights for leaders seeking to navigate challenges, overcome adversity, and endure in their roles with strength and determination.

♦ **Faith and Trust in God:**

Central to the Biblical foundation for resilience and perseverance is the concept of faith and trust in God.

Throughout the Bible, individuals faced daunting trials and tribulations, yet their unwavering trust in God enabled them to persevere. For instance, the story of Job exemplifies resilience in the face of immense suffering, as Job remained faithful despite losing everything he had. This principle encourages leaders to trust in God's providence even amidst uncertainty and difficulty.

♦ Endurance through Adversity:

Biblical figures often endured significant hardships, yet they remained steadfast in their commitment to God's will. The Apostle Paul, for example, faced numerous challenges, including persecution, imprisonment, and shipwrecks, yet he persisted in spreading the gospel. His resilience serves as a powerful example of enduring adversity with grace and perseverance. Leaders can draw inspiration from Paul's example, recognizing that trials can strengthen character and lead to growth and resilience.

♦ Perseverance in Pursuit of Purpose:

Biblical narratives emphasize the importance of perseverance in fulfilling one's calling or purpose. Moses spent forty years leading the Israelites through the wilderness, facing numerous obstacles along the way, yet he remained steadfast in his mission to lead God's people to the Promised Land. Similarly, leaders are called to persevere in pursuing their vision and goals, even when faced with challenges or setbacks.

♦ Learning from Failure and Resilience:

The Bible is replete with stories of individuals who experienced failure yet found redemption through resilience and perseverance. Peter, one of Jesus' disciples, famously denied knowing Jesus three times, yet he later became a key leader in the early Christian church. His story highlights the transformative power of resilience and the opportunity for growth and redemption in the face of failure.

♦ **Hope and Encouragement:**

Biblical teachings offer abundant encouragement and hope for those facing adversity. The Apostle Paul writes in Romans 5:3-4, **"We also glory in our sufferings, because we know that suffering produces perseverance; perseverance, character; and character, hope."** This passage underscores the transformative nature of perseverance and the hope that emerges from enduring trials. Leaders can inspire and uplift others by sharing messages of hope and encouragement grounded in Biblical truths.

In summary, the Biblical foundation for resilience and perseverance as leadership principles offers timeless wisdom and guidance for leaders facing adversity. By cultivating faith, enduring challenges with grace, persevering in pursuit of purpose, learning from failure, and embracing hope, leaders can navigate difficulties with strength, resilience, and unwavering determination.

Job's endurance in the face of adversity

The phrase "Job's endurance in the face of adversity" typically refers to the biblical figure Job, whose story is found in the Book of Job in the Old Testament. Job is often cited as an example of unwavering faith and endurance in extreme suffering and adversity.

According to the biblical narrative, Job was a wealthy man who faced a series of calamities, including the loss of his wealth, the death of his children, and a severe illness. Despite these hardships, Job maintained his faith in God and did not curse Him. Instead, he questioned and debated with God, seeking understanding and justice.

Job's endurance in the face of adversity has become a symbol of resilience, patience, and faith in the face of life's trials. The story is often interpreted as a lesson in trusting God's wisdom even when faced with circumstances that seem unjust or incomprehensible.

People may use the phrase "Job's endurance" more broadly to refer to anyone who demonstrates remarkable perseverance and resilience in the face of challenges. It has become a metaphor for enduring hardship with faith and patience, and the story continues to inspire individuals facing difficulties in various aspects of life.

The Bible contains several verses that highlight the endurance and perseverance of Job in the face of adversity. Here are a few key verses:

- **Job 1:20-22 (NIV):**

At this, Job got up, tore his robe, and shaved his head. Then he fell to the ground in worship and said: 'Naked I came from my mother's womb, and naked I will depart. The Lord gave and the Lord has taken away; may the name of the Lord be praised.' In all this, Job did not sin by charging God with wrongdoing."

- **Job 2:9-10 (NIV):**

"His wife said to him, 'Are you still maintaining your integrity? Curse God and die!' He replied, 'You are talking like a foolish woman. Shall we accept good from God, and not trouble?' In all this, Job did not sin in what he said."

- **Job 13:15 (NIV):**

"Though he slay me, yet will I hope in him; I will surely defend my ways to his face."
- Job 23:10-12 (NIV):

"But he knows the way that I take; when he has tested me, I will come forth as gold. My feet have closely followed his steps; I have kept to his way without turning aside. I have not departed from the commands of his lips; I have treasured the words of his mouth more than my daily bread."
- James 5:11 (NIV):

"As you know, we count as blessed those who have persevered. You have heard of Job's perseverance and have seen what the Lord finally brought about. The Lord is full of compassion and mercy."

These verses reflect Job's resilience, unwavering trust in God, and his refusal to curse God despite the immense suffering he endured. Job's story serves as a powerful example of faith and endurance in the face of adversity.

Key Lessons

The biblical figure Job, from the Book of Job in the Old Testament, provides several valuable lessons on leadership. While Job is often remembered for his patience and endurance through suffering, there are also leadership principles that can be gleaned from his story:

♦ **Resilience and Perseverance:** Job faced immense challenges, including the loss of his wealth, health, and family. Despite these hardships, he remained resilient and persevered through his trials. Leaders can learn from Job's ability to endure difficulties without losing hope or giving up.

♦ **Integrity and Righteousness:** Job was known for his integrity and righteousness. He maintained his faith and moral character even in the face of adversity. Leaders should strive to lead with integrity, making ethical decisions and upholding a powerful sense of morality.

♦ **Humility:** Job demonstrated humility by acknowledging the limits of his understanding and questioning God's ways. Leaders can learn the importance of humility, recognizing that they may not have all the answers and being open to learning from others.

♦ **Faith and Trust:** Job's story is a testament to his faith and trust in God, even in the darkest moments. Leaders can cultivate a sense of faith, whether it be in a higher power, their team, or the vision they are pursuing. Trust is essential for effective leadership.

♦ **Empathy and Compassion:** Job's friends initially came to comfort him but ended up blaming him for his misfortunes. Job, however, showed empathy for others and maintained compassion even in his suffering. Leaders should strive to understand and empathize with the challenges faced by their team members.

♦ **Communication and Transparency:** Job openly expressed his feelings, frustrations, and questions to God. Effective leaders communicate openly with their team, fostering an environment of transparency. This helps build trust and promotes a culture of openness.

♦ **Patience:** Job's patience during his trials is a central theme in the Book of Job. Leaders can benefit from cultivating patience, especially during challenging times. Patience allows leaders to make thoughtful decisions and navigate difficulties with a steady hand.

♦ **Faith in the Face of Uncertainty:** Job faced uncertainty and unanswered questions, yet he maintained his faith. Leaders often encounter ambiguity and unforeseen challenges. Having faith in the vision and mission, even when the path is unclear, can inspire and guide a team through uncertainty.

Leaders can draw inspiration from the biblical story of Job, incorporating these principles into their own leadership style to build resilience, foster integrity, and inspire those they lead.

30 Daily Meditation on Resilience and Perseverance

1. **Proverbs 16:24 - "Gracious words are like a honeycomb, sweetness to the soul and health to the body."**

2. **Proverbs 15:1 - "A gentle answer turns away wrath, but a harsh word stirs up anger."**

3. **Ephesians 4:29 - "Do not let any unwholesome talk come out of your mouths, but only what is helpful for building others up according to their needs, that it may benefit those who listen."**

4. **Proverbs 18:21 - "The tongue has the power of life and death, and those who love it will eat its fruit."**

5. James 1:19 - "My dear brothers and sisters, take note of this: Everyone should be quick to listen, slow to speak and slow to become angry."

6. Proverbs 25:11 - "A word fitly spoken is like apples of gold in settings of silver."

7. Colossians 4:6 - "Let your conversation be always full of grace, seasoned with salt, so that you may know how to answer everyone."

8. Proverbs 12:18 - "The words of the reckless pierce like swords, but the tongue of the wise brings healing."

9. Proverbs 13:3 - "Those who guard their lips preserve their lives, but those who speak rashly will come to ruin."

10. Proverbs 17:27-28 - "The one who has knowledge uses words with restraint, and whoever has understanding is even-tempered. Even fools are thought wise if they keep silent, and discerning if they hold their tongues."

11. Matthew 5:37 - "Let your 'Yes' be 'Yes,' and your 'No,' 'No.' For whatever is more than these is from the evil one."

12. Proverbs 15:4 - "Gentle words are a tree of life; a deceitful tongue crushes the spirit."

13. Ephesians 4:15 - "Instead, speaking the truth in love, we will grow to become in every respect the mature body of him who is the head, that is, Christ."

14. Proverbs 21:23 - "Whoever keeps his mouth, and his tongue keeps himself out of trouble."

15. Matthew 12:36-37 - "But I tell you that everyone will have to give an account on the day of judgment for every empty word they have spoken. For by your words, you will be acquitted, and by your words you will be condemned."

16. Psalm 19:14 - "May these words of my mouth and this meditation of my heart be pleasing in your sight, Lord, my Rock and my Redeemer."

17. Proverbs 16:23 - "The hearts of the wise make their mouths prudent, and their lips promote instruction."

18. Proverbs 20:15 - "Gold there is, and rubies in abundance, but lips that speak knowledge are a rare jewel."

19. James 3:1-12 - (A passage on the power and responsibility of the tongue)

20. Matthew 15:11 - "What goes into someone's mouth does not defile them, but what comes out of their mouth, that is what defiles them."

21. Proverbs 15:28 - "The heart of the righteous weighs its answers, but the mouth of the wicked gushes evil."

22. Ephesians 5:4 - "Nor should there be obscenity, foolish talk or coarse joking, which are out of place, but rather thanksgiving."

23. Proverbs 18:20 - "From the fruit of their mouth a person's stomach is filled; with the harvest of their lips, they are satisfied."

24. Proverbs 25:15 - "Through patience a ruler can be persuaded, and a gentle tongue can break a bone."

25. Proverbs 29:11 - "Fools give full vent to their rage, but the wise bring calm in the end."

26. Proverbs 31:26 - "She speaks with wisdom, and faithful instruction is on her tongue."

27. Proverbs 10:19 - "Sin is not ended by multiplying words, but the prudent hold their tongues."

28. Proverbs 15:2 - "The tongue of the wise adorns knowledge, but the mouth of the fool gushes folly."

29. 1 Peter 3:10 - "For, whoever would love life and see good days must keep their tongue from evil and their lips from deceitful speech."

30. Colossians 3:8 - "But now you must also rid yourselves of all such things as these: anger, rage, malice, slander, and filthy language from your lips."

These verses offer guidance on the power of words, the importance of wise communication, and the impact our speech can have on others.

TEAM BUILDING AND EMPOWERMENT

Team building and empowerment are crucial elements for creating a positive and productive work environment. They contribute to the overall success of an organization by fostering collaboration, boosting morale, and enhancing individual and team performance. Some key aspects to consider when focusing on team building and empowerment include:

♦ **Clear Goals and Objectives:** Ensure that the team understands the organization's overall goals and how their work contributes to these objectives.

♦ **Effective Communication:** Establish open and transparent communication channels within the team. Encourage regular team meetings and ensure everyone has a chance to voice their opinions and concerns.

♦ **Trust Building:** Foster trust among team members by promoting honesty, reliability, and accountability. Trust is the foundation of strong teamwork.

- **Collaboration:** Create opportunities for collaboration and teamwork. Encourage sharing of ideas and expertise to solve problems collectively.

- **Team Building Activities:** Organize team-building activities that are both fun and purposeful. These activities can improve communication, build trust, and strengthen interpersonal relationships.

- **Diversity and Inclusion:** Embrace diversity within the team. A mix of skills, experiences, and perspectives can lead to more creative solutions and better problem-solving.

- **Recognition and Rewards:** Acknowledge and celebrate team achievements. Recognition reinforces positive behavior and motivates team members.

Empowerment:
- **Clear Roles and Responsibilities:** Clearly define roles and responsibilities, ensuring that each team member understands their contribution to the team's success.

- **Autonomy:** Empower team members by giving them a degree of autonomy. This fosters a sense of ownership and responsibility for their work.

- **Skill Development:** Invest in training and development programs to enhance the skills of team members. This not only benefits the individual but also contributes to the overall team competence.

- **Feedback and Coaching:** Provide constructive feedback regularly. Offer coaching and guidance to help team members improve their performance and grow professionally.

◆ **Decision-Making Involvement:** Include team members in decision-making processes when possible. This not only empowers them but also leads to better decisions by tapping into diverse perspectives.

◆ **Resources and Support:** Ensure that the team has the necessary resources, tools, and support to carry out their responsibilities effectively.

◆ **Encourage Innovation:** Foster a culture of innovation by encouraging team members to propose and implement new ideas. Recognize and reward innovative thinking.

◆ **Conflict Resolution:** Provide a framework for resolving conflicts within the team. Addressing conflicts constructively prevents negativity from impacting team dynamics.

By focusing on team building and empowerment, organizations can create a positive and dynamic workplace where individuals are motivated, engaged, and working together toward common goals.

Biblical Foundation for Team Building and Empowerment

The Bible offers numerous principles and examples that can be applied to team building and empowerment within a leadership context. While the Bible is not a modern leadership manual, it contains timeless wisdom that transcends eras and cultures. Here is an exploration of some biblical foundations for team building and empowerment:

◆ **Unity and Diversity:** The Bible emphasizes the importance of unity within diversity. Just as the body has many parts but is one entity (1 Corinthians 12:12-

27), teams are composed of individuals with diverse talents, backgrounds, and perspectives. Effective team building involves recognizing and celebrating these differences while working towards a common goal.

◆ **Servant Leadership**: Jesus Christ's model of leadership is characterized by humility and service. In Mark 10:45, Jesus states, **"For even the Son of Man did not come to be served, but to serve, and to give his life as a ransom for many."** Leaders in the workplace can emulate this by prioritizing the needs of their team members, empowering them to succeed, and providing support and resources for their development.

◆ **Equipping and Empowering Others**: In Ephesians 4:11-12, it is written, **"So Christ himself gave the apostles, the prophets, the evangelists, the pastors and teachers, to equip his people for works of service, so that the body of Christ may be built up."** Effective leaders in teams follow this example by equipping their team members with the necessary skills, resources, and authority to fulfill their roles effectively. Empowering others leads to a sense of ownership, responsibility, and motivation.

◆ **Encouragement and Support**: The Bible encourages believers to **"encourage one another and build each other up" (1 Thessalonians 5:11)**. In a team setting, leaders should provide positive reinforcement, constructive feedback, and emotional support to cultivate a culture of trust, collaboration, and growth.

♦ **Clear Vision and Purpose**: Proverbs 29:18 states, **"Where there is no vision, the people perish."** Effective team building requires a clear vision and purpose that inspire and align team members towards a common objective. Leaders must communicate this vision effectively, ensuring that each team member understands their role in achieving it.

♦ **Conflict Resolution and Reconciliation**: Conflict is inevitable in any team setting, but the Bible provides principles for resolving conflicts peacefully and promoting reconciliation. In Matthew 18:15-17, Jesus outlines a process for addressing grievances within the community of believers. Leaders can apply these principles by promoting open communication, active listening, and seeking mutually beneficial solutions to conflicts.

♦ **Stewardship and Accountability**: In the Parable of the Talents (Matthew 25:14-30), Jesus teaches about stewardship and accountability. Leaders are entrusted with resources, responsibilities, and people, and they are accountable for how they manage them. Team building involves delegating authority, setting clear expectations, and holding team members accountable for their actions and contributions.

♦ **Continuous Learning and Improvement**: The Bible emphasizes the importance of wisdom, knowledge, and continuous learning. Proverbs 1:5 states, **"Let the wise listen and add to their learning, and let the discerning get guidance."** Effective leaders encourage a culture of learning, innovation, and continuous improvement within their teams, fostering creativity, adaptability, and resilience.

In conclusion, the Bible provides a rich foundation for team building and empowerment principles, offering timeless wisdom that can guide leaders in various organizational contexts. By applying these biblical principles, leaders can cultivate healthy, productive teams that glorify God through their unity, service, and stewardship.

The wisdom of selecting and empowering the twelve disciples

The selection and empowerment of the twelve disciples by Jesus Christ is a significant aspect of Christian tradition and has been widely interpreted for its spiritual and symbolic meaning. While interpretations may vary among different Christian denominations, several key themes and lessons can be gleaned from this event:

♦ **Symbolism of Twelve:**

The number twelve holds symbolic significance in the Bible, representing completeness and authority. In the Old Testament, there were twelve tribes of Israel, and in the New Testament, Jesus chose twelve disciples. The selection of twelve disciples mirrored the twelve tribes of Israel, emphasizing the continuity and fulfillment of God's covenant.

♦ **Diverse Backgrounds:**

The disciples came from various backgrounds and professions, such as fishermen, tax collectors, and zealots. This diversity highlights the inclusivity of Jesus' message, showing that His teachings were meant for people from all walks of life. It also serves as a reminder that God can use individuals with different skills and backgrounds to accomplish His purposes.

♦ Training and Empowerment:

Jesus spent considerable time teaching and training His disciples. They were given the opportunity to witness His miracles, hear His parables, and learn the principles of the Kingdom of God. The disciples were empowered by receiving the authority to heal the sick, cast out demons, and preach the message of repentance. This empowerment demonstrated Jesus' trust in them and prepared them for their future mission.

♦ Leadership Development:

The disciples were not only followers but also future leaders of the early Christian community. The training they received under Jesus equipped them to lead and spread the Gospel after His departure. Each disciple had unique strengths and weaknesses, illustrating that God's transformative power can work in individuals with diverse personalities and backgrounds.

♦ Commissioning for a Purpose:

Jesus sent the disciples on a mission to proclaim the Kingdom of God, heal the sick, and cast out demons. This mission emphasized the active participation of believers in spreading the message of salvation. The disciples' commissioning reflects the Christian concept of evangelism and the Great Commission, urging believers to share the good news and make disciples of all nations.

Mark 3:13-19 (New Living Translation):

"Afterward Jesus went up on a mountain and called out the ones he wanted to go with him. And they came to him. Then he appointed twelve of them and called them his apostles. They were to accompany him, and he would send them out to preach, giving them authority to cast out demons."

Luke 6:12-16 (English Standard Version):

"In these days he went out to the mountain to pray, and all night he continued in prayer to God. And when day came, he called his disciples and chose from them twelve, whom he named apostles: Simon, whom he named Peter, and Andrew his brother, and James and John, and Philip, and Bartholomew, and Matthew, and Thomas, and James the son of Alphaeus, and Simon who was called the Zealot, and Judas the son of James, and Judas Iscariot, who became a traitor."

These verses highlight Jesus' deliberate choice of twelve individuals, whom he empowered to carry out specific tasks such as preaching, healing, and casting out demons. The selection of the twelve disciples played a crucial role in the spread of Jesus' teachings and the establishment of the early Christian community.

In summary, the selection and empowerment of the twelve disciples by Jesus symbolize themes of completeness, diversity, training, empowerment, leadership development, and commissioning for a purpose. These aspects contribute to the rich tapestry of Christian theology and serve as lessons for believers on their own spiritual journeys.

30 Days Meditation on unity, teamwork, empowerment, and leadership

1. Ecclesiastes 4:9-10 - "Two are better than one because they have a good return for their labor: If either of them falls down, one can help the other

up. But pity anyone who falls and has no one to help them up."

2. Proverbs 27:17 - "As iron sharpens iron, so one person sharpens another."

3. Philippians 2:3-4 - "Do nothing out of selfish ambition or vain conceit. Rather, in humility value others above yourselves, not looking to your own interests but each of you to the interests of the others."

4. Romans 12:4-5 - "For just as each of us has one body with many members, and these members do not all have the same function, so in Christ, we, though many, form one body, and each member belongs to all the others."

5. 1 Corinthians 12:12-14 - "Just as a body, though one, has many parts, but all its many parts forms one body, so it is with Christ."

6. Proverbs 15:22 - "Plans fail for lack of counsel, but with many advisers, they succeed."

7. Ephesians 4:16 - "From him the whole body, joined and held together by every supporting ligament, grows and builds itself up in love, as each part does its work."

8. Proverbs 11:14 - "For lack of guidance a nation falls, but victory is won through many advisers."

9. Hebrews 10:24-25 - "And let us consider how we may spur one another on toward love and good deeds, not giving up meeting together, as some are in the habit of doing, but encouraging one

another—and all the more as you see the Day approaching."

10. 1 Thessalonians 5:11 - "Therefore encourage one another and build each other up, just as in fact you are doing."

11. Colossians 3:16 - "Let the message of Christ dwell among you richly as you teach and admonish one another with all wisdom through psalms, hymns, and songs from the Spirit, singing to God with gratitude in your hearts."

12. Romans 15:5-6 - "May the God who gives endurance and encouragement give you the same attitude of mind toward each other that Christ Jesus had, so that with one mind and one voice you may glorify the God and Father of our Lord Jesus Christ."

13. 1 Corinthians 3:9 - "For we are co-workers in God's service; you are God's field, God's building."

14. 1 Corinthians 12:20-22 - "As it is, there are many parts, but one body. The eye cannot say to the hand, 'I don't need you!' And the head cannot say to the feet, 'I don't need you!' On the contrary, those parts of the body that seem to be weaker are indispensable."

15. Romans 12:6-8 - "We have different gifts, according to the grace given to each of us. If your gift is prophesying, then prophesy in accordance with your faith; if it is serving, then serve; if it is teaching, then teach; if it is to encourage, then give encouragement; if it is giving, then give

generously; if it is to lead, do it diligently; if it is to show mercy, do it cheerfully."

16. Galatians 6:2 - "Carry each other's burdens, and in this way, you will fulfill the law of Christ."

17. Philippians 2:1-2 - "Therefore if you have any encouragement from being united with Christ, if any comfort from his love, if any common sharing in the Spirit, if any tenderness and compassion, then make my joy complete by being like-minded, having the same love, being one in spirit and of one mind."

18. 1 Peter 4:10-11 - "Each of you should use whatever gift you have received to serve others, as faithful stewards of God's grace in its various forms. If anyone speaks, they should do so as one who speaks the very words of God. If anyone serves, they should do so with the strength God provides, so that in all things God may be praised through Jesus Christ."

19. Proverbs 16:3 - "Commit to the LORD whatever you do, and he will establish your plans."

20. Proverbs 27:9 - "Perfume and incense bring joy to the heart, and the pleasantness of a friend springs from their heartfelt advice."

21. James 3:13 - "Who is wise and understanding among you? Let them show it by their good life, by deeds done in the humility that comes from wisdom."

22. 1 Corinthians 1:10 - "I appeal to you, brothers and sisters, in the name of our Lord Jesus Christ, that

all of you agree with one another in what you say and that there be no divisions among you, but that you be perfectly united in mind and thought."

23. Proverbs 12:15 - "The way of fools seems right to them, but the wise listen to advice."

24. Proverbs 19:20 - "Listen to advice and accept discipline, and at the end, you will be counted among the wise."

25. 1 Thessalonians 5:14 - "And we urge you, brothers and sisters, warn those who are idle and disruptive, encourage the disheartened, help the weak, be patient with everyone."

26. Galatians 6:9-10 - "Let us not become weary in doing good, for at the proper time, we will reap a harvest if we do not give up. Therefore, as we have opportunity, let us do good to all people, especially to those who belong to the family of believers."

27. Proverbs 27:17 - "As iron sharpens iron, so one person sharpens another."

28. Proverbs 15:22 - "Plans fail for lack of counsel, but with many advisers, they succeed."

29. Philippians 4:13 - "I can do all this through him who gives me strength."

30. Matthew 18:20 - "For where two or three gather in my name, there am I with them."

These verses emphasize the importance of unity, humility, mutual support, and the utilization of individual gifts for the greater good, all of which are foundational to effective team building and empowerment.

DECISION-MAKING AND JUDGEMENT

Decision-making and judgment are critical aspects of leadership and play a pivotal role in determining the success of an organization or a team. Effective leaders must be able to make sound decisions, assess situations accurately, and exercise good judgment to navigate complex and dynamic environments. Some key considerations for decision-making and judgment in leadership:

Information Gathering

Leaders should gather relevant and reliable information before making decisions. This involves seeking input from various sources, considering different perspectives, and staying well-informed about industry trends and changes.

Analytical Thinking

Leaders need to critically analyze information, identify patterns, and understand the implications of their decisions.

This involves assessing the potential risks and benefits and considering both short-term and long-term consequences.

Strategic Vision

Decision-making should be aligned with the organization's mission, vision, and strategic goals. Leaders must ensure that their decisions contribute to the overall success and sustainability of the organization.

Decision-Making Models

Some leaders use decision-making models, such as SWOT analysis, cost-benefit analysis, or decision trees, to structure their thinking and ensure a systematic approach to decision-making.

Inclusive Decision-Making

Involving team members in the decision-making process fosters collaboration and can lead to more well-rounded decisions. Leaders should seek input from those with diverse perspectives and expertise.

Decisiveness

Procrastination can lead to missed opportunities or exacerbated problems. Leaders must strike a balance between gathering enough information and making timely decisions to maintain momentum.

Adaptability

Circumstances can change rapidly, and leaders must be adaptable. Being open to adjusting decisions based on new information or changing conditions is a sign of effective leadership.

Emotional Intelligence

Leaders with high emotional intelligence can better understand the emotions of themselves and others, which is crucial for making decisions that consider the human impact and maintain positive team dynamics.

Risk Management

Leaders must assess and manage risks associated with their decisions. This involves understanding the acceptable level of risk for the organization and taking steps to mitigate potential negative outcomes.

Learning from Mistakes

Effective leaders view mistakes as learning opportunities. They reflect on both successful and unsuccessful decisions to continuously improve their judgment and decision-making skills.

Ethical Considerations

Leaders should make decisions based on ethical principles and values. Upholding integrity builds trust among team members and stakeholders.

In summary, effective decision-making and judgment in leadership require a combination of analytical skills, emotional intelligence, strategic thinking, and adaptability. Leaders who can navigate these aspects successfully are more likely to guide their teams and organizations toward sustainable success.

Biblical Foundation for Decision-Making and Judgement

The Bible serves as a foundational guide for decision-making and judgment in leadership, offering timeless principles that have been revered and followed for millennia. From the Old Testament to the New Testament, numerous stories, teachings, and commandments provide insight into effective leadership, decision-making, and judgment. Here is a detailed exploration of the biblical foundation for decision-making and judgment as principles of leadership:

♦ Wisdom Literature:

The Bible contains several books classified as Wisdom Literature, such as Proverbs, Ecclesiastes, and Job. These texts offer profound insights into decision-making, judgment, and leadership principles. Proverbs, in particular, is filled with practical wisdom for leaders, emphasizing the importance of seeking counsel (Proverbs 11:14), exercising discernment (Proverbs 3:5-6), and prioritizing integrity and righteousness (Proverbs 11:3).

♦ Examples of Leadership:

Throughout the Bible, various leaders exemplify both good and bad decision-making and judgment. For instance, King Solomon, renowned for his wisdom, faced a critical decision when two women claimed to be the mother of the same child (1 Kings 3:16-28). His judgment to discern the true mother demonstrated his wisdom and leadership. Conversely, King Saul's impulsive decisions and disobedience to God's commands led to his downfall, highlighting the consequences of poor judgment in leadership (1 Samuel 13:8-14).

♦ **Godly Counsel:**

The Bible emphasizes the importance of seeking godly counsel in decision-making and judgment. Proverbs 15:22 states, **"Plans fail for lack of counsel, but with many advisers, they succeed."** Leaders are encouraged to surround themselves with wise and trustworthy individuals who can provide guidance and perspective in navigating complex situations.

♦ **The Ten Commandments and Moral Principles:**

The Ten Commandments (Exodus 20:1-17) serve as foundational moral guidelines for decision-making and judgment in leadership. These commandments, including directives such as **"You shall not steal"** and **"You shall not bear false witness,"** establish ethical standards that leaders are called to uphold. Additionally, Jesus summarized the commandments into two overarching principles: **loving God and loving others (Matthew 22:37-40),** which further guide decision-making from a moral standpoint.

♦ **Prayer and Seeking God's Will:**

Biblical leaders frequently sought divine guidance through prayer and seeking God's will in decision-making. Jesus Himself exemplified this practice, often retreating to solitary places for prayer and seeking direction from the Father (Luke 5:16). Leaders are encouraged to pray for wisdom (James 1:5) and align their decisions with God's purposes.

♦ **Accountability and Responsibility:**

The Bible emphasizes the accountability and responsibility of leaders for their decisions and actions. Leaders are called to stewardship, managing resources and people entrusted to them with integrity and accountability

(Luke 12:48). Additionally, leaders are warned against arrogance and self-reliance, recognizing their dependence on God's guidance and grace (Proverbs 16:18).

In conclusion, the Bible provides a rich foundation for decision-making and judgment in leadership through its teachings, examples, principles, and moral guidelines. Leaders who integrate these biblical principles into their decision-making processes can cultivate wisdom, integrity, and effectiveness in their leadership roles, ultimately fulfilling their responsibilities with humility and obedience to God's will.

King Solomon's legendary wisdom in judgment

King Solomon is often celebrated for his legendary wisdom, particularly in the context of his renowned judgment in the Bible. The most famous story illustrating his wisdom is the Judgment of Solomon, which is found in the First Book of Kings **(1 Kings 3:16-28).** *Top of Form*
According to the story, two women came to Solomon, each claiming to be the mother of the same baby. They had given birth to their babies within days of each other and were living in the same house. One of the infants had died, and both women were now asserting that the living child was theirs. Unable to determine the true mother based on their conflicting claims, Solomon devised a clever and wise solution.

He proposed to cut the baby in half and give each woman half of the child. One of the women immediately agreed to this proposal, while the other begged Solomon not to harm the baby and instead suggested giving the baby to the other woman. Solomon, recognizing the true mother's selfless love for the child, declared her as the real mother and awarded her custody.

The story is often cited as an example of Solomon's divine wisdom and his ability to discern the deeper truths of human nature. It highlights his clever use of a harsh decision to reveal the genuine mother's love and sacrifice for her child.

In addition to this story, King Solomon is also credited with other displays of wisdom, such as his vast knowledge, writings (including the Book of Proverbs, Ecclesiastes, and Song of Solomon), and his reputation for resolving disputes and providing wise counsel to his subjects. The biblical accounts emphasize Solomon's wisdom as a gift from God, granted to him when he famously asked for wisdom to govern the people effectively (1 Kings 3:5-14).

Other Leadership Lessons from Solomon

Some leadership lessons drawn from King Solomon's experiences:

♦ **Listening and Empathy:** Solomon's ability to listen and understand the concerns of the people was evident in his judgments. Leaders should listen to their team, empathize with their struggles, and consider diverse perspectives before making decisions.

♦ **Building Alliances:** Solomon's strategic alliances, including his marriage to the daughter of Pharaoh and his partnerships with neighboring kings, helped establish stability and prosperity in his kingdom. Leaders should recognize the importance of building positive relationships and alliances, both internally and externally.

♦ **Effective Communication:** Solomon's communication skills were crucial in maintaining order and unity. Leaders should strive for clarity and effective communication to ensure that their vision and expectations are understood by all members of the organization.

♦ **Innovation and Infrastructure:** Solomon's construction projects, such as the building of the Temple in Jerusalem, highlighted his commitment to innovation and infrastructure development. Leaders should invest in the long-term growth and stability of their organizations, implementing innovative solutions and building a solid foundation.

♦ **Financial Management:** Solomon's reign was marked by economic prosperity. Leaders can learn from his emphasis on financial management and the importance of wise stewardship in ensuring the sustainability and success of their organizations.

♦ **Humility and Gratitude:** Despite his wisdom and wealth, Solomon acknowledged his dependence on God and expressed gratitude. Leaders should remain humble, recognizing the contributions of others and expressing gratitude for the support and resources that contribute to their success.

♦ **Long-Term Vision:** Solomon's focus on long-term vision is evident in his efforts to secure peace and prosperity for his kingdom. Leaders should adopt a forward-thinking approach, considering the future impact of their decisions and actions.

♦ **Crisis Management:** Solomon faced various challenges during his reign, including internal conflicts and external threats. Leaders should be adept at crisis management, staying calm under pressure and making well-informed decisions to navigate challenging situations.

♦ **Legacy and Succession Planning:** Solomon's efforts in building the Temple and organizing the kingdom contributed to his legacy. Leaders should engage in succession planning and work towards leaving a positive and enduring impact on their organizations.

While King Solomon's experiences are rooted in a historical and religious context, the leadership lessons derived from them can be applicable and valuable for leaders in various contemporary settings.

King Saul Decision-Making and Judgement

King Saul, a prominent figure in the biblical narrative, serves as a compelling example of decision-making and judgment in leadership. His story, as depicted in the Old Testament of the Bible, offers valuable insights into the complexities and challenges of leadership, particularly in contexts of uncertainty, pressure, and moral dilemmas.

♦ **Background of King Saul:**

Saul was the first king of Israel, chosen by God through the prophet Samuel. His reign marked a significant transition in Israel's governance, shifting from a loose confederation of tribes led by judges to a centralized monarchy. Saul was from the tribe of Benjamin and was described as tall, handsome, and initially humble.

♦ Decision-Making in Early Reign:

Saul's early decisions as king portrayed prudence and wisdom. For instance, when faced with the threat of Nahash the Ammonite, who intended to gouge out the right eye of the inhabitants of Jabesh-Gilead, Saul demonstrated decisive leadership by rallying the Israelites to defeat Nahash and deliver the besieged city (1 Samuel 11).

♦ Mistakes and Judgment:

Despite his early successes, Saul's leadership was marred by moments of impatience, disobedience, and flawed judgment. One significant instance is his handling of the situation before a battle with the Philistines. Saul, anxious due to the delay of Samuel's arrival for offering sacrifices, took matters into his own hands and performed the sacrifice himself, a role reserved for Samuel as the prophet. This impulsive action reflected Saul's lack of trust in God's timing and authority (1 Samuel 13).

♦ Overlooked Instructions:

Another critical lapse in judgment occurred when Saul was instructed by Samuel, under divine guidance, to destroy the Amalekites and all their possessions as punishment for their past atrocities against Israel. However, Saul spared King Agag and the best of the livestock, justifying his actions by intending to offer sacrifices to God. Samuel rebuked Saul for his disobedience, emphasizing the importance of obedience over religious rituals (1 Samuel 15).

♦ Consequences of Poor Judgment:

Saul's failure to adhere to divine commands had severe consequences. Samuel prophesied that because of his disobedience, God had rejected Saul as king over Israel, signaling the eventual loss of his dynasty and kingdom. Saul's actions not only resulted in personal downfall but also had broader implications for the nation he led.

♦ Psychological and Emotional Struggles:

Saul's decision-making was influenced by his psychological and emotional state. He experienced bouts of jealousy and insecurity, particularly in relation to David, a young warrior who gained popularity and favor among the people. Saul's irrational jealousy led him to pursue David relentlessly, even though David remained loyal and served Saul faithfully.

♦ Legacy and Lessons:

King Saul's leadership legacy is complex. While he demonstrated initial promise and capability, his flawed judgment and moral lapses led to his downfall. His story serves as a cautionary tale about the importance of obedience, humility, and discernment in leadership. Saul's failures highlight the significance of moral integrity, reliance on divine guidance, and accountability in decision-making processes.

In conclusion, King Saul's leadership journey offers a nuanced exploration of decision-making and judgment in leadership, displaying both commendable traits and critical mistakes. His story underscores the timeless principles of humility, obedience, and ethical leadership, which remain relevant for leaders across diverse contexts and epochs.

30 Days Meditation on decision-making and judgment

1. Proverbs 11:14 - "Where there is no guidance, a people fall, but in an abundance of counselors there is safety."

2. Proverbs 15:22 - "Without counsel plans fail, but with many advisers they succeed."

3. Proverbs 16:3 - "Commit your work to the Lord, and your plans will be established."

4. Proverbs 16:9 - "The heart of man plans his way, but the Lord establishes his steps."

5. Proverbs 20:18 - "Plans are established by counsel; by wise guidance wage war."

6. Proverbs 24:6 - "For by wise guidance you can wage your war, and in abundance of counselors there is victory."

7. James 1:5 - "If any of you lacks wisdom, let him ask God, who gives generously to all without reproach, and it will be given him."

8. James 3:17 - "But the wisdom from above is first pure, then peaceable, gentle, open to reason, full of mercy and good fruits, impartial and sincere."

9. Psalm 25:9 - "He leads the humble in what is right, and teaches the humble his way."

10. Psalm 37:5 - "Commit your way to the Lord; trust in him, and he will act."

11. Proverbs 3:5-6 - "Trust in the Lord with all your heart, and do not lean on your own understanding. In all your ways acknowledge him, and he will make straight your paths."

12. Psalm 119:105 - "Your word is a lamp to my feet and a light to my path."

13. Proverbs 2:6 - "For the Lord gives wisdom; from his mouth come knowledge and understanding."

14. Isaiah 30:21 - "And your ears shall hear a word behind you, saying, 'This is the way, walk in it,' when you turn to the right or when you turn to the left."

15. Colossians 3:16 - "Let the word of Christ dwell in you richly, teaching and admonishing one another in all wisdom, singing psalms and hymns and spiritual songs, with thankfulness in your hearts to God."

16. Proverbs 12:15 - "The way of a fool is right in his own eyes, but a wise man listens to advice."

17. Proverbs 19:20 - "Listen to advice and accept instruction, that you may gain wisdom in the future."

18. Proverbs 24:14 - "Know that wisdom is such to your soul; if you find it, there will be a future, and your hope will not be cut off."

19. Matthew 7:24 - "Everyone then who hears these words of mine and does them will be like a wise man who built his house on the rock."

20. Romans 12:2 - "Do not be conformed to this world, but be transformed by the renewal of your mind, that by testing you may discern what is the will of God, what is good and acceptable and perfect."

21. 1 Corinthians 2:16 - "For who has understood the mind of the Lord so as to instruct him? But we have the mind of Christ."

22. Ephesians 5:15-17 - "Look carefully then how you walk, not as unwise but as wise, making the best use of the time, because the days are evil. Therefore, do not be foolish but understand what the will of the Lord is."

23. James 4:13-15 - "Come now, you who say, 'Today or tomorrow we will go into such and such a town and spend a year there and trade and make a profit'— yet you do not know what tomorrow will bring. What is your life? For you are a mist that appears for a little time and then vanishes. Instead you ought to say, 'If the Lord wills, we will live and do this or that.'"

24. Proverbs 21:5 - "The plans of the diligent lead surely to abundance, but everyone who is hasty comes only to poverty."

25. Proverbs 29:18 - "Where there is no prophetic vision the people cast off restraint, but blessed is he who keeps the law."

26. Luke 14:28 - "For which of you, desiring to build a tower, does not first sit down and count the cost, whether he has enough to complete it?"

27. Hebrews 13:7 - "Remember your leaders, those who spoke to you the word of God. Consider the outcome of their way of life, and imitate their faith."

28. Titus 1:7-9 - "For an overseer, as God's steward, must be above reproach. He must not be arrogant or quick-tempered or a drunkard or violent or greedy for gain, but hospitable, a lover of good, self-controlled, upright, holy, and disciplined. He must hold firm to the trustworthy word as taught so that he may be able to give instruction in sound doctrine and rebuke those who contradict it.

29. 1 Peter 5:2-3 - "Shepherd the flock of God that is among you, exercising oversight, not under compulsion, but willingly, as God would have you; not for shameful gain, but eagerly; not domineering over those in your charge, but being examples to the flock."

30. Ecclesiastes 8:6 - "For there is a time and a way for everything, although man's trouble lies heavy on him."

These verses emphasize seeking wisdom, trusting in God's guidance, seeking counsel, and exercising discernment in decision-making, all crucial qualities for effective leadership.

ADAPTATION AND CHANGE

Adaptation and change in leadership are crucial aspects in today's dynamic and fast-paced business environment. Leaders must be able to navigate through uncertainties, embrace innovation, and respond effectively to evolving challenges. Some key considerations regarding adaptation and change in leadership are:

◆ **Continuous Learning:**

Effective leaders embrace a mindset of continuous learning. They stay informed about industry trends, technological advancements, and management best practices. Engaging in ongoing education and professional development helps leaders acquire new skills and knowledge, enabling them to adapt to changing circumstances.

◆ **Agility and Flexibility:**

Leaders need to be agile and flexible in their approach. This involves being open to new ideas, adjusting strategies when necessary, and quickly responding to emerging opportunities or threats. Adaptable leaders encourage a culture of flexibility within their teams, fostering an environment where change is seen as an opportunity rather than a threat.

♦ Effective Communication:

Transparent and open communication is essential during times of change. Leaders must communicate the reasons for change, the vision for the future, and how individuals and teams fit into the broader picture. Actively seeking feedback and maintaining a two-way communication channel helps leaders understand concerns and address potential resistance.

♦ Building a Resilient Team:

Leaders play a crucial role in building resilient teams that can thrive in the face of change. This involves developing a culture of adaptability and resilience, where team members are encouraged to learn from setbacks and view challenges as learning opportunities. Providing support and resources for skill development helps team members adapt to new technologies and methodologies.

♦ Strategic Vision:

Successful leaders have a clear strategic vision that guides their decision-making. This vision serves as a roadmap for the organization and helps align efforts during times of change. Leaders should be able to articulate the purpose and direction of the organization, ensuring that everyone understands the long-term goals and objectives.

♦ Innovation and Creativity:

Leaders should foster a culture of innovation and creativity within their organizations. This involves encouraging employees to think creatively, experiment with innovative ideas, and contribute to the evolution of products, processes, and services. Creating an environment where calculated risks are accepted can lead to breakthroughs and a more adaptable organization.

♦ **Leading by Example:**

Leaders must lead by example, demonstrating the behaviors and attitudes they expect from their teams. If leaders exhibit a positive attitude towards change, it is more likely that their teams will follow suit. Modeling adaptability, resilience, and a willingness to learn sets the tone for the entire organization.

♦ **Data-Driven Decision Making:**

Utilizing data to inform decision-making is crucial in an adaptive leadership approach. Leaders should leverage data analytics and insights to make informed choices and monitor the effectiveness of strategies. Regularly reviewing performance metrics and adjusting courses based on data helps leaders stay ahead of challenges and capitalize on opportunities.

In conclusion, effective leaders must be adaptable, forward-thinking, and capable of leading their teams through change. By fostering a culture of continuous learning, agility, and innovation, leaders can position their organizations for long-term success in an ever-evolving business landscape.

Biblical Foundation for Adaptation and Change

Leading with adaptation and change is a concept that can be observed throughout the Bible, as leaders faced various challenges and circumstances that required them to adapt their strategies and embrace change to fulfill their missions. Here are some examples:

♦ **Moses:**

One of the most prominent leaders in the Bible, Moses led the Israelites out of slavery in Egypt. Throughout their journey in the wilderness, Moses encountered numerous situations that demanded adaptation and change. For instance, when the Israelites complained about the lack of water, Moses followed God's instructions to strike a rock, bringing forth water for the people to drink (**Exodus 17:1-7**). This event demonstrates Moses' ability to adapt to the circumstances and find solutions to meet the needs of his followers.

♦ **David:**

As a young shepherd boy, David was anointed by Samuel to be the future king of Israel. However, David's path to kingship was filled with challenges and obstacles that required him to adapt and change his approach. When facing the giant Goliath, David rejected King Saul's armor and instead opted for his sling and stones, a choice that demonstrated his willingness to rely on his own strengths and methods rather than conforming to traditional expectations (1 Samuel 17).

♦ **Paul:**

Known for his missionary journeys and writings in the New Testament, the apostle Paul exemplifies leadership through adaptation and change. Initially a persecutor of Christians, Paul underwent a radical transformation after encountering Jesus on the road to Damascus. Throughout his ministry, Paul faced opposition, persecution, and changing circumstances, yet he remained steadfast in his commitment to spreading the gospel. He adapted his approach to different audiences, preaching in synagogues, marketplaces, and even addressing the Athenian philosophers on Mars Hill (**Acts 17:16-34**).

♦ Jesus:

The ultimate example of leading with adaptation and change is Jesus Christ himself. In his earthly ministry, Jesus encountered people from all social classes and addressed a wide range of issues. He adapted his teachings to the cultural context of his audience, using parables and metaphors that resonated with them. Jesus also demonstrated flexibility in his methods, performing miracles in numerous ways depending on the situation and the needs of those he encountered.

These examples from the Bible illustrate the importance of leading with adaptation and change. Effective leaders recognize the need to be flexible and responsive to changing circumstances, while remaining grounded in their core values and principles. By following the examples set by biblical figures like Moses, David, Paul, and Jesus, leaders can navigate challenges with wisdom, courage, and humility, fulfilling their purpose and impacting the lives of those they lead.

Joseph

Joseph, a prominent figure in the Bible, provides a compelling example of leadership characterized by adaptability and resilience. His narrative, found primarily in the book of **Genesis (chapters 37-50),** highlights a journey marked by unexpected twists, adversity, and eventual triumph. Through it all, Joseph demonstrates remarkable leadership qualities that are rooted in his ability to adapt to changing circumstances and embrace transformation.

♦ **Vision and Resilience in the Face of Adversity:**

Joseph begins his journey as a dreamer, envisioning his future greatness. However, his brothers' jealousy leads them to sell him into slavery, setting off a chain of events that would test Joseph's resilience. Despite the injustice he faces, Joseph does not lose sight of his dreams or his faith in God. His ability to hold onto his vision in adversity sets the stage for his eventual rise to leadership.

♦ **Adaptability in Different Environments:**

Throughout his life, Joseph finds himself in various environments, each requiring him to adapt and thrive. From being a slave in Potiphar's household to serving as a prisoner in Egypt, Joseph demonstrates versatility and resourcefulness. He excels in whatever role he is given, earning the trust and respect of those around him. His willingness to adapt to different circumstances enables him to navigate the complexities of his journey and eventually emerge as a leader.

♦ **Integrity and Ethical Leadership:**

Even in the face of temptation and injustice, Joseph remains steadfast in his commitment to integrity and ethical conduct. When falsely accused by Potiphar's wife, Joseph chooses to uphold his principles rather than compromise his values. This unwavering integrity earns him favor in the eyes of God and leads to his exaltation to a position of leadership in Egypt.

♦ **Forgiveness and Reconciliation:**

One of the most remarkable displays of Joseph's leadership is his ability to forgive and reconcile with his brothers, who had betrayed him years earlier. Rather than seeking revenge, Joseph extends grace and compassion to his family, recognizing that their actions were part of God's larger plan. His capacity for forgiveness not only demonstrates strength of character but also paves the way for healing and reconciliation within his family.

♦ **Strategic Planning and Crisis Management:**

As a leader in Egypt, Joseph demonstrates astute strategic planning and crisis management skills during times of prosperity and famine. Through his interpretation of Pharaoh's dreams, Joseph predicts seven years of abundance followed by seven years of famine and develops a comprehensive plan to mitigate the impact of the impending crisis. His foresight and proactive approach not only save Egypt from starvation but also position him as a wise and capable leader.

♦ **Empowering Others and Building Trust:**

Joseph's leadership is characterized by his ability to empower others and build trust among his colleagues and subordinates. Whether overseeing the distribution of food during the famine or managing Pharaoh's household affairs, Joseph delegates responsibilities effectively and fosters a culture of collaboration and mutual respect. His inclusive leadership style fosters loyalty and commitment among those he leads.

In summary, Joseph's leadership journey in the Bible serves as a timeless example of leading with adaptation and change. His ability to navigate adversity, adapt to new environments, uphold integrity, and foster forgiveness embodies the qualities of a resilient and visionary leader. Joseph's story continues to inspire individuals across generations, illustrating the transformative power of faith, perseverance, and ethical leadership.

Moses

The story of Moses in the Bible offers profound insights into leadership, adaptation, and change. Moses' journey, as depicted in the Old Testament, highlights his remarkable ability to lead his people through transformative periods while adapting to various challenges and circumstances. Here is a detailed exploration of Moses as a leader who exemplified adaptation and change:

Context of Moses' Leadership:

Moses emerges as a central figure in the Book of Exodus, leading the Israelites out of slavery in Egypt to the Promised Land. His leadership journey begins with his reluctant acceptance of his divine calling at the burning bush, where God commissions him to confront Pharaoh and demand the release of the Israelites.

Adaptation to Circumstances:

♦ **From Prince to Shepherd:** Moses was born into a privileged position as an Egyptian prince but fled to Midian after killing an Egyptian taskmaster. In Midian, he adapted to a vastly different lifestyle, becoming a shepherd. This experience humbled him and equipped him with valuable skills necessary for leading a nomadic people.

♦ **Learning from Jethro:** During his time in Midian, Moses married and worked for Jethro, his father-in-law. Jethro's wisdom and guidance provided Moses with practical leadership lessons, preparing him for the challenges ahead. Moses adapted his leadership style by heeding Jethro's advice to delegate tasks and establish a system of governance among the Israelites.

Leading Through Change:

♦ **Navigating Resistance:** Moses faced resistance from both Pharaoh and his own people. Despite the Israelites' initial skepticism, Moses persevered, convincing them to trust in God's plan for their deliverance. His unwavering faith and determination inspired confidence and unity among the Israelites during times of uncertainty.

♦ **Managing Crisis:** Throughout the Exodus journey, Moses encountered numerous crises, including scarcity of resources, internal discord, and external threats. His ability to remain calm under pressure and seek divine guidance enabled him to lead the Israelites through these challenges. Whether parting the Red Sea or providing manna from heaven, Moses demonstrated resourcefulness and resilience in the face of adversity.

Embracing Transformation:

♦ **Receiving the Law:** At Mount Sinai, Moses received the Ten Commandments and other laws that would govern the Israelites' conduct. As the mediator between God and his people, Moses facilitated a transformative covenant, guiding the Israelites toward spiritual renewal and moral accountability.

♦ **Passing the Baton:** Despite his pivotal role, Moses knew that he would not lead the Israelites into the Promised Land. His acceptance of this reality and his anointing of Joshua as his successor exemplify humility and foresight. By gracefully transitioning leadership, Moses ensured continuity and stability for the Israelites' future.

Leadership Lessons from Moses:

♦ **Adaptability:** Moses' willingness to adapt to changing circumstances and embrace new roles underscores the importance of flexibility in leadership.

♦ **Courage:** Despite facing formidable challenges, Moses remained steadfast in his convictions and confronted adversity with courage and conviction.

♦ **Vision:** Moses' vision of a Promised Land guided his leadership, inspiring hope, and perseverance among the Israelites.

♦ **Humility:** Despite his remarkable achievements, Moses remained humble, recognizing his dependence on God's guidance and the support of others.

Conclusion:

Moses' leadership exemplifies the power of adaptation and change in navigating complex and uncertain environments. His journey from reluctant shepherd to revered prophet offers timeless lessons for leaders across diverse contexts. By embracing transformation, navigating resistance, and leading with vision and humility, Moses demonstrated the enduring qualities of effective leadership in the face of adversity.

David

David, one of the most iconic figures in biblical history, offers a compelling narrative of leadership characterized by adaptation and change. From his humble beginnings as a shepherd boy to his reign as king of Israel, David's journey is replete with challenges, victories, and transformative experiences that highlight his ability to lead amidst changing circumstances.

David's Early Years: Adaptation in the Face of Adversity

David's story begins with his anointment by the prophet Samuel as the future king of Israel while he was still a young shepherd. Despite his youth and lack of experience, David displays remarkable adaptability when he faces Goliath, the giant Philistine warrior. Instead of conforming to conventional expectations of warfare, David adapts his approach by using a sling and stones, demonstrating ingenuity and courage in the face of overwhelming odds.

Leadership Amidst Peril and Betrayal

As David rises to prominence, he faces numerous challenges, including persecution by King Saul, who sees him as a threat to his reign. Forced to flee for his life, David finds refuge in the wilderness, where he gathers a band of loyal followers. In this hostile environment, David's leadership is tested as he navigates shifting alliances and scarce resources, demonstrating resilience and strategic acumen.

The Dynamics of Change: David's Ascension to the Throne

Despite Saul's relentless pursuit, David refrains from taking matters into his own hands, respecting the established order and God's timing. When Saul is eventually killed in battle, David mourns his death, exemplifying humility, and respect for authority even in the face of personal vindication. This transition of power underscores David's willingness to adapt to changing circumstances while upholding moral integrity.

Reigning with Wisdom and Flexibility

As king, David's leadership was characterized by both triumphs and tribulations. He expands Israel's territory through military conquests, establishes Jerusalem as the capital, and brings the Ark of the Covenant into the city, symbolizing the spiritual unity of the nation. However, David also grapples with personal failings, such as his affair with Bathsheba and the subsequent murder of her husband, Uriah. Despite these moral lapses, David demonstrates the capacity for repentance and growth, acknowledging his wrongdoing and seeking reconciliation with God.

Legacy of Adaptation and Change

David's legacy endures not only for his military prowess and political achievements but also for his ability to adapt to changing circumstances with humility, courage, and resilience. His story serves as a timeless example of leadership characterized by moral integrity, strategic flexibility, and a willingness to embrace transformation. Whether facing giants on the battlefield or navigating the complexities of governance, David's journey inspires leaders to lead with adaptability and change, guided by principles of righteousness and humility.

Paul

The story of Paul in the Bible provides numerous insights into leadership, particularly in the context of adaptation and change. Paul, originally known as Saul of Tarsus, underwent a profound transformation from a persecutor of Christians to one of the most influential figures in the early Christian church. His journey exemplifies principles of adaptive leadership, resilience, and the ability to embrace change.

♦ **Adaptability in Purpose**:

Paul's encounter with Jesus on the road to Damascus (Acts 9:1-19) marks a pivotal moment of change in his life. Prior to this event, Paul zealously persecuted Christians, believing he was serving God. However, his encounter with Christ led to a radical shift in his purpose. He adapted his understanding of his mission, recognizing that his previous actions were misguided. This adaptability in purpose allowed him to embrace a new direction and become a key advocate for Christianity.

♦ **Flexibility in Methods**:

Throughout his missionary journeys, Paul encountered diverse cultures, beliefs, and challenges. His approach to spreading the Gospel demonstrates a remarkable flexibility in methods. He adapted his preaching style, language, and strategies to effectively communicate with different audiences. For example, in Athens (Acts 17:16-34), he engaged with the philosophical and cultural context of the Athenians, using their own religious references to introduce them to the Christian faith. This ability to adapt his methods enabled Paul to effectively connect with diverse communities and spread the message of Christianity across various regions.

◆ **Resilience in Adversity**:

Paul faced numerous trials and hardships in his ministry, including persecution, imprisonment, and opposition from both Jewish authorities and Roman officials. Despite these challenges, he remained steadfast in his faith and commitment to his mission. His resilience in adversity serves as a powerful example of perseverance and determination in the face of obstacles. Instead of being deterred by setbacks, Paul used them as opportunities for growth and continued to proclaim the Gospel with unwavering resolve.

◆ **Embracing Change**:

Paul's leadership was characterized by a willingness to embrace change and adapt to new circumstances. He recognized the importance of contextualizing the Gospel message to diverse cultural and social contexts, rather than rigidly adhering to traditional practices. This adaptability enabled the early Christian church to thrive and expand beyond its Jewish roots, welcoming Gentiles into the faith community. Paul's letters, which comprise a sizable portion of the New Testament, reflect his ability to address emerging issues and guide believers through times of change.

In summary, Paul's leadership exemplifies the principles of adaptation and change. His transformative journey, flexibility in methods, resilience in adversity, and willingness to embrace change offer valuable lessons for leaders in navigating complexity and uncertainty. Paul's legacy continues to inspire individuals to lead with courage, adaptability, and a steadfast commitment to their mission.

Jesus Christ

When considering leadership through adaptation and change, the biblical figure of Jesus Christ provides a profound and timeless example. Throughout the New Testament, Jesus demonstrates remarkable adaptability and an ability to navigate change in various contexts. His leadership style, grounded in compassion, humility, and a steadfast commitment to his mission, offers valuable insights for leaders in any era.

♦ Flexibility in Approach:

Jesus exhibited flexibility in his approach to different situations and people. He tailored his teachings and actions to meet the specific needs and circumstances of individuals and communities. For example, in his interactions with the Pharisees, Jesus often engaged in intellectual debate, challenging their rigid interpretations of the law. However, when ministering to the marginalized or the sick, he showed compassion and offered healing without judgment.

♦ Embracing Diversity:

Jesus welcomed diversity and embraced individuals from all social classes. He associated with tax collectors, sinners, and social outcasts, breaking societal norms of his time. His inclusive leadership model transcended boundaries of ethnicity, socio-economic status, and religion, emphasizing the intrinsic value and dignity of every person.

◆ Resilience in the Face of Opposition:

Despite facing considerable opposition from religious authorities and political leaders, Jesus remained steadfast in his mission. He navigated challenges with resilience, responding to adversity with grace and wisdom. Jesus' ability to stay focused on his purpose amidst opposition serves as a powerful example of resilience and determination for leaders facing obstacles.

◆ Empowering Others:

Jesus empowered his disciples and followers to carry on his message and mission. He invested time in mentoring and equipping them for leadership roles, encouraging them to develop their strengths and abilities. Through parables, teachings, and personal example, Jesus instilled values of servanthood, humility, and love, empowering others to become agents of change in their communities.

◆ Leading by Servant Example:

The most profound aspect of Jesus' leadership is his embodiment of servant leadership. He washed the feet of his disciples, demonstrating humility and a willingness to serve others. Jesus challenged conventional notions of power and authority, emphasizing the importance of selflessness and sacrificial love in leadership.

◆ Adaptation to Changing Circumstances:

Jesus displayed remarkable adaptability in response to changing circumstances. He adjusted his ministry approach based on the needs and dynamics of different situations. Whether he was teaching crowds, engaging in one-on-one conversations, or performing miracles, Jesus demonstrated a keen understanding of context and a willingness to adapt his methods accordingly.

♦ **Visionary Leadership**:

Jesus exemplified visionary leadership, articulating a compelling vision of God's kingdom, and inviting others to participate in its realization. His vision was transformative, offering hope, healing, and redemption to a broken world. Jesus' unwavering commitment to his vision inspired countless followers then and continues to do so today.

In summary, the leadership of Jesus Christ embodies adaptability, resilience, empathy, and a servant-hearted approach. His example challenges leaders to embrace change, empower others, and lead with humility and compassion. By following the principles exemplified by Jesus, leaders can navigate complexity, inspire others, and make a positive impact in their spheres of influence.

30 Days Adaptation and Change Meditation

1. Ecclesiastes 3:1 - "To everything there is a season, and a time for every purpose under heaven."

2. Romans 12:2 - "Do not conform to the pattern of this world but be transformed by the renewing of your mind."

3. Isaiah 43:19 - "See, I am doing a new thing! Now it springs up; do you not perceive it? I am making a way in the wilderness and streams in the wasteland."

4. Proverbs 3:5-6 - "Trust in the Lord with all your heart and lean not on your own understanding; in

all your ways submit to him, and he will make your paths straight."

5. Philippians 4:13 - "I can do all things through him who gives me strength."

6. Joshua 1:9 - "Have I not commanded you? Be strong and courageous. Do not be afraid; do not be discouraged, for the Lord your God will be with you wherever you go."

7. 2 Corinthians 5:17 - "Therefore, if anyone is in Christ, the new creation has come: The old has gone, the new is here!"

8. Psalm 32:8 - "I will instruct you and teach you in the way you should go; I will counsel you with my loving eye on you."

9. Romans 8:28 - "And we know that in all things God works for the good of those who love him, who have been called according to his purpose."

10. Proverbs 16:9 - "In their hearts humans plan their course, but the Lord establishes their steps."

11. Isaiah 40:31 - "But those who hope in the Lord will renew their strength. They will soar on wings like eagles; they will run and not grow weary; they will walk and not be faint."

12. Matthew 6:34 - "Therefore do not worry about tomorrow, for tomorrow will worry about itself. Each day has enough trouble of its own."

13. Jeremiah 29:11 - "For I know the plans I have for you," declares the Lord, "plans to prosper you

and not to harm you, plans to give you hope and a future."

14. Psalm 119:105 - "Your word is a lamp for my feet, a light on my path."

15. Proverbs 19:21 - "Many are the plans in a person's heart, but it is the Lord's purpose that prevails."

16. James 1:5 - "If any of you lacks wisdom, you should ask God, who gives generously to all without finding fault, and it will be given to you."

17. Hebrews 13:8 - "Jesus Christ is the same yesterday and today and forever."

18. Ephesians 4:22-24 - "You were taught, with regard to your former way of life, to put off your old self, which is being corrupted by its deceitful desires; to be made new in the attitude of your minds; and to put on the new self, created to be like God in true righteousness and holiness."

19. Romans 15:13 - "May the God of hope fill you with all joy and peace as you trust in him, so that you may overflow with hope by the power of the Holy Spirit."

20. Colossians 3:23-24 - "Whatever you do, work at it with all your heart, as working for the Lord, not for human masters, since you know that you will receive an inheritance from the Lord as a reward. It is the Lord Christ you are serving."

21. Psalm 23:1-3 - "The Lord is my shepherd, I lack nothing. He makes me lie down in green pastures, he leads me beside quiet waters, he

refreshes my soul. He guides me along the right paths for his name's sake."

22. Proverbs 24:14 - "Know also that wisdom is like honey for you: If you find it, there is a future hope for you, and your hope will not be cut off."

23. Matthew 16:24 - "Then Jesus said to his disciples, 'Whoever wants to be my disciple must deny themselves and take up their cross and follow me.'"

24. Isaiah 41:10 - "So do not fear, for I am with you; do not be dismayed, for I am your God. I will strengthen you and help you; I will uphold you with my righteous right hand."

25. Philippians 3:13-14 - "Brothers and sisters, I do not consider myself yet to have taken hold of it. But one thing I do: Forgetting what is behind and straining toward what is ahead, I press on toward the goal to win the prize for which God has called me heavenward in Christ Jesus."

26. 1 Corinthians 10:31 - "So whether you eat or drink or whatever you do, do it all for the glory of God."

27. Galatians 6:9 - "Let us not become weary in doing good, for at the proper time we will reap a harvest if we do not give up."

28. Psalm 37:23-24 - "The Lord makes firm the steps of the one who delights in him; though he may stumble, he will not fall, for the Lord upholds him with his hand."

29. Hebrews 12:1-2 - "Therefore, since we are surrounded by such a great cloud of witnesses, let

us throw off everything that hinders and the sin that so easily entangles. And let us run with perseverance the race marked out for us, fixing our eyes on Jesus, the pioneer and perfecter of faith. For the joy set before him he endured the cross, scorning its shame, and sat down at the right hand of the throne of God."

30. Psalm 119:11 - "I have hidden your word in my heart that I might not sin against you."

CONFLICT RESOLUTION

Conflict resolution is a critical skill for leaders to possess, as conflicts are inevitable in any workplace or team. Effectively addressing and resolving conflicts can foster a positive work environment and improve team productivity. Some strategies and principles for conflict resolution in leadership include:

♦ **Early Intervention:** Address conflicts as soon as they arise. Procrastinating can allow the issue to escalate and become more difficult to resolve.

♦ **Open Communication:** Encourage open and honest communication. Create an environment where team members feel comfortable expressing their concerns without fear of retaliation.

♦ **Active Listening:** Leaders should actively listen to all parties involved in the conflict. This involves giving full attention, paraphrasing to confirm understanding, and asking clarifying questions.

♦ **Empathy:** Try to understand the perspectives and emotions of those involved. Empathy can help build rapport and demonstrate that their concerns are being taken seriously.

♦ **Neutral Mediation:** If appropriate, consider bringing in a neutral third party to mediate the conflict. This could be an HR professional or a trained mediator. Their objectivity can help facilitate a resolution.

♦ **Clarify Expectations:** Ensure that everyone involved has a clear understanding of expectations, roles, and responsibilities. Misunderstandings in these areas can often lead to conflicts.

♦ **Identify Common Goals:** Emphasize shared objectives and goals to remind team members of their common purpose. This can help shift the focus from personal differences to collective success.

♦ **Explore Solutions Collaboratively:** Encourage the parties involved to brainstorm and discuss potential solutions together. This collaborative approach can lead to more sustainable resolutions.

♦ **Establish Ground Rules:** Define acceptable behavior and communication norms within the team. Having clear guidelines can prevent future conflicts and provide a framework for addressing issues when they arise.

♦ **Follow-Up:** After a resolution has been reached, follow up to ensure that the agreed-upon solutions are being implemented. This helps prevent a recurrence of the same conflict.

♦ **Learn from Conflicts:** View conflicts as opportunities for growth and improvement. Analyze the root causes of conflicts to identify systemic issues that may need attention.

♦ **Provide Training:** Equip your team with conflict resolution skills through training programs. This can empower individuals to address and resolve conflicts independently.

Remember that each conflict is unique, and the chosen approach may vary based on the nature of the conflict and the personalities involved. Effective conflict resolution requires a combination of interpersonal skills, emotional intelligence, and a commitment to maintaining a positive team culture.

Biblical Foundation for Conflict Resolution

Conflict resolution in the Bible is a multifaceted topic that encompasses various principles, narratives, and teachings aimed at resolving disputes and fostering reconciliation. Throughout the Old and New Testaments, there are numerous instances where characters face conflicts, and the Bible offers guidance on how to navigate and resolve these conflicts in a manner consistent with God's will. Here, we will explore some key principles and examples of conflict resolution found in the Bible:

♦ **Seeking Peace:**

The Bible emphasizes the importance of seeking peace and reconciliation. In Matthew 5:9, Jesus says, **"Blessed are the peacemakers, for they will be called children of God."** This verse underscores the value of actively working towards resolving conflicts rather than perpetuating discord.

♦ Communication:

Effective communication plays a vital role in resolving conflicts. In Matthew 18:15, Jesus provides a model for conflict resolution within the Christian community: **"If your brother or sister sins, go and point out their fault, just between the two of you. If they listen to you, you have won them over."** This verse highlights the importance of addressing conflicts directly and privately, rather than gossiping or involving others unnecessarily.

♦ Forgiveness:

Forgiveness is central to Christian ethics and is essential for resolving conflicts. Ephesians 4:32 states, **"Be kind and compassionate to one another, forgiving each other, just as in Christ God forgave you."** By extending forgiveness to those who have wronged us, we can break the cycle of retaliation and promote reconciliation.

♦ Humility:

Humility is another key principle in conflict resolution. Proverbs 13:10 states, **"Pride only breeds quarrels, but wisdom is found in those who take advice."** By humbly acknowledging our own faults and limitations, we can approach conflicts with a spirit of openness and receptivity to resolution.

♦ Seeking Mediation:

In cases where conflicts cannot be resolved directly between the parties involved, seeking mediation can be beneficial. In Matthew 18:16, Jesus advises**, "But if they will not listen, take one or two others along, so that 'every matter may be established by the testimony of two or three witnesses."** Mediators can help facilitate communication, foster understanding, and guide parties towards a mutually acceptable resolution.

♦ **Love Your Enemies:**

One of the most challenging teachings on conflict resolution in the Bible is found in Matthew 5:44, where Jesus says, **"But I tell you, love your enemies and pray for those who persecute you."** This radical command challenges believers to respond to conflict with love and compassion rather than hostility or vengeance.

Examples of Conflict Resolution in the Bible

♦ **The Reconciliation of Jacob and Esau:**

In Genesis 32-33, we see the story of Jacob, who had deceived his brother Esau to obtain his birthright and blessing. After many years, Jacob prepares to meet Esau, fearing his anger. However, Esau embraces Jacob with forgiveness and reconciliation, illustrating the power of forgiveness in resolving deep-seated conflicts.

♦ **The Dispute Resolution in Acts 15:**

In Acts 15, the early Christian community faces a conflict regarding whether Gentile converts must be circumcised according to Jewish law. The apostles and elders gather in Jerusalem to discuss the issue, and through open dialogue, prayer, and discernment, they reach a consensus that Gentiles do not need to be circumcised. This example demonstrates the importance of communal discernment and seeking God's guidance in resolving doctrinal disputes.

♦ **Paul's Instructions on Conflict Resolution:**

In several of his letters, the Apostle Paul provides practical guidance on resolving conflicts within the Christian community. For example, in Ephesians 4:25-27, Paul admonishes believers to speak truthfully, avoid sinful anger, and not let the sun go down while still angry, emphasizing the importance of addressing conflicts promptly and constructively.

In conclusion, conflict resolution in the Bible encompasses principles such as seeking peace, effective communication, forgiveness, humility, seeking mediation, and loving one's enemies. Through various narratives and teachings, the Bible offers timeless wisdom on how individuals and communities can navigate conflicts in a manner that honors God and promotes reconciliation.

Abraham and Lot

The conflict between Abraham and Lot in the Bible is a fascinating narrative found in the Book of Genesis, primarily in chapters 13 and 14. This story provides valuable lessons in conflict resolution, negotiation, and maintaining familial harmony.

Abraham (originally named Abram) and Lot were uncle and nephew, respectively. They had journeyed together from Ur of the Chaldeans to Canaan, following God's call to Abraham. As they traveled, both Abraham and Lot accumulated wealth in terms of livestock, servants, and possessions. However, as their herds grew, tensions began to arise due to the limited resources available for grazing.

The pivotal conflict occurred when their herdsmen quarreled over grazing land. The situation had the potential to escalate into a larger dispute that could damage their family relationship. Recognizing the importance of resolving the conflict peacefully, Abraham took the initiative to address the issue directly.

Abraham's approach to conflict resolution can be analyzed in several key steps:

♦ **Initiating Dialogue**: Rather than allowing tensions to simmer or resorting to aggression, Abraham initiated a conversation with Lot. He recognized the need to address the conflict openly and honestly. By communicating directly, Abraham set the stage for constructive dialogue.

♦ **Prioritizing Peace**: Abraham prioritized maintaining peace and unity within the family. He understood the significance of preserving familial bonds over material possessions. This mindset guided his approach to resolving the conflict in a manner that would benefit both parties.

♦ **Offering Options**: Abraham presented Lot with viable options to resolve the conflict. He proposed that they separate and offered Lot the first choice of land. This gesture demonstrated Abraham's willingness to compromise and his commitment to finding a mutually agreeable solution.

♦ **Exercising Humility**: Despite being the elder and patriarch of the family, Abraham approached the conflict with humility. He did not assert his authority or demand his own preferences. Instead, he humbly deferred to Lot and allowed him to make the decision that best suited his needs.

♦ **Trusting God**: Throughout the negotiation process, Abraham demonstrated his trust in God's provision and guidance. He was confident that God would bless him and Lot regardless of the outcome. This faith empowered Abraham to approach the conflict with confidence and grace.

Lot chose the fertile plain of the Jordan Valley, leaving Abraham to dwell in the land of Canaan. Abraham's willingness to prioritize peace, communicate effectively, and seek a mutually beneficial resolution exemplifies timeless principles of conflict resolution.

Furthermore, this narrative serves as a reminder of the importance of humility, trust, and prioritizing relationships over material gain. By following Abraham's example, individuals can navigate conflicts in a manner that promotes understanding, reconciliation, and unity.

Jacob and Esau

The story of Jacob and Esau in the Bible, found primarily in the book of **Genesis (chapters 25-33)**, is a profound example of conflict resolution, forgiveness, and reconciliation between brothers. The narrative begins with the birth of Jacob and Esau, twin sons of Isaac and Rebekah. From their birth, the brothers' lives were marked by rivalry and conflict, culminating in a significant confrontation later in their lives.

♦ **Sibling Rivalry and Deception:**

Jacob and Esau were fraternal twins, but they were vastly different in temperament and interests. Esau was a skilled hunter and favored by his father, Isaac, while Jacob was more inclined towards domestic affairs and was favored by his mother, Rebekah. The conflict escalated when Jacob, with the help of his mother, deceived his blind father, Isaac, into giving him the blessing intended for Esau, which was traditionally reserved for the eldest son. This act of deception fueled Esau's anger and led him to vow revenge against Jacob.

◆ Jacob's Flight and Reconciliation:

Fearing Esau's wrath, Jacob fled to his uncle Laban's house in Haran. During his time there, Jacob experienced his share of trials and blessings, including marrying Laban's daughters and acquiring wealth. After many years, Jacob decided to return to Canaan, his homeland. Aware of the potential danger posed by Esau, he sent messengers ahead to inform Esau of his return and to gauge his brother's disposition.

Learning that Esau was approaching with a large company, Jacob prepared for the encounter with a mixture of fear and anticipation. He divided his family and possessions into two camps, hoping that if one were attacked, the other might escape. In a pivotal moment, Jacob wrestled with a mysterious figure, traditionally interpreted as an angel or manifestation of God. This encounter symbolized Jacob's struggle with his past and his readiness to confront whatever lay ahead.

◆ Reconciliation and Forgiveness:

When Jacob finally met Esau, he bowed down to him seven times, a gesture of humility and respect. This act contrasted sharply with Jacob's earlier deception and symbolized his willingness to reconcile with his brother. Esau's response was unexpected. Instead of seeking revenge, he ran to embrace Jacob, weeping and expressing genuine joy at their reunion. Esau forgave Jacob and refused his brother's extravagant gifts, declaring that he had enough.

The brothers' reconciliation was genuine and heartfelt, marking the end of their long-standing conflict. They parted ways amicably, with Esau returning to his land and Jacob continuing his journey to Canaan.

♦ **Lessons Learned:**

- ♦ The story of Jacob and Esau teaches valuable lessons about conflict resolution, forgiveness, and reconciliation. It illustrates the importance of humility, honesty, and willingness to confront past wrongs in the pursuit of peace.

- ♦ Jacob's transformation from a deceitful schemer to a humble seeker of reconciliation demonstrates the power of repentance and personal growth.

- ♦ Esau's forgiveness and generosity highlight the transformative power of grace and the ability to let go of past hurts.

In summary, the story of Jacob and Esau is a timeless example of conflict resolution and reconciliation. It emphasizes the importance of forgiveness, humility, and reconciliation in resolving familial conflicts and restoring broken relationships.

Joseph and His Brothers

The story of Joseph and his brothers in the Bible, found in the book of Genesis, is a timeless narrative that encapsulates various themes, including conflict resolution, forgiveness, and reconciliation. It provides valuable insights into human nature, family dynamics, and the complexities of resolving conflicts, even in the face of betrayal and adversity.

Overview of the Story:

The narrative begins with Joseph, the favored son of Jacob, who is gifted a coat of many colors by his father, symbolizing his special status within the family. Joseph's brothers become jealous of him due to his favored position, exacerbated by Joseph's dreams that suggest he will one day rule over them. This jealousy leads them to conspire against Joseph.

The brothers plot to kill Joseph but eventually decide to sell him into slavery instead. Joseph is taken to Egypt, where he faces numerous trials and tribulations, including being falsely accused and imprisoned. However, through his unwavering faith and divine intervention, Joseph rises to prominence in Egypt, eventually becoming the second most powerful man in the land, only second to Pharaoh himself.

Meanwhile, a famine strikes the region, leading Joseph's brothers to travel to Egypt in search of food. Unbeknownst to them, they encounter Joseph, who recognizes them but conceals his identity. Through a series of tests and trials, Joseph orchestrates a plan to reunite with his family, revealing himself to his brothers and reconciling with them.

Conflict Resolution Themes:

♦ Forgiveness

Despite the immense betrayal and suffering Joseph endured at the hands of his brothers, he demonstrates remarkable forgiveness. Rather than seeking revenge, Joseph chooses to forgive his brothers, recognizing that their actions were part of a greater divine plan. His ability to let go of past grievances and extend forgiveness is a central theme of the story.

♦ Reconciliation

Joseph's reconciliation with his brothers serves as a powerful example of healing and restoration within fractured relationships. Through open communication, vulnerability, and genuine remorse, Joseph and his brothers can confront their past and move towards reconciliation. Their reunion symbolizes the restoration of familial bonds and the possibility of healing even the deepest wounds.

♦ **Divine Providence**

Throughout the story, divine intervention plays a significant role in shaping events and guiding the characters towards resolution. Despite the brothers' malicious intentions, God works behind the scenes to bring about reconciliation and redemption. Joseph recognizes this divine providence, acknowledging that what his brothers meant for evil, God intended for good.

♦ **Communication and Understanding**

Effective communication and mutual understanding are crucial elements in resolving conflicts. Joseph employs strategic communication techniques to test his brothers' sincerity and assess their remorse. By fostering open dialogue and creating a safe space for honest expression, Joseph facilitates the process of reconciliation and lays the foundation for rebuilding trust.

Lessons and Applications:

The story of Joseph and his brothers offers timeless lessons in conflict resolution and interpersonal relationships:

- ♦ **Forgiveness:** Holding onto grudges and seeking revenge only perpetuates cycles of conflict and suffering. **True healing and resolution often begin with forgiveness and letting go of past hurts.**

- ♦ **Reconciliation:** Rebuilding trust and repairing relationships requires humility, empathy, and a willingness to confront difficult truths. **Reconciliation is a journey that requires effort and commitment from all parties involved.**

♦ **Divine Providence:** Trusting in a higher power and recognizing that adversity can lead to growth and transformation can provide solace and perspective during challenging times.

♦ **Communication:** Effective communication, characterized by honesty, empathy, and active listening, is essential for resolving conflicts and fostering understanding.

In summary, the story of Joseph and his brothers exemplifies the power of forgiveness, reconciliation, and divine intervention in resolving conflicts and healing fractured relationships. It serves as a timeless testament to the human capacity for redemption and the transformative power of love and forgiveness.

David and Saul

The story of David and Saul in the Bible is a gripping narrative of conflict, power struggles, jealousy, and, redemption. It is found primarily in the books of 1 Samuel and 2 Samuel, offering profound insights into the complexities of human relationships and the dynamics of leadership. At its core, the tale of David and Saul exemplifies various methods of conflict resolution and the consequences of different approaches.

Background

Saul was the first king anointed by the prophet Samuel, chosen by God to lead the Israelites. Initially, Saul enjoyed divine favor and military success. However, as his reign progressed, he became increasingly disobedient to God's commands, leading to his eventual rejection by God. David, a young shepherd, enters the scene as a skilled musician summoned to soothe Saul's troubled spirit with his harp playing. David's rise to prominence begins when he slays the Philistine giant Goliath, earning him widespread acclaim and the favor of the people.

Conflict Emergence

The conflict between David and Saul emerges gradually. Saul's jealousy is sparked by the people's praise for David's military victories, which he perceives as a threat to his own kingship. This jealousy festers into deep-seated animosity as Saul repeatedly attempts to kill David out of fear and envy. David, despite being anointed as Saul's successor by Samuel, refuses to harm Saul, acknowledging him as God's chosen king.

Conflict Resolution Attempts:

♦ Evasion and Avoidance

Initially, David attempts to resolve the conflict by evading Saul's attempts on his life. He seeks refuge in the wilderness, hiding in caves and remote areas to escape Saul's pursuit. This strategy allows David to survive immediate threats but fails to address the underlying issues between them.

♦ Direct Confrontation

On multiple occasions, David has opportunities to retaliate against Saul, even having him at his mercy.

However, he refuses to harm Saul, emphasizing his loyalty to God's anointed king. Instead of escalating the conflict through violence, David confronts Saul verbally, appealing to his sense of reason and mercy.

♦ Seeking Mediation

At one point, David's presence is requested by Saul's son, Jonathan, who serves as a mediator between the two. Jonathan tries to reconcile his father Saul with David, recognizing David's innocence and loyalty. Despite Jonathan's efforts, Saul's irrational jealousy persists, leading to further conflict.

♦ Divine Intervention

Throughout the narrative, divine intervention plays a crucial role in shaping the conflict resolution process. God's providence protects David from Saul's schemes and guides him through the turmoil. David consistently acknowledges God's sovereignty over the situation, trusting in divine justice rather than taking matters into his own hands.

Resolution and Lessons Learned

The conflict between David and Saul culminates tragically with Saul's death in battle against the Philistines. Despite Saul's downfall, David mourns his former king, demonstrating forgiveness and compassion. David's refusal to retaliate against Saul, his commitment to integrity, and his reliance on divine guidance led to his vindication and ascension to the throne of Israel.

The story of David and Saul offers several profound lessons in conflict resolution:

♦ **Restraint and Forgiveness:** David's refusal to seek vengeance against Saul highlights the importance of restraint and forgiveness in resolving conflicts. Despite being wronged, David chooses to extend mercy rather than perpetuate the cycle of violence.

♦ **Wisdom and Patience:** David demonstrates wisdom and patience in navigating the complexities of interpersonal conflict. He trusts in God's timing and providence, refusing to take hasty or impulsive actions that could exacerbate the situation.

♦ **Leadership and Humility:** David's leadership qualities shine through his humility and respect for authority, even in the face of injustice. His willingness to submit to God's will and honor Saul's kingship sets a powerful example of ethical leadership.

♦ **Seeking Mediation:** The story underscores the importance of seeking mediation and reconciliation in resolving conflicts. Jonathan's attempts to bridge the gap between David and Saul highlight the potential for dialogue and understanding, even in irreconcilable situations.

The conflict resolution journey of David and Saul serves as timeless narrative rich in moral lessons and profound insights into human nature. It illustrates the transformative power of forgiveness, the importance of ethical leadership, and the enduring value of trust in divine guidance.

Paul and Barnabas

The conflict between Paul and Barnabas, as recorded in the Bible, provides valuable insights into human relationships, leadership dynamics, and the complexities of resolving conflicts within Christian communities. This incident is primarily documented in **Acts 15:36-41**. Paul and Barnabas were both prominent figures in the early Christian church, playing crucial roles in spreading the message of Jesus Christ.

Background

Paul, formerly known as Saul, was a fervent persecutor of Christians until his conversion on the road to Damascus. Barnabas, however, was an early disciple known for his generosity and encouragement within the community (**Acts 4:36-37**). The two came together during Paul's early ministry in Antioch (**Acts 11:25-26**) and later embarked on missionary journeys together, spreading the Gospel across different regions.

♦ **The Dispute**:

The conflict between Paul and Barnabas arose over John Mark, who accompanied them on their first missionary journey but left them midway (**Acts 13:13**). When planning their next journey, Barnabas proposed taking John Mark along again, but Paul objected due to Mark's previous desertion. The disagreement between the two was sharp, leading to a division in their partnership.

♦ **Key Issues**: The conflict highlighted several underlying issues:

- ♦ **Trust**: Paul questioned John Mark's reliability and commitment to the mission, while Barnabas believed in giving him a second chance.

- ♦ **Priorities**: Paul prioritized the effectiveness of the mission and the commitment of fellow workers, while Barnabas emphasized grace and restoration.

159

♦ **Leadership Styles**: Paul tended to be more assertive and focused on the task, whereas Barnabas was known for his compassion and willingness to invest in people.

♦ **Resolution**

Despite their disagreement, the narrative does not end with bitterness or estrangement. Instead, they choose to part ways amicably. Barnabas takes John Mark with him to Cyprus, while Paul selects Silas as his new companion and continues his missionary journey **(Acts 15:39-41)**. This decision allowed both parties to pursue their respective paths while maintaining their commitment to the Gospel.

♦ **Lessons Learned**

♦ **Grace and Forgiveness**: Barnabas exemplified the principle of giving second chances and extending grace, recognizing the potential for growth and redemption in others.

♦ **Pragmatism in Mission**: Paul's decision reflected the necessity of prioritizing the effectiveness of the mission and the reliability of fellow workers, albeit at the cost of personal relationships.

♦ **Diversity in Ministry**: The separation of Paul and Barnabas resulted in the expansion of their missionary efforts, demonstrating that different approaches to ministry can lead to greater impact when pursued separately.

♦ **Continued Impact**

Despite their separation, both Paul and Barnabas continued to play significant roles in the early church, with

Paul's missionary journeys furthering the spread of Christianity, and Barnabas contributing to the growth of believers in Cyprus and beyond.

In conclusion, the conflict between Paul and Barnabas serves as a poignant reminder of the complexities of human relationships and the importance of handling disagreements with grace, humility, and a focus on the overarching mission. Their story provides valuable lessons for Christians navigating conflicts within communities and underscores the possibility of reconciliation and continued service despite differences.

Dispute Resolution Between Jews and Gentiles (Acts 15)

Conflict resolution between Jews and Gentiles regarding circumcision in the Bible is a topic that reflects the tensions and negotiations between diverse cultural and religious groups in the ancient world. Circumcision, a central ritual in Judaism, became a point of contention as early Christian communities, primarily composed of Gentiles, emerged and interacted with Jewish communities.

♦ Background of Circumcision in Judaism:

Circumcision holds significant religious and cultural importance in Judaism, dating back to the covenant between God and Abraham as described in the Book of Genesis **(Genesis 17:9-14).** According to Jewish tradition, circumcision is a symbol of the covenant between God and the Jewish people, marking them as the chosen people.

♦ Early Christian Attitudes:

In the early Christian community, comprised mostly of Gentiles, circumcision became a matter of debate and conflict. While Jewish Christians adhered to circumcision as a continuation of their Jewish identity alongside their faith in Jesus as the Messiah, Gentile converts questioned the necessity of this practice for salvation.

♦ **Scriptural References and Debates**:

The New Testament addresses the issue of circumcision extensively, particularly in the letters of Paul, who played a crucial role in shaping early Christian theology. In his letters, such as Galatians and Romans, Paul argues against the requirement of circumcision for Gentile believers, emphasizing faith in Jesus Christ as the primary criterion for salvation rather than adherence to Jewish laws and customs.

♦ **The Council of Jerusalem**:

Acts 15 describes the Council of Jerusalem, where early Christian leaders convened to address the issue of circumcision and the inclusion of Gentiles in the Christian community. The decision reached at this council, guided by the Holy Spirit according to Christian belief, was that Gentile believers did not need to be circumcised to be saved, but they were expected to abstain from certain practices, such as idolatry, sexual immorality, and consuming blood.

♦ **Continued Tensions and Resolutions**:

Despite the decision of the Council of Jerusalem, tensions between Jewish and Gentile Christians persisted in the early Christian communities. Over time, as Christianity spread beyond Jewish territories and became increasingly Gentile-dominated, the significance of circumcision diminished within the Christian faith.

♦ **Modern Perspectives and Interpretations:**

In contemporary times, the debate over circumcision in religious contexts continues among different denominations of Christianity and between Christians and Jews. While some Christian denominations practice infant baptism as a replacement for circumcision, others view circumcision as a cultural rather than a religious practice. Jewish perspectives affirm circumcision as a fundamental aspect of Jewish identity and covenantal relationship with God.

♦ **Interfaith Dialogue and Understanding:**

In addressing conflicts related to circumcision, interfaith dialogue plays a crucial role in fostering understanding and respect between Jewish and Christian communities. Recognizing the diversity of beliefs and practices within both traditions can lead to mutual appreciation and cooperation while acknowledging historical differences.

In summary, the conflict resolution between Jews and Gentiles regarding circumcision in the Bible reflects a complex interplay of theological, cultural, and historical factors. Through dialogue, interpretation, and mutual respect, communities can navigate these differences while upholding their respective religious identities and traditions.

30 Days Conflict Resolution Meditation

1. **"Blessed are the peacemakers, for they will be called children of God." - Matthew 5:9**

2. **"If it is possible, as far as it depends on you, live at peace with everyone." - Romans 12:18**

3. "Do not repay anyone evil for evil. Be careful to do what is right in the eyes of everyone." - Romans 12:17

4. "A gentle answer turns away wrath, but a harsh word stirs up anger." - Proverbs 15:1

5. "Bearing with one another and, if one has a complaint against another, forgiving each other; as the Lord has forgiven you, so you also must forgive." - Colossians 3:13

6. "Finally, all of you, be like-minded, be sympathetic, love one another, be compassionate and humble." - 1 Peter 3:8

7. "But I tell you, love your enemies and pray for those who persecute you." - Matthew 5:44

8. "And let the peace of Christ rule in your hearts, to which indeed you were called in one body. And be thankful." - Colossians 3:15

9. "If your brother or sister sins, go and point out their fault, just between the two of you. If they listen to you, you have won them over." - Matthew 18:15

10. "Do not let the sun go down while you are still angry." - Ephesians 4:26

11. "Let us therefore make every effort to do what leads to peace and to mutual edification." - Romans 14:19

12. "When a man's ways please the Lord, he makes even his enemies to be at peace with him." - Proverbs 16:7

13. "So, in everything, do to others what you would have them do to you, for this sums up the Law and the Prophets." - Matthew 7:12

14. "A hot-tempered person stirs up conflict, but the one who is patient calms a quarrel." - Proverbs 15:18

15. "Make every effort to keep the unity of the Spirit through the bond of peace." - Ephesians 4:3

16. "Hatred stirs up conflict, but love covers over all wrongs." - Proverbs 10:12

17. "If it is possible, as far as it depends on you, live at peace with everyone." - Romans 12:18

18. Let all bitterness, wrath, anger, clamor, and slander be put away from you, along with all malice. Be kind to one another, tenderhearted, forgiving one another, as God in Christ forgave you." - Ephesians 4:31-32

19. "With all humility and gentleness, with patience, bearing with one another in love." - Ephesians 4:2

20. "Do nothing out of selfish ambition or vain conceit. Rather, in humility value others above yourselves." - Philippians 2:3

21. "The Lord is near to the brokenhearted and saves the crushed in spirit." - Psalm 34:18

22. "Better is open rebuke than hidden love." - Proverbs 27:5

23. "Whoever is slow to anger has great understanding, but he who has a hasty temper exalts folly." - Proverbs 14:29

24. "And the Lord's servant must not be quarrelsome but must be kind to everyone, able to teach, not resentful." - 2 Timothy 2:24

25. "But love your enemies, do good to them, and lend to them without expecting to get anything back. Then your reward will be great, and you will be children of the Most High, because he is kind to the ungrateful and wicked." - Luke 6:35

26. "Do not repay evil for evil or reviling for reviling, but on the contrary, bless, for to this you were called, that you may obtain a blessing." - 1 Peter 3:9

27. "Whoever covers an offense seeks love, but he who repeats a matter separates close friends." - Proverbs 17:9

28. "Strive for peace with everyone, and for the holiness without which no one will see the Lord." - Hebrews 12:14

29. "And above all this put-on love, which binds everything together in perfect harmony." - Colossians 3:14

30. "Let the word of Christ dwell in you richly, teaching and admonishing one another in all wisdom, singing psalms and hymns and spiritual songs, with thankfulness in your hearts to God." - Colossians 3:16

These verses offer timeless wisdom on how to handle conflicts with grace, humility, and love, reflecting the principles taught in the Bible.

LEADING WITH COMPASSION

Leading with compassion is an approach to leadership that emphasizes empathy, understanding, and a genuine concern for the well-being of others. Compassionate leaders prioritize the needs of their team members and create a positive and supportive work environment. Some key principles and practices associated with leading with compassion are:

♦ **Empathy**

Compassionate leaders seek to understand the perspectives, feelings, and challenges of their team members. They listen actively, show genuine interest, and demonstrate that they care about the well-being of others.

♦ **Understanding Individual Needs**

Recognizing that each team member is unique, compassionate leaders take the time to understand the individual needs, strengths, and aspirations of their team members. This allows them to tailor their leadership approach to support each person effectively.

◆ Open Communication

Compassionate leaders foster an open and transparent communication environment. They encourage team members to express their thoughts, concerns, and ideas without fear of judgment. Honest and constructive feedback is valued.

◆ Supporting Personal Growth:

Compassionate leaders are invested in the personal and professional growth of their team members. They provide opportunities for learning and development, mentorship, and skill-building, fostering an environment that encourages continuous improvement.

◆ Work-Life Balance:

Recognizing the importance of work-life balance, compassionate leaders strive to create a culture that supports the well-being of their team members. They understand that a healthy balance leads to increased productivity, creativity, and job satisfaction.

◆ Recognition and Appreciation:

Compassionate leaders acknowledge and appreciate the contributions of their team members. Recognizing achievements, milestones, and hard work helps create a positive and motivating work atmosphere.

◆ Adaptability:

Compassionate leaders are adaptable and responsive to the changing needs of their team. They are willing to adjust their leadership style and strategies based on the circumstances, and they provide support during challenging times.

♦ Inclusive Leadership:

Compassionate leaders promote diversity and inclusion. They create an inclusive environment where everyone feels valued, respected, and able to contribute their unique perspectives.

♦ Conflict Resolution:

When conflicts arise, compassionate leaders address them with empathy and a solution-oriented mindset. They seek to understand the root causes of conflicts and work towards resolutions that benefit the team.

♦ Leading by Example:

Compassionate leaders lead by example, demonstrating the values and behaviors they expect from their team. They model authenticity, integrity, and a commitment to ethical leadership.

In summary, leading with compassion involves cultivating a positive and supportive leadership style that prioritizes the well-being and growth of individuals within the team. This approach not only contributes to a healthier work environment but also enhances team morale, engagement, and overall organizational success.

Biblical Foundation for Leading with Compassion

Leading with compassion is a central theme in the Bible, exemplified by the actions and teachings of various biblical figures, including Jesus Christ. Compassion, in the biblical context, refers to a deep awareness of and sympathy for the suffering of others, coupled with a strong desire to alleviate that suffering. It is a fundamental attribute of God and is repeatedly emphasized as a characteristic to be embodied by

His followers. Here, we will explore this concept in detail, highlighting key examples from the Bible:

Prophetic Call to Compassion:

Throughout the Old Testament, prophets frequently called upon the people to show compassion and justice, especially towards the marginalized and oppressed. For example, Isaiah 58:6-7 emphasizes the importance of breaking the chains of injustice, sharing food with the hungry, and providing shelter for the homeless.

New Testament Apostles

Following Jesus's example, the apostles also emphasized compassion in their teachings and actions. The early Christian community in Acts demonstrated compassion by caring for one another's needs **(Acts 4:32-35)** and reaching out to those in distress.

Paul's Letter's

The apostle Paul, in his letters to various churches, repeatedly stressed the importance of compassion and kindness among believers. For example, in **Colossians 3:12,** he urges them to clothe themselves with compassion, kindness, humility, gentleness, and patience.

In summary, leading with compassion is not just a moral virtue advocated in the Bible; it lies at the heart of Christian faith and practice. The examples provided throughout the biblical narratives serve as timeless reminders of the transformative power of compassion in building a more just, loving, and merciful world.

Jesus Christ: The Ultimate Example

Jesus Christ stands out as the ultimate example of leading with compassion. Throughout the New Testament, numerous accounts depict Jesus demonstrating compassion in various forms:

♦ **Healing the Sick:** Jesus showed compassion by healing the sick and afflicted. In Matthew 14:14, it is written, **"When Jesus landed and saw a large crowd, he had compassion on them and healed their sick."**

♦ **Feeding the Hungry:** In the well-known miracle of feeding the multitude **(Matthew 14:13-21),** Jesus displayed compassion by recognizing the physical needs of the people and providing for them.

♦ **Forgiving Sinners:** Jesus showed compassion not only through physical healing but also by forgiving sins and offering spiritual restoration. One notable example is the story of the woman caught in adultery **(John 8:1-11),** where Jesus responds with mercy and compassion rather than condemnation.

♦ **Teaching and Encouraging:** Jesus's teachings often emphasized compassion, instructing his followers to love one another, care for the needy, and show mercy. The parable of the Good Samaritan (Luke 10:25-37) illustrates the importance of compassion in action.

Leading with compassion is a central theme in the life and teachings of Jesus as depicted in the Bible. Throughout the

New Testament, Jesus exemplifies compassion through his interactions with various individuals, including the marginalized, the sick, the oppressed, and even his adversaries. His compassionate leadership serves as a model for believers and leaders alike, emphasizing the importance of empathy, kindness, and selflessness in guiding and serving others.

One of the most well-known examples of Jesus's compassion is his ministry to the poor and needy. In the Gospel accounts, Jesus frequently demonstrates care and concern for those who are marginalized or suffering. He feeds the hungry, heals the sick, and comforts the downtrodden. One notable instance is the feeding of the five thousand, where Jesus multiplies loaves and fishes to ensure that a large crowd of hungry people is fed (Matthew 14:13-21). This act of compassion not only addresses the physical needs of the people but also symbolizes Jesus's ability to provide abundantly for those who trust in him.

Additionally, Jesus shows compassion towards individuals who are often ostracized or mistreated by society. He interacts with sinners, tax collectors, and other social outcasts, demonstrating acceptance and love rather than judgment. For example, Jesus dines with Zacchaeus, a despised tax collector, and offers him forgiveness and salvation (Luke 19:1-10). Through these actions, Jesus challenges societal norms and teaches that every individual is worthy of compassion and redemption.

Moreover, Jesus's ministry is characterized by his willingness to heal the sick and alleviate suffering. Countless times in the Gospels, we see Jesus healing the blind, the lame, the lepers, and those possessed by demons. His miracles not only highlight his divine power but also underscore his deep compassion for those who are afflicted. In these acts of healing, Jesus not only restores physical health but also offers spiritual wholeness, emphasizing the holistic nature of his compassion.

Furthermore, Jesus's compassion extends even to his adversaries and those who persecute him. On the cross, Jesus prays for forgiveness for those who crucify him, saying, **"Father, forgive them, for they know not what they do"** **(Luke 23:34)**. This act of forgiveness exemplifies the radical extent of Jesus's compassion, as he extends grace and mercy even in the face of extreme suffering and injustice.

In addition to his actions, Jesus also teaches about the importance of compassion through his parables and teachings. In the parable of the Good Samaritan (Luke 10:25-37), Jesus illustrates the concept of compassion through the story of a Samaritan who shows kindness to a wounded stranger, regardless of racial or social barriers. Through this parable, Jesus teaches that compassion knows no bounds and challenges his listeners to do likewise.

The parable of the Good Samaritan

The Parable of the Good Samaritan is a well-known story from the Bible, specifically found in the Gospel of **Luke 10:25-37**. It is a narrative that Jesus uses to illustrate the principle of loving one's neighbor and the concept of compassion.

The parable begins with a legal expert questioning Jesus about the way to inherit eternal life. In response, Jesus prompts the expert to recite the two greatest commandments: to love God with all one's heart, soul, strength, and mind, and to love one is neighbor as oneself. Seeking to justify himself, the expert then asks, **"And who is my neighbor?"**

In reply, Jesus tells the story of a man who is traveling from Jerusalem to Jericho and is attacked by robbers. They strip him of his clothes, beat him, and leave him half-dead by the side of the road. A priest and a Levite, both respected figures in Jewish society, come across the wounded man but pass by without helping. However, a Samaritan, someone traditionally despised by the Jews, stops to help. The Samaritan tends to the man's wounds, puts him on his own donkey, takes him to an inn, and pays for his care.

Through this parable, Jesus challenges the narrow definition of "neighbor" held by the legal expert and emphasizes that one's neighbor is anyone in need, regardless of race, ethnicity, or social status. The Samaritan, who would have been considered an outsider, becomes the exemplar of compassion and mercy. **The lesson is clear: love and compassion should extend beyond familiar boundaries and should be shown to all, especially to those society might overlook or reject.**

In a broader sense, the Parable of the Good Samaritan serves as a timeless reminder for people to lead with compassion, demonstrating kindness and care for others, irrespective of differences. It encourages individuals to break down societal barriers, challenge prejudices, and prioritize empathy in their interactions with those in need.

Overall, the life and teachings of Jesus in the Bible serve as a powerful example of leading with compassion. His ministry to the marginalized, his acts of healing and forgiveness, and his teachings on love and mercy all emphasize the transformative power of compassion in leadership. By following Jesus's example, believers are called to embody compassion in their own lives, leading with empathy, kindness, and selflessness in service to others.

Joseph

Joseph is a prominent figure in the Bible, known for his story of resilience, forgiveness, and, leadership marked by compassion. His narrative is primarily found in the book of Genesis, chapters 37 to 50.

Joseph's Early Life

Joseph was the eleventh son of Jacob and the first son of Rachel. His father favored him, which fueled jealousy among his brothers. The situation worsened when Joseph had dreams of his family bowing down to him, further angering his brothers. In a fit of jealousy, they plotted against him, stripped him of his coat of many colors, and sold him into slavery to a passing caravan.

Slavery and Imprisonment:

Joseph found himself in Egypt, sold to Potiphar, an officer of Pharaoh. Despite the hardships, Joseph's qualities of integrity and hard work shone through, and he rose to a position of trust within Potiphar's household. However, falsely accused by Potiphar's wife, he was unjustly thrown into prison.

Even in prison, Joseph's character and abilities stood out. He interpreted dreams for fellow prisoners, foreshadowing his future role in interpreting Pharaoh's dreams.

Interpretation of Pharaoh's Dreams

Pharaoh had troubling dreams that none of his wise men could interpret. The chief cupbearer, whom Joseph had helped in prison, remembered Joseph's gift of dream interpretation. Joseph was summoned, and he explained that Egypt would experience seven years of abundance followed by seven years of famine. Impressed by Joseph's wisdom, Pharaoh appointed him as second-in-command to manage the upcoming crisis.

Compassion in Leadership

As the famine struck, Joseph's brothers, desperate for food, traveled to Egypt seeking help. They bowed before Joseph, not recognizing him. Despite the wrongs done to him, Joseph harbored no bitterness. His compassion and forgiveness are evident when he revealed his identity, saying, **"Do not be distressed and do not be angry with yourselves for selling me here because it was to save lives that God sent me ahead of you" (Genesis 45:5).**

Joseph's leadership during the famine displayed compassion, as he not only provided for the Egyptians but also ensured the survival of his own family. He reconciled with his brothers and invited them to settle in Egypt, illustrating his ability to lead with empathy and forgiveness.

Legacy of Compassion

Joseph's life is a powerful testament to the transformative power of compassion and forgiveness. Despite facing adversity and betrayal, he maintained his faith and integrity. His leadership in Egypt not only saved lives but also reconciled a broken family.

The story of Joseph serves as a timeless example of how compassion and forgiveness can be powerful tools in leadership, fostering reconciliation and creating a legacy that transcends personal suffering.

King David

King David, one of the most prominent figures in the Bible, is often remembered not only for his military prowess and political leadership but also for his deep compassion and empathy. His story, as depicted in the Old Testament, illustrates how compassion can be a powerful force in leadership, influencing not just individual lives but entire nations.

David's journey begins in the Book of Samuel, where he is introduced as a shepherd boy chosen by God to succeed King Saul as the ruler of Israel. Despite facing numerous trials and tribulations, David's compassion shines through in various instances throughout his life:

♦ Compassion towards Saul

Despite being anointed as the next king, David shows immense respect and compassion towards Saul, his predecessor. Even when Saul becomes jealous and seeks to kill him, David refuses to harm Saul, emphasizing his reverence for God's anointed king.

♦ Friendship with Jonathan

David shares a deep bond of friendship with Jonathan, Saul's son, which is marked by mutual respect, loyalty, and compassion. Their relationship serves as a testament to David's ability to cultivate meaningful connections based on empathy and understanding.

♦ Mercy towards Enemies

David demonstrates compassion even towards his enemies. For instance, when he could kill Saul, he spares his life, unwilling to harm someone whom God had anointed.

Similarly, when he becomes king, he extends mercy to Saul's grandson, Mephibosheth, showing kindness and compassion to the house of Saul.

◆ **Caring for the Vulnerable:**

As king, David exhibits compassion by caring for the vulnerable within his kingdom. He shows kindness to the lame and the blind, as seen in his interactions with Mephibosheth. Additionally, he takes steps to ensure justice and fairness, listening to the grievances of his people and acting with compassion to address their needs.

◆ **Repentance and Forgiveness:**

Despite his flaws and moral failings, David's willingness to acknowledge his mistakes and seek forgiveness demonstrates his compassionate nature. The story of his affair with Bathsheba and the subsequent murder of her husband, Uriah, highlights his capacity for repentance and his reliance on God's mercy.

David's leadership is characterized by a balance of strength and compassion. While he is a formidable warrior and a shrewd political leader, his actions are guided by a deep sense of empathy and concern for others. His example teaches us that **true leadership is not just about power and authority but also about humility, empathy, and compassion.**

In conclusion, King David's life serves as a profound example of leading with compassion. His ability to empathize with others, show mercy to his enemies, and care for the vulnerable highlights the transformative power of compassion in leadership. Through his actions, David leaves a legacy that continues to inspire generations, reminding us of the importance of kindness, forgiveness, and empathy in all aspects of life and leadership.

30 Days Leading with Compassion Meditation Challenge

1. Colossians 3:12 - "Therefore, as God's chosen people, holy and dearly loved, clothe yourselves with compassion, kindness, humility, gentleness and patience."

2. Proverbs 11:25 - "A generous person will prosper; whoever refreshes others will be refreshed."

3. Ephesians 4:32 - "Be kind and compassionate to one another, forgiving each other, just as in Christ God forgave you."

4. Matthew 9:36 - "When he saw the crowds, he had compassion on them, because they were harassed and helpless, like sheep without a shepherd."

5. Psalm 145:9 - "The Lord is good to all; he has compassion on all he has made."

6. Micah 6:8 - "He has shown you, O mortal, what is good. And what does the Lord require of you? To act justly and to love mercy and to walk humbly with your God."

7. Luke 6:36 - "Be merciful, just as your Father is merciful."

8. 1 Peter 3:8 - "Finally, all of you, be like-minded, be sympathetic, love one another, be compassionate and humble."

9. Isaiah 30:18 - "Yet the Lord longs to be gracious to you; therefore, he will rise up to show you compassion. For the Lord is a God of justice. Blessed are all who wait for him!"

10. Romans 12:15 - "Rejoice with those who rejoice; mourn with those who mourn."

11. Zechariah 7:9 - "This is what the Lord Almighty said: 'Administer true justice; show mercy and compassion to one another.'"

12. Galatians 6:2 - "Carry each other's burdens, and in this way, you will fulfill the law of Christ."

13. James 3:17 - "But the wisdom from heaven is first pure; then peace-loving, considerate, submissive, full of mercy and good fruit, impartial and sincere."

14. Psalm 103:13 - "As a father has compassion on his children, so the Lord has compassion on those who fear him."

15. 2 Corinthians 1:3-4 - "Praise be to the God and Father of our Lord Jesus Christ, the Father of compassion and the God of all comfort, who comforts us in all our troubles, so that we can comfort those in any trouble with the comfort we ourselves receive from God."

16. Matthew 5:7 - "Blessed are the merciful, for they will be shown mercy."

17. Ephesians 2:4 - "But because of his great love for us, God, who is rich in mercy, made us alive with Christ even when we were dead in

transgressions—it is by grace you have been saved."

18. Psalm 112:4 - "Even in darkness light dawns for the upright, for those who are gracious and compassionate and righteous."

19. Proverbs 19:17 - "Whoever is kind to the poor lends to the Lord, and he will reward them for what they have done."

20. 2 Corinthians 4:1-2 - "Therefore, since through God's mercy we have this ministry, we do not lose heart. Rather, we have renounced secret and shameful ways; we do not use deception, nor do we distort the word of God. On the contrary, by setting forth the truth plainly we commend ourselves to everyone's conscience in the sight of God."

21. Matthew 14:14 - "When Jesus landed and saw a large crowd, he had compassion on them and healed their sick."

22. Psalm 82:3-4 - "Defend the weak and the fatherless; uphold the cause of the poor and the oppressed. Rescue the weak and the needy; deliver them from the hand of the wicked."

23. Hebrews 4:16 - "Let us then approach God's throne of grace with confidence, so that we may receive mercy and find grace to help us in our time of need."

24. 1 John 3:17 - "If anyone has material possessions and sees a brother or sister in need but has no pity

on them, how can the love of God be in that person?"

25. Luke 10:33-34 - "But a Samaritan, as he traveled, came where the man was; and when he saw him, he took pity on him. He went to him and bandaged his wounds, pouring on oil and wine. Then he put the man on his own donkey, brought him to an inn and took care of him."

26. Romans 9:15 - "For he says to Moses, 'I will have mercy on whom I have mercy, and I will have compassion on whom I have compassion.'"

27. Proverbs 14:31 - "Whoever oppresses the poor shows contempt for their Maker, but whoever is kind to the needy honors God."

28. Matthew 18:27 - "The servant's master took pity on him, cancelled the debt and let him go."

29. Psalm 112:5 - "Good will come to those who are generous and lend freely, who conduct their affairs with justice."

30. Proverbs 21:13 - "Whoever shuts their ears to the cry of the poor will also cry out and not be answered."

LEADING WITH LOVE

Leading with love is a leadership approach that emphasizes compassion, empathy, understanding, and kindness in guiding and managing individuals or teams. It involves prioritizing the well-being and growth of those you lead, fostering an environment of trust, respect, and support.

At its core, leading with love recognizes that people are not just resources to be managed but individuals with emotions, aspirations, and needs. It goes beyond traditional hierarchical structures and focuses on building strong relationships based on care and mutual respect. Here is a detailed exploration of what leading with love entails:

♦ Empathy and Understanding

Leaders who lead with love seek to understand the perspectives, feelings, and challenges of their team members. They actively listen, put themselves in others' shoes, and show genuine concern for their well-being. By empathizing with their struggles and celebrating their successes, leaders create a sense of belonging and trust within the team.

♦ Compassionate Communication

Effective communication is a cornerstone of leading with love. Leaders communicate openly, honestly, and with empathy. They provide feedback constructively, focusing on growth and improvement rather than criticism. Compassionate communication fosters a culture of transparency, where team members feel safe expressing their thoughts and concerns.

♦ Support and Encouragement

Leading with love involves offering support and encouragement to help individuals reach their full potential. Leaders provide resources, guidance, and mentorship, empowering their team members to overcome challenges and achieve their goals. By acknowledging and celebrating their achievements, leaders boost morale and motivation within the team.

♦ Building Trust and Respect

Trust is essential in any relationship, including the relationship between leaders and their team members. Leaders who lead with love prioritize building trust through integrity, consistency, and reliability. They demonstrate respect for everyone's contributions, regardless of their role or position, creating an inclusive and supportive work environment.

♦ Servant Leadership

Leading with love often aligns with the principles of servant leadership, where leaders prioritize serving the needs of others above their own. They focus on empowering and enabling their team members to succeed, rather than exerting authority or control. By serving as role models and advocates for their team, leaders inspire loyalty and commitment.

♦ **Cultivating a Positive Culture**

Leaders who lead with love actively cultivate a positive organizational culture based on kindness, appreciation, and collaboration. They promote teamwork, mutual support, and a sense of community, fostering a workplace where individuals feel valued and motivated to contribute their best efforts.

♦ **Personal Growth and Development**

Leading with love involves investing in the personal growth and development of team members. Leaders encourage continuous learning, provide opportunities for skill-building and advancement, and support individuals in achieving their career aspirations. By investing in their team's growth, leaders not only enhance individual performance but also strengthen the overall capabilities of the organization.

♦ **Resilience and Compassion**

In times of adversity or crisis, leaders who lead with love demonstrate resilience and compassion. They offer reassurance, guidance, and emotional support to help their team navigate challenges and overcome obstacles. By staying grounded in empathy and understanding, leaders foster a sense of unity and solidarity that enables the team to weather difficult times together.

In summary, leading with love is a leadership approach centered on empathy, compassion, and support. By prioritizing the well-being and growth of their team members, leaders create a positive work environment where individuals feel valued, respected, and inspired to achieve their full potential. This approach not only enhances organizational performance but also fosters stronger relationships and a sense of fulfillment among all stakeholders.

Biblical Foundation on Leading with Love

"Leading with love" is a concept deeply rooted in the teachings of the Bible, particularly in the New Testament, where love is emphasized as the foundation of Christian faith and leadership. The Bible teaches that love is not merely an emotion or feeling but an active and sacrificial commitment to the well-being of others. **Leading with love involves displaying compassion, kindness, humility, patience, forgiveness, and selflessness in all interactions and decision-making processes**. Let us explore this concept further:

♦ **The Greatest Commandment**

In the New Testament, Jesus emphasizes the importance of love as the greatest commandment. In Matthew 22:37-39 (NIV), Jesus says, **"'Love the Lord your God with all your heart and with all your soul and with all your mind.' This is the first and greatest commandment. And the second is like it: 'Love your neighbor as yourself.'"** Here, Jesus teaches that love for God and love for others are inseparable and foundational to living a life of faith.

♦ **The Example of Jesus**:

Jesus Christ, as the perfect embodiment of God's love, provides the ultimate example of leading with love. Throughout his ministry, Jesus demonstrated compassion, mercy, and forgiveness towards all people, regardless of their social status, ethnicity, or background. His teachings on servant leadership highlight the importance of humility and self-sacrifice in leadership **(Mark 10:45).**

♦ 1 Corinthians 13: The Way of Love

Often referred to as the "love chapter," 1 Corinthians 13 outlines the characteristics of love. Verses 4-7 (NIV) state, **"Love is patient, love is kind. It does not envy, it does not boast, it is not proud. It does not dishonor others, is not self-seeking, is not easily angered, or keeps no record of wrongs. Love does not delight in evil but rejoices with the truth. It always protects, always trusts, always hopes, always perseveres."** These verses provide a blueprint for how leaders should conduct themselves with love at the forefront of their actions and decisions.

♦ Leading by Serving

Jesus taught his disciples that true greatness comes from serving others. In John 13:14-15 (NIV), Jesus says**, "Now that I, your Lord and Teacher, have washed your feet, you also should wash one another's feet. I have set you an example that you should do as I have done for you."** This act of humility and service exemplifies the essence of leading with love, where leaders prioritize the needs of others over their own desires.

♦ Forgiveness and Reconciliation

Love also encompasses forgiveness and reconciliation. In Matthew 18:21-22 (NIV), Jesus instructs his followers to forgive others not just seven times but seventy-seven times, emphasizing the importance of extending grace and mercy to others, even in the face of repeated offenses. **Leading with love means fostering an environment of** reconciliation and restoration, where conflicts are resolved with compassion and understanding.

♦ **Fruit of the Spirit:**

Galatians 5:22-23 (NIV) lists the fruits of the Spirit, which include **love, joy, peace, patience, kindness, goodness, faithfulness, gentleness, and self-control.** These qualities are essential for effective leadership rooted in love. When leaders are guided by the Holy Spirit, they naturally exhibit these attributes in their interactions with others, fostering unity, harmony, and mutual respect within their communities or organizations.

In conclusion, **leading with love in the Bible is not merely a suggestion but a commandment and a model set forth by Jesus Christ himself.** It involves embodying the selfless, sacrificial, and transformative love that Jesus demonstrated throughout his life and ministry. By prioritizing love in leadership, individuals can inspire, empower, and positively impact those around them, creating environments characterized by grace, compassion, and unity.

Examples of Leading with Love

"Leading with love" can be interpreted as acting with compassion, empathy, and kindness towards others. In the Bible, there are numerous examples of this principle in action. Here are a few:

♦ **The Good Samaritan (Luke 10:25-37)**

In this parable, a man is beaten and left for dead on the side of the road. While a priest and a Levite pass by without helping, a Samaritan stops to assist him, showing mercy and compassion regardless of racial or cultural differences.

♦ Jesus' teachings on love (Matthew 22:37-40)

When asked which commandment is the greatest, Jesus responds by saying, **"Love the Lord your God with all your heart and with all your soul and with all your mind... And... love your neighbor as yourself."** This encapsulates the essence of leading with love, emphasizing love for both God and others.

♦ Forgiveness of sins (Luke 7:36-50)

When a sinful woman washes Jesus' feet with her tears and anoints them with perfume, the Pharisee hosting Jesus questions his identity as a prophet. Jesus responds by illustrating the depth of her love and forgiveness, teaching that those who are forgiven much, love much.

♦ The Prodigal Son (Luke 15:11-32)

This parable illustrates the unconditional love and forgiveness of a father towards his wayward son who squandered his inheritance. Despite the son's mistakes, the father welcomes him back with open arms, demonstrating love and mercy.

♦ Jesus washing the disciples' feet (John 13:1-17)

Before his crucifixion, Jesus humbly washes his disciples' feet, demonstrating servanthood and love. He encourages them to follow his example of serving one another with love and humility.

♦ The Beatitudes (Matthew 5:3-12)

In these teachings, Jesus highlights the qualities of those who are blessed, including the meek, merciful, and peacemakers. These qualities reflect a disposition of leading with love, showing kindness and compassion towards others.

These examples emphasize the importance of leading with love in relationships, interactions, and service to others, reflecting the core teachings of Christianity.

Jesus Teaching on Love

"Leading with Love: Matthew 22:37-40" encapsulates one of the fundamental teachings of Jesus Christ, emphasizing the primacy of love in guiding one's actions and relationships. This passage from the Gospel of Matthew is part of a dialogue between Jesus and a Pharisee who asks him about the greatest commandment in the Law. Jesus responds with a twofold commandment that summarizes the essence of the entire Law:

"Jesus replied: 'Love the Lord your God with all your heart and with all your soul and with all your mind.' This is the first and greatest commandment. And the second is like it: 'Love your neighbor as yourself.' All the Law and the Prophets hang on these two commandments." (Matthew 22:37-40, NIV)

◆ Love for God

The first part of Jesus' response underscores the importance of loving God wholeheartedly. This love is described as comprehensive, involving all aspects of one being—heart, soul, and mind. It signifies a deep, intimate, and sincere devotion to God, acknowledging His supremacy, goodness, and sovereignty over all things. Loving God with all one's heart involves passion and commitment, loving Him with all one's soul involves a profound spiritual connection, and loving Him with all one's mind involves intellectual engagement and understanding of His will and teachings.

♦ Love for Neighbor

The second part of Jesus' response highlights the inseparable connection between loving God and loving others. Jesus instructs his followers not only to love God fervently but also to demonstrate that love by loving their neighbors as themselves. This commandment reflects the principle of treating others with the same care, compassion, and respect that one desires for oneself. It encompasses acts of kindness, empathy, forgiveness, and service towards others, regardless of their background, status, or beliefs. Loving one's neighbor as oneself requires a selfless attitude and a willingness to prioritize the well-being and interests of others.

♦ The Fulfillment of the Law and Prophets

Jesus concludes by asserting that these two commandments encapsulate the entirety of the Law and the Prophets, which constituted the religious and ethical framework for the Jewish people. In other words, all the commandments, teachings, and principles found in the Old Testament scriptures find their ultimate fulfillment and expression in the commandments to love God and love others. Thus, by faithfully adhering to these two overarching principles, individuals fulfill the divine requirements of the Law and honor the prophetic vision of a community characterized by righteousness, justice, and love.

"Leading with Love" based on Matthew 22:37-40, therefore, serves as a guiding principle for Christians in their personal lives, relationships, and interactions with the world. It underscores the transformative power of love in shaping individuals and communities, fostering unity, reconciliation, and the realization of God's kingdom on earth. By prioritizing love for God and love for neighbor, Christians emulate the example of Jesus Christ and participate in the ongoing work of God's redemptive love in the world.

The Good Samaritan

The parable of the Good Samaritan is one of the most well-known and impactful stories in the Bible, found in the Gospel of **Luke 10:25-37.** It is a timeless narrative that transcends religious boundaries, conveying a profound message about compassion, empathy, and the universal call to love one another. At its core, the parable illustrates what it means to lead with love and emphasizes the importance of kindness and generosity towards others, regardless of their background or circumstances.

The story unfolds with a conversation between Jesus and a legal expert who seeks to test him by asking**, "Teacher, what must I do to inherit eternal life?"** Jesus responds by prompting the expert to reflect on the law, to which the expert replies with the dual commandment to love God with all one's heart, soul, strength, and mind, and to love one's neighbor as oneself. Seeking to justify himself, the expert then asks Jesus**, "And who is my neighbor?"**

In response, Jesus tells the parable of the Good Samaritan:

"A man was going down from Jerusalem to Jericho when he was attacked by robbers. They stripped him of his clothes, beat him and went away, leaving him half dead. A priest happened to be going down the same road, and when he saw the man, he passed by on the other side. So too, a Levite, when he came to the place and saw him, passed by on the other side. But a Samaritan, as he traveled, came where the man was; and when he saw him, he took pity on him. He went to him and bandaged his wounds, pouring on oil and wine. Then he put the man on his own donkey, brought him to an inn, and took care of him. The next day he took out two denarii and gave them to the inn-keeper. 'Look after him,' he said, 'and when I return, I will reimburse you for any extra expense you may have.'"

Jesus concludes the parable by asking the legal expert, "Which of these three do you think was a neighbor to the man who fell into the hands of robbers?" The expert responds, "The one who had mercy on him." Jesus then instructs him, **"Go and do likewise."**

The significance of the Good Samaritan parable lies in its profound teachings about love, compassion, and the true meaning of neighborliness. It challenges conventional notions of social boundaries and exposes the innate human tendency to overlook the suffering of others. The Samaritan, traditionally considered an outsider and even despised by the Jewish community, demonstrates exemplary love and mercy by selflessly aiding a stranger in need.

In this parable, Jesus conveys several essential lessons about leading with love:

♦ **Compassion knows no boundaries:** The Samaritan's compassion transcends ethnic and religious divisions. He extends help to a stranger regardless of their background, challenging prejudice, and discrimination.

♦ **Action over ritual:** The priest and the Levite, who represent religious figures, prioritize ritual purity over human compassion. Their failure to act serves as a cautionary tale, emphasizing the importance of practical love over religious formalities.

♦ **Practical love:** The Samaritan's love is not merely sentimental but practical. He tends to the wounded man's needs, providing immediate assistance and ensuring ongoing care, demonstrating that love manifests in tangible actions.

♦ **Self-sacrifice:** The Samaritan sacrifices his time, resources, and comfort to help the injured man. His willingness to inconvenience himself for the sake of another exemplifies the sacrificial nature of love.

♦ **Inclusive love:** The parable challenges listeners to broaden their definition of neighborliness and extend love and compassion to all, irrespective of social status, ethnicity, or religion.

The Good Samaritan parable serves as a powerful reminder of the transformative power of love and the imperative to embody that love through compassionate action. It calls for individuals to transcend self-interest and embrace a lifestyle characterized by empathy, kindness, and generosity. Leading with love, as exemplified by the Samaritan, not only enriches the lives of others but also fosters a more just, compassionate, and interconnected society.

Prodigal Son

The story of the Prodigal Son, found in the Gospel of **Luke 15:11-32**, is one of the most famous parables taught by Jesus Christ. It is narrative rich with symbolism and profound teachings on love, forgiveness, redemption, and the nature of God's relationship with humanity.

The story begins with a man who has two sons. The younger son asks for his inheritance in advance, which his father grants. The younger son then leaves home and squanders his wealth in reckless living, finding himself impoverished and hungry.

Realizing his mistake, the younger son decides to return home, repentant, and willing to serve his father as a hired servant. As he approaches, his father, filled with compassion, runs to greet him, embraces him, and orders a celebration to mark his return.

Meanwhile, the elder son, who has stayed loyal and worked diligently for his father, becomes resentful and refuses to join the celebration. He feels that his years of faithful service have gone unappreciated, while his brother, who squandered his inheritance, is being honored.

The father, seeing the elder son's bitterness, goes out to plead with him. He reassures him of his love and explains that they should celebrate because the lost son has returned, symbolizing repentance and redemption.

Unconditional Love

The central theme of the parable is the unconditional love of the father. Despite the younger son's betrayal and irresponsible behavior, the father's love remains steadfast. His response to his son's return is one of joy and forgiveness, exemplifying the boundless love and mercy of God.

Forgiveness and Redemption

The story illustrates the transformative power of forgiveness and redemption. The younger son, after experiencing the consequences of his actions, humbly returns seeking forgiveness. His father not only welcomes him back but also restores him to his former status as a beloved son. This demonstrates God's willingness to forgive those who repent and turn back to Him.

Compassion and Empathy

The father's compassionate response to his wayward son contrasts with the elder son's lack of empathy. It highlights the importance of compassion and understanding in our relationships with others, especially those who have made mistakes or gone astray.

Gratitude and Humility

The parable also teaches the importance of gratitude and humility. The younger son's realization of his folly leads him to humble himself before his father, acknowledging his need for grace. Likewise, the elder son's self-righteous attitude prevents him from experiencing the joy of reconciliation.

Equality and Inclusion

The father's actions challenge societal norms of the time by treating both sons equally. He emphasizes that both sons are loved and valued, regardless of their differences or past mistakes. This underscores the inclusive nature of God's love, which transcends human judgments and prejudices.

Application in Leadership

♦ Leading with Love

In the context of leadership, the parable encourages leaders to embody love and compassion in their interactions with others. Just as the father in the story demonstrates unwavering love for his sons, effective leaders prioritize empathy, forgiveness, and reconciliation in their relationships with their team members.

♦ Forgiveness and Second Chances

Leaders can also learn from the father's willingness to forgive and offer second chances. Recognizing that people make mistakes, compassionate leaders provide opportunities for growth and redemption, fostering an environment where individuals feel valued and supported.

♦ Building Inclusive Communities

The parable underscores the importance of building inclusive communities where all individuals are embraced and celebrated. Leaders who promote diversity, equity, and inclusion cultivate environments where every member feels accepted and appreciated, regardless of their background or past experiences.

♦ Humility and Servant Leadership

Furthermore, the parable highlights the virtue of humility and servant leadership. Leaders who humbly acknowledge their own imperfections and serve others with love and selflessness inspire loyalty and trust among their followers, fostering a culture of collaboration and mutual respect.

The story of the Prodigal Son serves as a timeless reminder of the transformative power of love, forgiveness, and redemption, offering profound insights for both personal growth and leadership development.

The Beatitude

The Beatitudes, found in the Gospel of Matthew, chapter 5, verses 3 to 12, are a set of teachings by Jesus that outline the qualities and attitudes that characterize those who are truly blessed by God. These teachings are often regarded as some of the most profound and challenging in the entire Bible, encapsulating the essence of Jesus' message of love, humility, and righteousness.

In these verses, Jesus delivers a series of blessings, each beginning with the phrase "Blessed are..." or "Happy are..." depending on the translation. These blessings are not necessarily about earthly prosperity or happiness in the conventional sense; rather, they speak to a deeper, spiritual blessedness that transcends worldly circumstances.

Let us explore each of the Beatitudes in turn:

♦ **Blessed are the poor in spirit, for theirs is the kingdom of heaven.**

This first Beatitude speaks to the virtue of humility and spiritual poverty. It suggests that those who recognize their own spiritual emptiness and dependence on God are the ones who will inherit the kingdom of heaven. It is a call to recognize our need for God's grace rather than relying solely on our own achievements or righteousness.

♦ **Blessed are those who mourn, for they will be comforted.**

Here, Jesus acknowledges the reality of pain and suffering in the world but promises comfort to those who mourn. This Beatitude speaks to the empathy and compassion that characterize the followers of Christ, as well as the hope of divine consolation in times of grief.

♦ **Blessed are the meek, for they will inherit the earth.**

Meekness is often misunderstood as weakness, but in this context, it refers to gentleness, humility, and a lack of arrogance. Jesus teaches that those who are humble and gentle will be exalted, inheriting not just earthly possessions but also spiritual blessings.

♦ **Blessed are those who hunger and thirst for righteousness, for they will be filled.**

This Beatitude emphasizes the importance of seeking righteousness with a passionate and earnest desire. It speaks to the longing for justice, both in personal conduct and in the world at large, and promises fulfillment to those who earnestly pursue it.

♦ **Blessed are the merciful, for they will be shown mercy.**

Mercy lies at the heart of the Christian ethic, and here Jesus highlights its reciprocal nature. Those who show compassion and forgiveness to others will themselves receive mercy from God.

♦ **Blessed are the pure in heart, for they will see God.**

Purity of heart refers to integrity, sincerity, and a single-minded devotion to God. Jesus teaches that those whose hearts are free from deceit and impurity will have a clear vision of God and His will.

♦ **Blessed are the peacemakers, for they will be called children of God.**

Peace is not merely the absence of conflict but the presence of harmony, reconciliation, and justice. Those who actively work towards peace, both in their relationships and in society, are identified as children of God, reflecting His nature as the ultimate peacemaker.

♦ **Blessed are those who are persecuted because of righteousness, for theirs is the kingdom of heaven.**

This final Beatitude acknowledges the reality of suffering and persecution that often accompanies a life committed to righteousness and truth. It reassures believers that their suffering is not in vain and that they will be rewarded in the kingdom of heaven.

Overall, the Beatitudes offer a radical vision of blessedness that challenges conventional wisdom and societal values. They call us to embody qualities such as humility, compassion, and righteousness, and to live in a way that reflects the love and grace of God. Leading with love, as exemplified in the Beatitudes, means embracing these attitudes and values as the foundation of our lives and relationships.

30 Days Challenge of Daily Leading with Love Meditation

1. **1 Corinthians 16:14 - "Let all that you do be done in love."**

2. Ephesians 4:2 - "Be completely humble and gentle; be patient, bearing with one another in love."

3. 1 Peter 4:8 - "Above all, love each other deeply, because love covers over a multitude of sins."

4. Colossians 3:14 - "And over all these virtues put on love, which binds them all together in perfect unity."

5. John 13:34-35 - "A new command I give you: Love one another. As I have loved you, so you must love one another. By this everyone will know that you are my disciples, if you love one another."

6. 1 John 4:7 - "Dear friends, let us love one another, for love comes from God. Everyone who loves has been born of God and knows God."

7. Romans 12:10 - "Be devoted to one another in love. Honor one another above yourselves."

8. Galatians 5:13 - "You, my brothers and sisters, were called to be free. But do not use your freedom to indulge the flesh; rather, serve one another humbly in love."

9. Ephesians 5:2 - "And walk in the way of love, just as Christ loved us and gave himself up for us as a fragrant offering and sacrifice to God."

10. 1 John 4:18 - "There is no fear in love. But perfect love drives out fear, because fear has to do with punishment. The one who fears is not made perfect in love."

11. Proverbs 10:12 - "Hatred stirs up conflict, but love covers over all wrongs."

12. 1 Thessalonians 3:12 - "May the Lord make your love increase and overflow for each other and for everyone else, just as ours does for you."

13. Romans 13:10 - "Love does no harm to a neighbor. Therefore, love is the fulfillment of the law."

14. 1 John 4:16 - "And so we know and rely on the love God has for us. God is love. Whoever lives in love lives in God, and God in them."

15. 1 Corinthians 13:4-8 - "Love is patient, love is kind. It does not envy, it does not boast, it is not proud. It does not dishonor others, it is not self-seeking, it is not easily angered, it keeps no record of wrongs. Love does not delight in evil but rejoices with the truth. It always protects, always trusts, always hopes, always perseveres. Love never fails."

16. 1 John 4:19 - "We love because he first loved us."

17. Romans 5:5 - "And hope does not put us to shame, because God's love has been poured out into our hearts through the Holy Spirit, who has been given to us."

18. 1 Corinthians 16:14 - "Do everything in love."

19. 1 Peter 1:22 - "Now that you have purified yourselves by obeying the truth so that you have sincere love for each other, love one another deeply, from the heart."

20. Hebrews 13:1 - "Keep on loving one another as brothers and sisters."

21. Matthew 5:44 - "But I tell you, love your enemies and pray for those who persecute you."

22. 1 John 4:21 - "And he has given us this command: Anyone who loves God must also love their brother and sister."

23. John 15:12 - "My command is this: Love each other as I have loved you."

24. 1 Corinthians 8:1 - "Now about food sacrificed to idols: We know that "We all possess knowledge." But knowledge puffs up while love builds up."

25. Romans 12:9 - "Love must be sincere. Hate what is evil; cling to what is good."

26. 1 John 3:18 - "Dear children, let us not love with words or speech but with actions and in truth."

27. Ephesians 3:17-19 - "So that Christ may dwell in your hearts through faith. And I pray that you, being rooted and established in love, may have power, together with all the Lord's holy people, to grasp how wide and long and high and deep is the love of Christ, and to know this love that surpasses knowledge—that you may be filled to the measure of all the fullness of God."

28. Philippians 2:2-3 - "Then make my joy complete by being like-minded, having the same love, being one in spirit and of one mind. Do nothing out of selfish ambition or vain conceit. Rather, in humility value others above yourselves."

29. 1 John 4:11 - "Dear friends, since God so loved us, we also ought to love one another."

30. Luke 6:31 - "Do to others as you would have them do to you."

HUMILITY AND SERVANT LEADERSHIP

Humility and servant leadership are interconnected concepts that emphasize the importance of putting others before oneself, serving the needs of others, and fostering a collaborative and supportive environment. While humility is often regarded as a personal trait or characteristic, servant leadership is a leadership philosophy or style that embodies humility and focuses on serving the needs of others.

Humility can be defined as a modest and respectful attitude towards oneself and others. It involves an acknowledgment of one's limitations, strengths, and weaknesses without arrogance or pride.

Humility is a fundamental aspect of servant leadership, as it underpins the servant leader's mindset, values, and behaviors. A servant leader's humility enables them to empathize with others, recognize their own limitations, and prioritize the needs of their followers. By embracing humility, servant leaders foster trust, collaboration, and a sense of purpose within their teams or organizations.

In summary, humility and servant leadership are intertwined concepts that emphasize the importance of self-awareness, empathy, service, and collaboration. Leaders who embody humility and embrace the principles of servant leadership are more likely to inspire and empower others, create a positive work environment, and achieve sustainable success.

Embracing Servant Leadership Principles

Embracing servant leadership principles involves adopting a leadership approach that prioritizes serving others, empowering team members, and fostering a culture of collaboration and growth. This leadership style, popularized by Robert K. Greenleaf in the 1970s, emphasizes the leader's role as a servant to their team rather than a commanding authority. Here is a detailed exploration of what it means to embrace servant leadership principles

♦ Putting Others First

Servant leadership begins with a fundamental shift in focus from self-interest to the well-being and development of others. Leaders who embrace this principle prioritize the needs of their team members above their own ambitions or desires. They actively listen to their team, empathize with their concerns, and work to address their needs.

♦ Empowering and Developing Others

Servant leaders empower their team members to reach their full potential. Instead of micromanaging, they provide guidance, support, and resources to help individuals grow and succeed. This involves delegating authority, encouraging autonomy, and providing opportunities for skill development and career advancement.

♦ Building Trust and Collaboration

Trust is essential in servant leadership. Leaders build trust by demonstrating integrity, transparency, and genuine concern for the well-being of their team. By fostering a culture of openness and collaboration, servant leaders encourage communication, idea-sharing, and teamwork, which leads to higher morale and productivity.

♦ **Servant Leadership in Decision-Making**:

Servant leaders involve their team members in the decision-making process whenever possible. They value diverse perspectives and seek input from those affected by decisions. This inclusive approach not only leads to better decisions but also promotes ownership and accountability among team members.

♦ **Leading by Example**:

Servant leaders lead by example, embodying the values and behaviors they wish to see in their team. They model humility, empathy, and a commitment to service. By demonstrating a willingness to roll up their sleeves and work alongside their team, they inspire trust, respect, and loyalty.

♦ **Caring for the Whole Person**

Servant leadership recognizes that individuals are more than just employees—they are whole persons with personal lives, aspirations, and challenges. Leaders who embrace this principle show genuine concern for the holistic well-being of their team members, supporting them not only professionally but also emotionally and personally when needed.

♦ **Serving the Greater Good**

Servant leaders are driven by a sense of purpose beyond individual or organizational success. They are committed to making a positive difference in the lives of their team members, the organization, and the broader community. By aligning their leadership efforts with a higher purpose, they inspire others to contribute to something meaningful and enduring.

In summary, embracing servant leadership principles involves a shift from traditional hierarchical leadership models to a more inclusive, compassionate, and service-oriented approach. By prioritizing the needs of others, empowering, and developing their team members, building trust and collaboration, involving others in decision-making, leading by example, caring for the whole person, and serving the greater good, servant leaders create environments where individuals thrive, teams excel, and organizations flourish.

Biblical Foundation for Humility and Servant Leadership

Humility and leadership are recurring themes throughout the Bible, with numerous examples of leaders who exemplified humility in their service to God and their people. The Bible teaches that true leadership involves serving others with humility, putting their needs above one's own, and recognizing that all authority comes from God. Let us explore some key examples:

♦ **Moses**: One of the most prominent examples of humility in leadership is Moses. Despite being chosen by God to lead the Israelites out of Egypt and receiving direct communication from God, Moses remained humble. In Numbers 12:3, it is written, "Now Moses was a very humble man, more humble than anyone else on the face of the earth." Despite his unique position of authority, Moses constantly deferred to God's guidance and sought His will above his own desires. One striking example is when Moses interceded on behalf of the rebellious Israelites, even offering to have his name blotted out of God's book if it meant sparing them (Exodus 32:30-32).

♦ **Jesus Christ**: Jesus is the ultimate example of humility in leadership. Though He was the Son of God, He took on the form of a servant and willingly sacrificed Himself for the salvation of humanity. Philippians 2:5-8 beautifully encapsulates this: "In your relationships with one another, have the same mindset as Christ Jesus: Who, being in very nature God, did not consider equality with God something to be used to his own advantage; rather, he made himself nothing by taking the very nature of a servant, being made in human likeness. And being found in appearance as a man, he humbled himself by becoming obedient to death—even death on a cross!" Throughout His ministry, Jesus consistently demonstrated humility by washing the feet of His disciples (John 13:1-17) and teaching that true greatness comes from serving others (Matthew 20:26-28).

♦ **David**: King David, despite his flaws, is often portrayed as a humble leader. He recognized that his strength and success came from God and frequently sought His guidance. In Psalm 18:35, David acknowledges, "You have given me the shield of your salvation, and your right hand supported me, and your gentleness made me great." Despite being anointed king, David endured persecution and exile before assuming the throne, demonstrating patience and trust in God's timing. Additionally, when confronted with his sins, such as his adultery with Bathsheba and the murder of her husband Uriah, David humbly repented and sought God's forgiveness (2 Samuel 12:13; Psalm 51).

◆ **Paul:** The apostle Paul, although a towering figure in early Christianity and responsible for spreading the gospel to the Gentiles, maintained a spirit of humility. In his letters, he often referred to himself as the least of the apostles and the chief of sinners (1 Corinthians 15:9; 1 Timothy 1:15). Despite enduring numerous hardships, including imprisonment and persecution, Paul remained steadfast in his commitment to serving God and others, exemplifying humility in his leadership.

These biblical examples emphasize that true leadership is rooted in humility, service, and a recognition of one's dependence on God. Leaders who emulate these qualities are not driven by self-interest or a desire for power but seek to uplift and serve those under their care, reflecting the character of Christ.

Moses

Humility and leadership are often seen as contradictory traits, but in the case of Moses as depicted in the Bible, they converge in a remarkable way. Moses is a central figure in the Hebrew Bible, revered not only for his role as a prophet and leader but also for his humility. His story offers profound lessons on the relationship between humility and effective leadership.

♦ Background and Early Life:

Moses was born in Egypt during a time when the Israelites were enslaved. Despite being raised as a prince in Pharaoh's household, he identified with his oppressed people. His early life reflects a sense of empathy and connection with those who suffer, a characteristic often associated with humility.

♦ Encounter with God at the Burning Bush:

One of the most iconic moments in Moses' life is his encounter with God at the burning bush (Exodus 3). Despite his initial reluctance and feelings of inadequacy, Moses accepts God's call to lead the Israelites out of Egypt. His humility is evident in his response to God's commission. Instead of boasting about his abilities or seeking glory for himself, Moses expresses doubt in his own capabilities, stating, "Who am I that I should go to Pharaoh and bring the Israelites out of Egypt?" (Exodus 3:11). This humility allows him to be open to God's guidance and direction.

♦ Servant Leadership:

Throughout his leadership of the Israelites, Moses embodies the concept of servant leadership. He prioritizes the needs of his people above his own ambitions or desires. Despite his position of authority, he is approachable and accessible, listening to the concerns of the Israelites and interceding on their behalf. This humility fosters trust and loyalty among his followers, essential qualities for effective leadership.

♦ Intercession for the Israelites:

On multiple occasions, Moses demonstrates humility through his willingness to intercede for the Israelites, even in the face of their disobedience and rebellion. For example, after the incident of the golden calf, when God expresses anger and threatens to destroy the Israelites, Moses pleads for mercy on their behalf (Exodus 32:11-14). His humility allows him to empathize with the shortcomings of his people and act as a mediator between them and God.

♦ **Moses' Final Days**:

In the book of Deuteronomy, as Moses prepares to pass leadership to Joshua and the Israelites prepare to enter the Promised Land, he delivers a series of speeches recounting their journey and emphasizing the importance of obedience to God's commands. Despite his pivotal role in leading the Israelites out of Egypt, Moses humbly acknowledges that he will not accompany them into the Promised Land due to his disobedience at Meribah (Deuteronomy 32:48-52). This act of humility serves as a reminder of the consequences of pride and the importance of obedience.

♦ **Legacy**:

Moses' humility and leadership leave a legacy that extends beyond his lifetime. He is remembered not only as a lawgiver and prophet but also as a humble servant of God. His example continues to inspire leaders in various fields to prioritize humility, empathy, and service to others.

In conclusion, Moses' story in the Bible illustrates the profound connection between humility and effective leadership. His willingness to put the needs of others before his own, his openness to God's guidance, and his humility in acknowledging his limitations all contribute to his remarkable legacy as a leader. Through his example, Moses teaches us that true greatness lies not in power or prestige but in service and humility.

Jesus Christ

Leading with humility is a profound concept deeply rooted in the teachings and life of Jesus Christ as portrayed in the Bible. Throughout the New Testament, Jesus exemplifies humility in his actions, words, and interactions with others, offering invaluable lessons on servant leadership and the virtues of humility.

♦ Servant Leadership:

Jesus introduced a revolutionary model of leadership that prioritized service over authority. In Matthew 20:28, Jesus said, **"the Son of Man came not to be served but to serve, and to give his life as a ransom for many."** This statement encapsulates his entire ministry, emphasizing the importance of selflessly serving others. He demonstrated this through acts such as washing the feet of his disciples (John 13:1-17), a task typically reserved for servants, to illustrate the humility and servitude expected of his followers.

♦ Leading by Example:

Jesus did not just preach humility; he embodied it in his own life. Despite being the Son of God, he chose a humble birth, born in a manger in Bethlehem, and lived a life of simplicity and modesty. He associated with the marginalized, including tax collectors, sinners, and the poor, demonstrating his compassion and humility. By living among the people, he served, Jesus showed that leadership is not about exalting oneself but lifting others up.

♦ Teaching Through Parables:

Jesus often used parables to convey profound truths about humility and leadership. The Parable of the Good

Samaritan (Luke 10:25-37), for instance, highlights the importance of compassion and selflessness. The Samaritan, despite social and religious differences, humbly assists a stranger in need, illustrating that true leadership involves caring for others without regard for personal gain or recognition.

♦ **Resisting Temptation:**

Jesus faced numerous temptations throughout his ministry, including the temptation for power and recognition. In the wilderness (Matthew 4:1-11), Satan tempted Jesus to assert his authority and demonstrate his divinity through miracles. However, Jesus rejected these temptations, choosing instead to remain obedient to God's will and serve humbly. His example teaches that humility involves resisting the allure of pride and worldly acclaim.

♦ **Sacrificial Love:**

The pinnacle of Jesus' humility is seen in his sacrificial death on the cross. Despite being innocent, he willingly endured humiliation, torture, and death to redeem humanity from sin. In Philippians 2:5-8, the apostle Paul writes, "Have this mind among yourselves, which is yours in Christ Jesus, who, though he was in the form of God, did not count equality with God a thing to be grasped, but emptied himself, by taking the form of a servant, being born in the likeness of men. And being found in human form, he humbled himself by becoming obedient to the point of death, even death on a cross." Jesus' ultimate act of humility and love serves as a powerful example for leaders, reminding them of the importance of self-sacrifice and putting the needs of others before their own.

In summary, Jesus Christ's life and teachings in the Bible offer a profound blueprint for leading with humility. By embodying servant leadership, leading by example, teaching through parables, resisting temptation, and demonstrating sacrificial love, Jesus exemplifies humility as the cornerstone of effective and virtuous leadership. His legacy continues to inspire countless individuals to lead with humility, compassion, and selflessness.

Washing the disciples' feet: A lesson in humility from Jesus

Washing the disciples' feet is a significant event in the New Testament, found in the Gospel of John, chapter 13, verses 1-17. This episode demonstrates a profound lesson in humility taught by Jesus Christ to his disciples during the Last Supper.

♦ Setting the Scene:

The event takes place just before the Passover festival, a significant Jewish holiday commemorating the liberation of the Israelites from slavery in Egypt. Jesus, aware of the approaching culmination of his earthly ministry, gathers with his disciples for a final meal.

♦ The Act of Foot Washing:

During the meal, Jesus, who is portrayed as the master and teacher, takes on the role of a servant by washing his disciples' feet. This act was traditionally performed by servants or slaves in ancient times, as guests would often enter a home with dusty feet due to the unpaved roads

♦ Peter's Resistance:

Initially, when Jesus approaches Peter to wash his feet, Peter is taken aback and refuses, expressing disbelief that Jesus, his revered teacher, would perform such a menial task. However, Jesus insists, explaining that unless Peter allows him to wash his feet, he will have no part with him.

♦ The Symbolism:

Jesus uses this act of foot washing to convey a deeper spiritual lesson about humility and service. He tells his disciples, "Now that I, your Lord and Teacher, have washed your feet, you also should wash one another's feet. I have set you an example that you should do as I have done for you" (John 13:14-15, NIV). Here, Jesus emphasizes the importance of serving others selflessly, regardless of one's social status or position.

♦ The Model of Leadership:

In washing his disciples' feet, Jesus redefines the concept of leadership. Instead of asserting authority through power and privilege, he exemplifies servant leadership, where the leader's primary role is to serve and uplift others. This contrasts sharply with the prevailing cultural norms of his time, where leaders were often authoritarian and sought to maintain their status through dominance.

♦ The Call to Humility:

Through this symbolic act, Jesus teaches his disciples— and by extension, all believers—that true greatness is found in humility. He challenges them to embrace a mindset of humility and servitude in their relationships with one another and with the world.

◆ Continued Relevance:

The lesson of washing the disciples' feet continues to resonate with Christians today as a powerful reminder of the values of humility, service, and love. Many Christian traditions observe foot washing ceremonies as part of their Maundy Thursday or Holy Thursday services, symbolizing the ongoing call to follow Jesus' example of servanthood.

In conclusion, the washing of the disciples' feet serves as a poignant illustration of Jesus' teachings on humility and service. It challenges believers to embody these virtues in their daily lives, following the example set by their Lord and Savior.

David

King David, one of the most prominent figures in the Bible, is often revered for his leadership qualities, among which humility stands out as a defining characteristic. His story, found in the Old Testament, particularly in the books of Samuel and Chronicles, offers numerous insights into how humility shaped his leadership style and contributed to his success.

Background of King David

David's story begins with his anointing by the prophet Samuel as the future king of Israel, while he was still a young shepherd. Despite this significant prophecy, David's journey to the throne was marked by trials and challenges, including his famous encounter with the giant Goliath, his time in Saul's court, and his years of exile as a fugitive from Saul's jealousy.

Demonstrations of Humility:

♦ **Acceptance of God's Will:** Throughout his life, David exhibited humility by acknowledging and accepting God's sovereignty over his circumstances. Despite being anointed king, he waited patiently for God's timing, refusing to take matters into his own hands, even when given the opportunity to kill Saul, who was hunting him.

♦ **Recognition of His Flaws:** David was not without faults, and he openly acknowledged his shortcomings. Most famously, his affair with Bathsheba and subsequent murder of her husband, Uriah, serve as a stark reminder of his humanity. However, when confronted by the prophet Nathan, David repented sincerely, displaying humility in acknowledging his sin and seeking forgiveness.

♦ **Dependence on God:** In times of both triumph and adversity, David turned to God for guidance and strength. His Psalms are filled with expressions of reliance on God's wisdom, protection, and grace, reflecting a humble recognition of his own limitations and a profound trust in God's providence.

♦ **Servant Leadership:** Despite his exalted status as king, David often exhibited the traits of a servant leader, prioritizing the well-being of his people above his own interests. He demonstrated compassion and empathy toward his subjects, seeking to rule with justice and integrity rather than exploiting his power for personal gain.

♦ **Respect for Authority:** Even when faced with persecution and injustice at the hands of King Saul, David maintained a respectful attitude toward Saul's position as God's anointed king. He refused to harm Saul, recognizing the sacredness of the office despite Saul's personal animosity toward him.

Lessons in Humility from David's Leadership

♦ **Authenticity:** David's humility stemmed from a genuine recognition of his place before God and his fellow human beings. He did not feign humility for the sake of appearances but lived it out sincerely in his actions and attitudes.

♦ **Strength in Vulnerability:** David's willingness to acknowledge his mistakes and vulnerabilities did not diminish his leadership; rather, it strengthened it by fostering trust and transparency among his followers. His example teaches us that true strength lies in humility and vulnerability.

♦ **Empathy and Compassion:** David's empathy toward others, especially the marginalized and oppressed, exemplifies how humility fosters a heart of compassion. As leaders, cultivating humility enables us to empathize with the struggles of those we lead and to govern with fairness and kindness.

♦ **Trust in God's Providence:** David's life is a testament to the transformative power of humility in fostering a deep trust in God's providence. By surrendering his own desires and ambitions to God's will, David found strength and guidance even in the most challenging circumstances.

In summary, King David's leadership exemplifies the profound impact of humility on shaping character, fostering trust, and guiding effective governance. His story serves as a timeless reminder of the enduring importance of humility in leadership, inspiring us to emulate his example in our own lives and endeavors.

Apostle Paul

Leading with humility is a concept deeply rooted in various religious and philosophical traditions, and the Apostle Paul in the Bible exemplifies this principle remarkably. Paul, originally known as Saul of Tarsus, was a fervent persecutor of early Christians before his dramatic conversion on the road to Damascus. After this transformative experience, Paul became one of the most influential figures in the spread of Christianity, not only through his missionary journeys but also through his letters, which form a significant portion of the New Testament.

Paul's approach to leadership was characterized by humility, which is evident in several aspects of his life and teachings

◆ Transformation and Redemption:

Paul's humility is evident in his acknowledgment of his own past as a persecutor of Christians. Despite his former role, he humbly accepted the transformative power of his encounter with Jesus Christ and dedicated his life to spreading the gospel. This willingness to acknowledge his past mistakes and embrace change serves as a powerful example of humility for Christian leaders.

◆ Service and Sacrifice:

Throughout his ministry, Paul emphasized the importance of serving others and sacrificing personal comfort for the greater good. In his letter to the Philippians, he writes, "Do nothing out of selfish ambition or vain conceit. Rather, in humility, value others above yourselves, not looking to your own interests but each of you to the interests of the others" (Philippians 2:3-4, NIV). This selfless attitude underscores Paul's humility as a leader who prioritized the needs of others over his own.

♦ **Reliance on God's Strength:**

Despite his considerable accomplishments and knowledge, Paul did not boast in his own abilities but instead relied on the strength and guidance of God. In his second letter to the Corinthians, he writes, "But he said to me, 'My grace is sufficient for you, for my power is made perfect in weakness.' Therefore, I will boast even more gladly about my weaknesses, so that Christ's power may rest on me" (2 Corinthians 12:9, NIV). This acknowledgment of human weakness and dependence on divine strength reflects Paul's humility as a leader who recognized his limitations and trusted in God's provision.

♦ **Identification with the Marginalized:**

Paul demonstrated humility by identifying with the marginalized and oppressed members of society. He often spoke out against injustice and advocated for the inclusion of Gentiles within the Christian community, challenging prevailing social norms and cultural barriers. In his letter to the Galatians, he famously declares, "There is neither Jew nor Gentile, neither slave nor free, nor is there male and female, for you are all one in Christ Jesus" (Galatians 3:28, NIV). This inclusive vision reflects Paul's humility as a leader who valued the dignity and equality of all people before God.

♦ **Emphasis on Unity and Reconciliation:**

Paul prioritized the unity of the church and worked tirelessly to reconcile divisions among believers. In his letter to the Ephesians, he writes, "Make every effort to keep the unity of the Spirit through the bond of peace" (Ephesians 4:3, NIV). Paul understood the importance of humility in fostering reconciliation and cooperation within the Christian community, setting aside personal pride and grievances for the sake of greater harmony.

Overall, the Apostle Paul's life and teachings serve as a powerful example of leading with humility. His willingness to acknowledge his own weaknesses, prioritize the needs of others, rely on God's strength, identify with the marginalized, and promote unity and reconciliation offer timeless lessons for leaders in both religious and secular contexts. Paul's legacy continues to inspire countless individuals to embrace humility as a foundational virtue in their leadership journey.

30 Days Meditation on Leading with Humility and Servanthood

1. **Philippians 2:3-4 - "Do nothing out of selfish ambition or vain conceit. Rather, in humility value others above yourselves, not looking to your own interests but each of you to the interests of the others."**

2. **Matthew 20:26-28 - "Instead, whoever wants to become great among you must be your servant, and whoever wants to be first must be your slave— just as the Son of Man did not come to be served, but to serve, and to give his life as a ransom for many."**

3. Luke 22:26 - "But you are not to be like that. Instead, the greatest among you should be like the youngest, and the one who rules like the one who serves."

4. Mark 10:43-45 - "Not so with you. Instead, whoever wants to become great among you must be your servant, and whoever wants to be first must be slave of all. For even the Son of Man did not come to be served, but to serve, and to give his life as a ransom for many."

5. 1 Peter 5:5-6 - "In the same way, you who are younger, submit yourselves to your elders. All of you, clothe yourselves with humility toward one another, because, 'God opposes the proud but shows favor to the humble.' Humble yourselves, therefore, under God's mighty hand, that he may lift you up in due time."

6. Proverbs 11:2 - "When pride comes, then comes disgrace, but with humility comes wisdom."

7. Colossians 3:12 - "Therefore, as God's chosen people, holy and dearly loved, clothe yourselves with compassion, kindness, humility, gentleness, and patience."

8. James 4:6 - "But he gives us more grace. That is why Scripture says: 'God opposes the proud but shows favor to the humble.'"

9. Micah 6:8 - "He has shown you, O mortal, what is good. And what does the Lord require of you? To act justly and to love mercy and to walk humbly with your God."

10. Ephesians 4:2 - "Be completely humble and gentle; be patient, bearing with one another in love."

11. Romans 12:10 - "Be devoted to one another in love. Honor one another above yourselves."

12. Galatians 5:13 - "You, my brothers and sisters, were called to be free. But do not use your freedom to indulge the flesh; rather, serve one another humbly in love."

13. Philippians 2:5-7 - "In your relationships with one another, have the same mindset as Christ Jesus: Who, being in very nature God, did not consider equality with God something to be used to his own advantage; rather, he made himself nothing by taking the very nature of a servant, being made in human likeness."

14. 1 Corinthians 10:24 - "No one should seek their own good, but the good of others."

15. Matthew 23:11-12 - "The greatest among you will be your servant. For those who exalt themselves will be humbled, and those who humble themselves will be exalted."

16. Proverbs 22:4 - "Humility is the fear of the Lord; its wages are riches and honor and life."

17. 1 Timothy 1:15-16 - "Here is a trustworthy saying that deserves full acceptance: Christ Jesus came into the world to save sinners—of whom I am the worst. But for that very reason I was shown mercy so that in me, the worst of sinners, Christ Jesus might display his immense patience as an

example for those who would believe in him and receive eternal life."

18. Hebrews 13:17 - "Have confidence in your leaders and submit to their authority, because they keep watch over you as those who must give an account. Do this so that their work will be a joy, not a burden, for that would be of no benefit to you."

19. John 13:14-15 - "Now that I, your Lord and Teacher, have washed your feet, you also should wash one another's feet. I have set you an example that you should do as I have done for you."

20. Galatians 6:2 - "Carry each other's burdens, and in this way, you will fulfill the law of Christ."

21. 1 Corinthians 9:19 - "Though I am free and belong to no one, I have made myself a slave to everyone, to win as many as possible."

22. Philippians 2:8 - "And being found in appearance as a man, he humbled himself by becoming obedient to death— even death on a cross!"

23. Ephesians 6:7 - "Serve wholeheartedly, as if you were serving the Lord, not people."

24. Romans 12:3 - "For by the grace given me I say to every one of you: Do not think of yourself more highly than you ought, but rather think of yourself with sober judgment, in accordance with the faith God has distributed to each of you."

25. Proverbs 18:12 - "Before a downfall the heart is haughty, but humility comes before honor."

26. Colossians 3:13 - "Bear with each other and forgive one another if any of you has a grievance against someone. Forgive as the Lord forgave you."

27. 1 Peter 3:8 - "Finally, all of you, be like-minded, be sympathetic, love one another, be compassionate and humble."

28. Matthew 5:5 - "Blessed are the meek, for they will inherit the earth."

29. Luke 14:11 - "For all those who exalt themselves will be humbled, and those who humble themselves will be exalted."

30. Isaiah 66:2 - "Has not my hand made all these things, and so they came into being?" declares the Lord. "These are the ones I look on with favor: those who are humble and contrite in spirit, and who tremble at my word.

LEADING WITH FAITH

Leading with faith can take on various meanings depending on the context in which it is applied. It can refer to leadership guided by religious faith, where individuals draw upon the principles, teachings, and values of their faith tradition to inform their leadership style and decision-making processes. Alternatively, it can also encompass a broader sense of faith, including trust, confidence, and belief in oneself, others, and the greater good.

Leadership Guided by Religious Faith

In this interpretation, leading with faith involves integrating one's religious beliefs into their leadership approach. Leaders who adhere to this perspective often draw inspiration from religious scriptures, teachings, and principles to guide their actions. They may prioritize values such as compassion, humility, integrity, and service to others, which are central tenets of many faith traditions.

Example:

A CEO who leads with faith might base their decisions on ethical principles derived from their religious teachings, such as treating employees with fairness and respect, prioritizing corporate social responsibility, and fostering a culture of inclusivity and diversity.

Trust and Belief in Others:

Leading with faith can also involve having trust and belief in the capabilities and potential of others. This approach emphasizes empowering and supporting team members to reach their full potential, even in the face of uncertainty or adversity. Leaders who adopt this perspective often cultivate an environment of trust, collaboration, and open communication.

Example:

A coach who leads with faith trusts in their players' abilities, providing encouragement, guidance, and mentorship to help them succeed on and off the field. They instill confidence in their team members, fostering a sense of unity and shared purpose.

Courage and Resilience:

Leading with faith can entail having the courage to pursue bold visions and goals, even without certainty or guarantees of success. It involves facing challenges with resilience, perseverance, and a steadfast belief in one's ability to overcome obstacles and achieve meaningful outcomes.

Example:

An entrepreneur who leads with faith ventures into uncharted territory, taking calculated risks and embracing failure as part of the learning process. They remain resilient in the face of setbacks, drawing strength from their belief in the vision they are pursuing and their capacity to adapt and innovate.

Spiritual and Moral Guidance:

For some, leading with faith involves seeking spiritual and moral guidance from sources beyond themselves. This can include prayer, meditation, reflection, or seeking counsel from spiritual advisors or mentors. By grounding their leadership in principles of wisdom, compassion, and justice, leaders can navigate complex ethical dilemmas and make decisions that align with their values and principles.

Example:

A nonprofit leader who leads with faith seeks guidance through prayer and reflection when faced with tough decisions about resource allocation or organizational priorities. They strive to uphold the organization's mission and values while remaining mindful of the needs and well-being of those they serve.

Overall, leading with faith encompasses a multifaceted approach that integrates religious or spiritual beliefs, trust in others, courage, resilience, and moral guidance. It is about aligning one's leadership practices with deeply held values and convictions, striving to inspire and uplift others while making a positive impact in the world.

Incorporating faith into your leadership style

Incorporating faith into your leadership style can profoundly impact how you lead, influence others, and make decisions. It involves integrating your religious or spiritual beliefs into your approach to leadership, guiding your actions, values, and interactions with others. Whether you adhere to a specific religion or hold personal spiritual beliefs, incorporating faith into your leadership style can contribute to creating a more compassionate, ethical, and purpose-driven environment. Here are some key aspects to consider when integrating faith into your leadership style:

♦ **Values Alignment:**

Faith often provides a set of core values and principles that guide behavior and decision-making. By aligning your leadership values with your faith principles, you create consistency and integrity in your actions. For example, if honesty and compassion are central to your faith, you should prioritize these values in your leadership interactions.

♦ **Servant Leadership:**

Many religious traditions emphasize the importance of service to others. Incorporating this aspect into your leadership style involves prioritizing the well-being and growth of your team members above your own interests. It means leading with humility, empathy, and a willingness to serve and support others in achieving their goals.

♦ **Ethical Decision-Making:**

Faith often provides a moral compass for decision-making. Leaders who incorporate their faith into their decision-making process may consider not only the practical implications but also the ethical and moral implications of their choices. This can lead to decisions that prioritize integrity, fairness, and the greater good.

♦ Inspiration and Motivation:

Faith can serve as a source of inspiration and motivation for both leaders and team members. Leaders who openly express their faith and share how it influences their leadership style can inspire others to align their actions with their own values and beliefs. This can foster a sense of purpose and cohesion within the team.

♦ Respect for Diversity:

While incorporating faith into leadership can be empowering, it is essential to respect the diversity of beliefs within your team. A good leader acknowledges and celebrates the various faith backgrounds and perspectives of their team members, creating an inclusive environment where everyone feels valued and respected.

♦ Mindfulness and Reflection:

Many faith traditions emphasize the importance of mindfulness, prayer, or meditation to center oneself and gain clarity. Leaders who incorporate these practices into their routine may find themselves better equipped to handle the challenges of leadership with patience, wisdom, and emotional resilience.

♦ Building Community and Trust:

Faith-based leadership often emphasizes the importance of building strong relationships based on trust, respect, and compassion. Leaders who incorporate faith into their leadership style prioritize nurturing a sense of community and belonging within their team, fostering trust and cooperation among team members.

◆ Balancing Work and Personal Life:

Faith-based leadership often encourages a comprehensive approach to life, recognizing the importance of balancing professional responsibilities with personal well-being, family, and spiritual growth. Leaders who incorporate faith into their leadership style prioritize maintaining this balance and encourage their team members to do the same.

In summary, incorporating faith into your leadership style involves aligning your values, decision-making process, and interactions with others with your religious or spiritual beliefs. By doing so, you can create a more ethical, compassionate, and purpose-driven work environment that fosters personal and professional growth for yourself and your team members.

Biblical Foundation for Leading with Faith

Leading with faith, as depicted in the Bible, is a profound concept rooted in the trust and belief in God's guidance and wisdom. Throughout the scriptures, numerous examples highlight individuals who exemplified leadership based on their unwavering faith in God. Here, we delve into some key examples and principles of leading with faith in the Bible:

◆ **Abraham**: Abraham is often regarded as the epitome of faith-based leadership. In Genesis 12, God calls Abraham to leave his homeland and go to a place that He would show him. Despite uncertainties and challenges, Abraham obeys God's command, demonstrating remarkable faith and trust in God's plan. His journey serves as a testament to the importance of obedience and reliance on God's guidance in leadership.

♦ **Moses**: Moses's leadership of the Israelites out of Egypt is another powerful example of leading with faith. When God calls Moses to lead His people out of slavery, Moses initially doubts his abilities. However, God assures him and provides miraculous signs to confirm His presence and power. Despite facing numerous obstacles, including the resistance of Pharaoh, Moses persists in his mission, guided by his faith in God's promises.

♦ **David**: King David's reign is characterized by his deep faith in God. Despite facing formidable enemies and personal failures, David consistently seeks God's guidance and relies on Him for strength and wisdom. In Psalm 23, David poetically illustrates his trust in God as a shepherd who leads and protects his flock, highlighting the intimate relationship between faith and leadership.

♦ **Esther**: Esther's story exemplifies courageous leadership grounded in faith. As queen of Persia, Esther risks her life by approaching the king to plead for the salvation of her people, the Jews, who faced annihilation. Esther's faith is evident in her declaration, "If I perish, I perish" (Esther 4:16), as she places her trust in God's providence while taking bold action to fulfill her role in His plan.

♦ **Jesus**: As the ultimate example of leadership, Jesus exemplifies unwavering faith in God's will. Throughout his ministry, Jesus demonstrates humility, compassion, and obedience to God's purposes, even in the face of persecution and death. His teachings emphasize the importance of faith, love, and servanthood in leadership, challenging conventional notions of power and authority.

In each of these examples, leading with faith involves a deep-seated trust in God's guidance, a willingness to obey His commands, and a reliance on His strength in times of trial. These biblical narratives offer timeless lessons for leaders today, inspiring them to cultivate faith-based leadership characterized by humility, integrity, and courage.

Abraham

Abraham, often referred to as the father of three major monotheistic religions—Judaism, Christianity, and Islam—stands out as an iconic figure of faith and leadership in the sacred texts of these traditions. His story, chronicled in the book of Genesis in the Hebrew Bible, presents narrative rich with lessons on faith, trust, and perseverance that continue to resonate across cultures and generations.

Abraham's journey begins in the land of Ur, where he receives a divine call from God to leave his homeland and embark on a journey to a land that God promises to show him. This call marks the inception of Abraham's journey of faith, where he demonstrates unwavering trust and obedience in the face of uncertainty and adversity.

One of the defining moments in Abraham's narrative is his willingness to sacrifice his son Isaac, as commanded by God. This test of faith, known as the binding of Isaac or the Akedah, displays Abraham's absolute devotion to God. Despite the emotional turmoil and moral conflict, Abraham exhibits a profound trust in the divine will, leading to the intervention of God, who provides a ram as a substitute sacrifice. This event underscores Abraham's unwavering faith and serves as a paradigmatic example of obedience and commitment to God's commands.

Abraham's leadership style is characterized by his ability to inspire and mobilize others through his example of faith and righteousness. His hospitality towards strangers, as depicted in the story of the three visitors who come to announce the birth of Isaac, exemplifies his generosity and kindness. Abraham's leadership extends beyond his immediate family to his role as a mediator and peacemaker within his community. He negotiates with God on behalf of the inhabitants of Sodom and Gomorrah, demonstrating his compassion and sense of justice.

Moreover, Abraham's journey is marked by numerous trials and tribulations, including famine, conflict, and personal struggles. Despite these challenges, Abraham remains steadfast in his faith, trusting in God's promises and providence. His perseverance in the face of adversity serves as a testament to the transformative power of faith and resilience.

Abraham's legacy reverberates throughout the ages, inspiring believers to emulate his example of faith and leadership. His story serves as a foundational narrative in the religious consciousness of Judaism, Christianity, and Islam, shaping theological doctrines and ethical principles. Moreover, Abraham's role as a patriarch symbolizes the unity and interconnectedness of the Abrahamic faiths, fostering dialogue and understanding among diverse religious communities.

The narrative of Abraham in the Bible offers profound insights into the nature of faith, leadership, and human resilience. His unwavering commitment to God's will, his compassion towards others, and his ability to navigate through life's uncertainties with faith and courage continue to resonate as timeless lessons for individuals and communities seeking guidance and inspiration in their own journeys of faith and leadership.

Leadership Lessons:

The narratives of Abraham and the Israelites offer timeless lessons in leadership:

♦ **Faith and Trust**: Effective leadership requires unwavering faith and trust in God's guidance and provision, even in the face of uncertainty and adversity.

♦ **Courage and Obedience**: Leaders must demonstrate courage and obedience in following God's commands, even when it requires personal sacrifice or goes against conventional wisdom.

♦ **Humility and Servant Leadership**: True leadership is marked by humility and a willingness to serve others, prioritizing the needs of the community over personal ambitions.

♦ **Resilience and Perseverance**: Leaders must persevere through challenges and setbacks, trusting in God's faithfulness and remaining steadfast in their commitment to the mission.

In summary, the faith of Abraham and the journey of the Israelites serve as profound examples of faith, leadership, and divine guidance, inspiring believers to emulate their virtues and trust in God's providence.

Moses

Moses is one of the most significant figures in the Bible, revered not only in Judaism but also in Christianity and

Islam. His leadership journey, marked by faith, courage, and obedience to God, serves as a profound example of divine guidance and human resilience. From his miraculous birth to his pivotal role in the liberation of the Israelites from Egyptian bondage, Moses epitomizes the archetype of a transformative leader, one who navigates adversity with unwavering faith and determination.

Early Life and Calling

Moses' narrative begins with his extraordinary birth during a time when Pharaoh ordered the death of all Hebrew male infants. His mother, guided by faith, concealed him in a basket and set him adrift on the Nile River, where he was discovered by Pharaoh's daughter and raised as royalty. Despite his privileged upbringing, Moses never forgot his Hebrew heritage. In a pivotal moment of identity realization, he witnessed an Egyptian taskmaster abusing a Hebrew slave and driven by a sense of justice, intervened, killing the taskmaster. Fearing punishment, Moses fled to the wilderness of Midian, where he would spend the next forty years in exile.

Encounter with the Divine

It was in the solitude of the wilderness that Moses encountered the Divine in the form of a burning bush. This iconic event marked the beginning of his divine commission as the deliverer of the Israelites. Despite initial hesitance and self-doubt, Moses accepted the monumental task set before him, trusting in God's promise of guidance and support. This encounter also revealed the sacred name of God, Yahweh, signifying a deeply personal and covenantal relationship between God and His chosen people.

Leadership in Exodus

Armed with newfound faith and resolve, Moses returned to Egypt to confront Pharaoh and demand the release of the Israelites. Through a series of miraculous signs and plagues, God demonstrated His power and sovereignty, compelling Pharaoh to relent. The Exodus, symbolizing liberation from oppression and bondage, became a defining moment in Israelite history, with Moses at its helm.

Challenges and Tests of Faith

However, leading the Israelites out of Egypt was not without its challenges. The journey through the wilderness tested the faith and patience of both Moses and the Israelites. Facing hunger, thirst, and the threat of enemy attacks, Moses relied on his unwavering trust in God's provision. Despite moments of doubt and rebellion among the people, Moses remained steadfast in his leadership, interceding on their behalf, and seeking divine guidance at every turn.

The Giving of the Law

At Mount Sinai, Moses received the Ten Commandments and the Law, establishing the moral and ethical framework for the Israelite community. As the mediator between God and His people, Moses played a crucial role in conveying divine revelation and fostering a covenantal relationship between the Israelites and their Creator.

Legacy and Final Days

Moses' leadership culminated at the edge of the Promised Land, overlooking the land flowing with milk and honey. Though he would not enter the land himself, Moses ensured the continuity of his mission by anointing Joshua as his successor. In his final moments, Moses delivered a poignant farewell address, exhorting the Israelites to remain faithful to God's commandments and promising them blessings for obedience.

Conclusion

The story of Moses serves as a timeless testament to the power of faith, perseverance, and obedience in the face of adversity. His journey from reluctant leader to liberator and lawgiver inspires countless generations to trust in God's providence and to lead with integrity and compassion. In leading with faith, Moses not only shaped the destiny of his people but also left an indelible mark on the collective consciousness of humanity, reminding us that true leadership is grounded in humility, courage, and an unwavering commitment to serving a higher purpose.

King David

"Leading with Faith: King in the Bible" encompasses a rich tapestry of narratives, teachings, and examples drawn from the lives of various kings depicted in the Bible. These accounts provide profound insights into leadership principles, the dynamics of power, and the intertwining relationship between faith and governance. Among the many kings featured in the Bible, none is as iconic and influential as King David, often regarded as a paradigmatic figure of leadership and faith.

David's story is one of triumph and tribulation, marked by his rise from humble beginnings as a shepherd to becoming the revered king of Israel. Central to David's leadership was his unwavering faith in God, which guided his decisions and actions throughout his reign. His faith was exemplified in numerous instances, including his defeat of the giant Goliath, his steadfast trust in God's promises, and his repentance in the face of moral failings.

One of the most renowned episodes in David's life is his confrontation with Goliath, a Philistine champion who taunted the Israelite army. While seasoned soldiers cowered in fear, David, armed with nothing but a sling and his faith in God, boldly faced Goliath on the battlefield. His victory not only demonstrated courage but also highlighted the potency of faith in overcoming insurmountable obstacles— a powerful lesson for leaders confronting daunting challenges.

David's faith also played a pivotal role in his ascent to the throne. Despite enduring persecution and exile at the hands of King Saul, David remained steadfast in his belief that God had chosen him to be the next king of Israel. This conviction sustained him through years of adversity and uncertainty, leading to his coronation as king—a testament to the divine providence that underpinned his reign.

However, David's leadership was not without flaws, as evidenced by his infamous affair with Bathsheba and the subsequent murder of her husband, Uriah. Yet, even in his moments of moral failing, David's faith remained a guiding force, prompting him to acknowledge his wrongdoing and seek repentance before God. His humility and contrition serve as a poignant reminder that true leadership is not immune to imperfection but is characterized by accountability and a willingness to learn from mistakes.

Beyond David, the Bible features a diverse array of kings whose leadership legacies offer valuable insights into the interplay between faith and governance. From Solomon's wisdom and administrative prowess to Hezekiah's faith-driven reforms, each king's story contributes to a multifaceted understanding of leadership informed by faith.

"Leading with Faith: King David in the Bible" encapsulates a profound exploration of leadership principles grounded in faith, courage, humility, and divine guidance. Through the lives of biblical kings, individuals are inspired to emulate their virtues, confront their shortcomings, and lead with unwavering trust in a higher purpose.

Queen Esther

Queen Esther is a prominent figure in the Bible, revered for her courage, wisdom, and faith. Her story, found in the Book of Esther in the Hebrew Bible or the Old Testament, is a tale of bravery and divine providence amidst adversity. Through her leadership, she saved her people, the Jews, from annihilation, illustrating how faith can guide and empower individuals to overcome insurmountable challenges.

Esther's story begins with her humble origins as an orphan raised by her cousin Mordecai in the Persian capital of Susa. Despite her modest background, Esther possesses remarkable beauty and grace, catching the eye of King Xerxes (Ahasuerus), who selects her as his queen through a beauty contest. However, Esther conceals her Jewish identity as instructed by Mordecai.

The crisis unfolds when Haman, the king's vizier, plots to exterminate the Jewish population of Persia out of personal animosity towards Mordecai. Learning of this dire threat, Mordecai implores Esther to intercede with the king on behalf of her people. Initially hesitant due to the danger of approaching the king without being summoned, Esther finds courage through prayer and fasting, declaring, "If I perish, I perish" (Esther 4:16). She approaches the king, risking her life to plead for the salvation of her people.

Esther's faith is evident in her trust in God's guidance and timing throughout this critical moment. Despite the uncertainty and peril, she faces, she remains steadfast in her belief that God will provide a way. This unwavering faith empowers her to take bold action, demonstrating her leadership underpinned by spiritual conviction.

Esther's leadership also exemplifies strategic wisdom and discernment. Rather than immediately revealing her request to the king, she employs shrewd tactics, inviting him and Haman to a series of banquets, gradually building rapport and setting the stage for her plea. In doing so, she navigates the complexities of court politics while staying true to her mission of saving her people.

Esther reveals her Jewish identity to the king and exposes Haman's treachery, leading to his downfall. Through her courage, faith, and diplomacy, she secures a decree allowing the Jews to defend themselves against their enemies. The Jewish people are saved from destruction, and Esther's role as their savior is commemorated in the festival of Purim, celebrated annually by Jews around the world.

Esther's leadership with faith offers timeless lessons for individuals and leaders alike. Her story illustrates the power of faith to embolden individuals in the face of adversity, the importance of strategic thinking and discernment in leadership, and the profound impact one person can have in shaping the course of history. Esther's example continues to inspire and resonate, reminding us of the transformative potential of faith-driven leadership.

Jesus Christ

"Leading with Faith: Jesus in the Bible" is a profound and

multifaceted topic that delves into the portrayal, teachings, and significance of Jesus Christ within the Christian scriptures, primarily the New Testament. Jesus, as depicted in the Bible, serves as a central figure not only in Christianity but also in Western civilization. His life, teachings, and the example he set for his followers offer a framework for understanding leadership, faith, and the human condition.

Birth and Early Life:

Jesus' birth, as narrated in the Gospels of Matthew and Luke, is a foundational story in Christianity. Born in Bethlehem to Mary and Joseph, his humble beginnings underscore themes of humility and the unexpected nature of divine intervention.

Ministry and Teachings:

The bulk of Jesus' story in the Bible revolves around his ministry, which began around the age of 30. His teachings, often delivered through parables and sermons, emphasized love, compassion, forgiveness, and service to others. Jesus challenged societal norms, confronted hypocrisy, and championed the marginalized, embodying a leadership style rooted in empathy and humility.

Miracles and Healing:

Throughout his ministry, Jesus performed various miracles, including healing the sick, feeding the hungry, and even raising the dead. These acts of compassion demonstrated his divine authority and reinforced the idea of servant leadership, where power is used not for personal gain but for the betterment of others.

Death and Resurrection:

The climax of Jesus' story in the Bible is his crucifixion and subsequent resurrection. According to Christian belief, Jesus willingly sacrificed himself to atone for humanity's sins, offering redemption and the promise of eternal life to those who believe in him. His resurrection serves as a testament to the power of faith and the triumph of life over death.

Leadership Lessons from Jesus

Servant Leadership:

Jesus' leadership style stands in stark contrast to traditional notions of power and authority. He washed his disciples' feet, prioritized the needs of the vulnerable, and led them by example rather than coercion. Jesus' model of servant leadership emphasizes humility, empathy, and a commitment to serving others.

Vision and Purpose:

Central to Jesus' leadership was a clear vision and purpose. He articulated a kingdom not of this world, characterized by justice, mercy, and righteousness. Jesus inspired his followers with a compelling vision of a better future and called them to participate actively in its realization.

Courage and Conviction:

Jesus demonstrated unwavering courage and conviction in the face of opposition and adversity. Despite knowing the consequences, he fearlessly challenged religious authorities, confronted injustice, and remained steadfast in his mission until the very end.

The Significance of Jesus in Christian Faith:

Savior and Redeemer:

For Christians, Jesus is more than just a moral teacher or exemplary leader; he is the Son of God and the savior of humanity. Through his death and resurrection, Jesus offers salvation and the forgiveness of sins, reconciling humanity with God and offering the hope of eternal life.

Role Model and Guide:

Jesus serves as a role model for Christians, providing a blueprint for how to live a life of faith, compassion, and service. His teachings on love, forgiveness, and humility continue to inspire countless individuals to this day.

Source of Hope and Comfort:

In times of struggle and uncertainty, many Christians turn to Jesus as a source of hope and comfort. His promise of presence, peace, and ultimate victory over sin and death provides solace and reassurance amid life's challenges.

Conclusion:

"Leading with Faith: Jesus in the Bible" encapsulates the profound impact of Jesus Christ on both Christian theology and the broader human experience. His life, teachings, and example offer invaluable insights into leadership, faith, and the enduring power of love and compassion. Whether as a historical figure, a religious icon, or a moral exemplar, Jesus continues to inspire countless individuals to lead lives of purpose, integrity, and service.

30 Daily Meditation on leading with faith:

1. Proverbs 3:5-6 - "Trust in the Lord with all your heart, and do not lean on your own understanding. In all your ways acknowledge him, and he will make straight your paths."

2. Hebrews 11:1 - "Now faith is the assurance of things hoped for, the conviction of things not seen."

3. Joshua 1:9 - "Have I not commanded you? Be strong and courageous. Do not be frightened, and do not be dismayed, for the Lord your God is with you wherever you go."

4. James 1:5 - "If any of you lacks wisdom, let him ask God, who gives generously to all without reproach, and it will be given him."

5. Proverbs 16:3 - "Commit your work to the Lord, and your plans will be established."

6. Philippians 4:13 - "I can do all things through him who strengthens me."

7. Psalm 37:23-24 - "The steps of a man are established by the Lord, when he delights in his way; though he fall, he shall not be cast headlong, for the Lord upholds his hand."

8. Colossians 3:23-24 - "Whatever you do, work heartily, as for the Lord and not for men, knowing that from the Lord you will receive the

inheritance as your reward. You are serving the Lord Christ."

9. Isaiah 41:10 - "Fear not, for I am with you; be not dismayed, for I am your God; I will strengthen you, I will help you, I will uphold you with my righteous right hand."

10. Romans 8:28 - "And we know that for those who love God all things work together for good, for those who are called according to his purpose."

11. Psalm 32:8 - "I will instruct you and teach you in the way you should go; I will counsel you with my eye upon you."

12. 1 Corinthians 16:13 - "Be watchful, stand firm in the faith, act like men, be strong."

13. Matthew 17:20 - "He said to them, 'Because of your little faith. For truly, I say to you, if you have faith like a grain of mustard seed, you will say to this mountain, 'Move from here to there,' and it will move, and nothing will be impossible for you.'"

14. Ephesians 6:10 - "Finally, be strong in the Lord and in the strength of his might."

15. Galatians 6:9 - "And let us not grow weary of doing good, for in due season we will reap, if we do not give up."

16. Hebrews 13:7 - "Remember your leaders, those who spoke to you the word of God. Consider the outcome of their way of life, and imitate their faith."

17. 1 Timothy 4:12 - "Let no one despise you for your youth, but set the believers an example in speech, in conduct, in love, in faith, in purity."

18. 1 Peter 5:6-7 - "Humble yourselves, therefore, under the mighty hand of God so that at the proper time he may exalt you, casting all your anxieties on him, because he cares for you."

19. Psalm 23:1-3 - "The Lord is my shepherd; I shall not want. He makes me lie down in green pastures. He leads me beside still waters. He restores my soul. He leads me in paths of righteousness for his name's sake."

20. 2 Corinthians 5:7 - "For we walk by faith, not by sight."

21. Romans 12:11-12 - "Do not be slothful in zeal, be fervent in spirit, serve the Lord. Rejoice in hope, be patient in tribulation, be constant in prayer."

22. Isaiah 43:2 - "When you pass through the waters, I will be with you; and through the rivers, they shall not overwhelm you; when you walk through fire you shall not be burned, and the flame shall not consume you."

23. Psalm 121:1-2 - "I lift up my eyes to the hills. From where does my help come? My help comes from the Lord, who made heaven and earth."

24. Proverbs 11:14 - "Where there is no guidance, a people falls, but in an abundance of counselors there is safety."

25. Matthew 6:33 - "But seek first the kingdom of God and his righteousness, and all these things will be added to you."

26. Hebrews 10:23 - "Let us hold fast the confession of our hope without wavering, for he who promised is faithful."

27. 2 Timothy 2:15 - "Do your best to present yourself to God as one approved, a worker who has no need to be ashamed, rightly handling the word of truth."

28. Psalm 20:7 - "Some trust in chariots and some in horses, but we trust in the name of the Lord our God."

29. John 14:27 - "Peace I leave with you; my peace I give to you. Not as the world gives do I give to you. Let not your hearts be troubled, neither let them be afraid."

30. 1 Corinthians 10:31 - "So, whether you eat or drink, or whatever you do, do all to the glory of God."

These verses can serve as guidance and inspiration for those seeking to lead with faith in various aspects of their lives.

LEADING WITH ETHICS AND INTEGRITY

Leading with ethics and integrity is a fundamental aspect of effective leadership that involves making decisions and taking actions based on principles of honesty, fairness, and accountability. This approach requires leaders to prioritize values over personal gain or short-term benefits, thereby fostering trust, respect, and credibility among team members, stakeholders, and the broader community.

Ethics refers to the moral principles that guide individuals' behavior and decision-making. Ethical leaders adhere to these principles even when faced with difficult choices while Integrity involves consistency between one's words, actions, and beliefs. Leaders with integrity are honest, transparent, and principled in their conduct.

Leaders must set an example by demonstrating ethical behavior in all aspects of their leadership roles. When leaders prioritize ethics and integrity, they create a culture where such values are valued and practiced by everyone in the organization.

Ethical leaders communicate clear expectations regarding ethical conduct and establish guidelines or codes of ethics that outline acceptable behavior within the organization. These standards serve as a reference point for decision-making and behavior.

Ethical leaders consider the potential impact of their decisions on various stakeholders, including employees, customers, shareholders, and the community. They weigh competing interests and strive to make choices that uphold ethical principles and values.

Ethical decision-making frameworks, such as the utilitarian approach, deontological ethics, and virtue ethics, may be used to evaluate the moral implications of different options.

Leaders foster transparency by openly communicating information about their decisions, actions, and the rationale behind them. Transparency builds trust and encourages stakeholders to hold leaders accountable for their conduct.

Ethical leaders willingly accept responsibility for their decisions and actions, acknowledging both successes and failures. They encourage a culture of accountability where individuals are held responsible for their behavior.

Leaders cultivate an environment where ethical behavior is valued and rewarded. This may involve recognizing and celebrating acts of integrity, providing ethics training and education, and integrating ethical considerations into performance evaluations and promotions.

Ethical leaders confront ethical dilemmas and instances of misconduct promptly and decisively. They prioritize resolving issues in a fair and equitable manner, upholding the organization's values and principles. When addressing ethical breaches, leaders emphasize corrective action, education, and support for those involved, rather than punitive measures alone.

By consistently demonstrating ethical behavior and upholding integrity, leaders earn the trust and respect of their followers, peers, and stakeholders. Trust is essential for effective leadership, as it fosters collaboration, loyalty, and commitment.

Ethical leadership is dynamic and responsive to evolving societal norms, cultural contexts, and business challenges. Leaders must continually reflect on their values and adapt their approach to ensure alignment with ethical principles in diverse circumstances.

Organizations may develop metrics and assessment tools to evaluate the effectiveness of ethical leadership practices, such as employee surveys, ethical audits, and compliance evaluations. Feedback mechanisms help leaders identify areas for improvement and reinforce positive behaviors.

In summary, leading with ethics and integrity involves embodying core values, making principled decisions, fostering a culture of trust and accountability, and continuously striving to uphold ethical standards in all aspects of leadership. By prioritizing ethics and integrity, leaders not only contribute to the success and sustainability of their organizations but also serve as role models for ethical conduct in society.

Biblical Foundation of Leading with Integrity

Leading with integrity is a recurring theme throughout the Bible, emphasizing the importance of honesty, righteousness, and moral uprightness in leadership.

Numerous biblical figures serve as examples, both positive and negative, of leadership qualities related to integrity. Here is an exploration of this theme along with examples:

♦ **Abraham**: Abraham is often considered the father of faith in the Bible. His story in Genesis portrays him as a man of integrity who obeyed God's commands even when they seemed impossible or contradictory. One notable example is his willingness to sacrifice his son Isaac as commanded by God, displaying unwavering obedience and trust.

♦ **Joseph**: Joseph's story in the book of Genesis illustrates integrity in the face of temptation and adversity. Despite being sold into slavery and facing false accusations, Joseph remained faithful to God and demonstrated integrity in his conduct, eventually rising to a position of authority in Egypt.

♦ **Moses**: Moses exemplifies integrity as a leader chosen by God to deliver the Israelites from slavery in Egypt. Despite his initial reluctance, Moses obeyed God's call and led the Israelites with courage and integrity, even in the face of opposition and challenges from his own people.

♦ **David**: King David, despite his flaws, is often celebrated for his integrity and devotion to God. His psalms reflect a deep commitment to righteousness and honesty, even as he acknowledges his own sins and failings. Despite his moral lapses, David's repentance, and desire to follow God's will demonstrate his integrity as a leader.

♦ **Daniel**: Daniel's story in the book of Daniel displays his unwavering commitment to God and his principles, even in the face of persecution and opposition. His refusal to compromise his beliefs or defile himself with the king's food demonstrates his integrity and loyalty to God.

♦ **Jesus Christ**: As the ultimate example of leadership with integrity, Jesus exemplified truth, love, and righteousness in all aspects of his life and ministry. He challenged religious hypocrisy and injustice, consistently speaking the truth with compassion and authority. Jesus' selflessness, humility, and sacrificial love epitomize the highest standards of integrity in leadership.

♦ **Paul**: The apostle Paul, known for his missionary journeys and letters to the early Christian churches, emphasized the importance of integrity in leadership. He encouraged leaders to be above reproach, demonstrating integrity in their character, conduct, and teaching.

These biblical examples emphasize the importance of leading with integrity, which involves honesty, righteousness, humility, and obedience to God's commands. Leaders who follow these principles can inspire trust, foster unity, and make a positive impact on their followers and communities, fulfilling God's purposes and glorifying Him.

Abraham

Abraham, revered as the patriarch of Judaism, Christianity, and Islam, is a central figure in the Bible, particularly in the book of Genesis. His life serves as a profound example of leading with integrity, marked by faith, obedience, and unwavering commitment to his values and beliefs. Through various trials and triumphs, Abraham's journey offers timeless lessons on leadership characterized by integrity.

◆ Faith and Trust:

Abraham's story begins with a call from God to leave his homeland and journey to a land that God would show him. Despite the uncertainties and challenges, Abraham exhibits unwavering faith and trust in God's guidance. This foundational trust forms the bedrock of his leadership. Leaders who lead with integrity must have faith not only in themselves but also in something greater than themselves, whether it be a higher power, a cause, or a set of values.

◆ Courage to Step into the Unknown:

Leaving behind familiarity and venturing into the unknown requires courage. Abraham's willingness to step out in faith, leaving behind his homeland and everything he knew, exemplifies courageous leadership. Leaders often face situations where they must make bold decisions with uncertain outcomes. Integrity demands the courage to pursue what is right, even when the path ahead is unclear.

◆ Commitment to Righteousness:

Throughout his life, Abraham demonstrates a commitment to righteousness and justice. He intercedes for the cities of Sodom and Gomorrah, bargaining with God for the righteous few within those cities. This commitment to righteousness underscores the importance of moral integrity in leadership. Leaders must prioritize ethical principles and stand up for what is right, even in the face of opposition or adversity.

◆ Humility and Hospitality:

Abraham's hospitality towards strangers, as seen in the story of the three visitors in Genesis 18, reflects his humility and generosity. Leaders who lead with integrity recognize the importance of humility and serving others. They are open to different perspectives, willing to listen, and generous in their dealings with others.

◆ Resilience in the Face of Challenges:

Abraham's journey is marked by various trials, including famine, conflicts with neighboring kings, and the challenge of childlessness. Despite these challenges, Abraham remains resilient, trusting in God's promises. Leaders often encounter setbacks and obstacles, but integrity demands perseverance and resilience in the pursuit of their goals.

◆ Faithful Stewardship:

Abraham is depicted as a faithful steward of the blessings and responsibilities entrusted to him by God. From his wealth to his family, Abraham manages his resources with integrity and wisdom. Leaders are called to be stewards, entrusted with the well-being of those under their care. Integrity in leadership involves responsibly managing resources and nurturing the growth and development of others.

◆ Submission to God's Will:

The ultimate test of Abraham's integrity comes in the story of the binding of Isaac (the Akedah). Despite the immense personal cost, Abraham is willing to obey God's command without question. His submission to God's will, even when it seems incomprehensible, demonstrates profound integrity and devotion. Leaders must be willing to submit their own desires and agendas to a higher purpose or calling.

In conclusion, Abraham's life serves as a powerful example of leading with integrity. His faith, courage, commitment to righteousness, humility, resilience, stewardship, and submission to God's will offer timeless lessons for leaders in any context. By embodying these qualities, leaders can inspire trust, foster collaboration, and make a positive impact on the world around them.

Joseph

The story of Joseph in the Bible, found primarily in the book of Genesis (chapters 37-50), is one of the most compelling narratives of integrity, resilience, and divine providence. Joseph, the eleventh son of Jacob, demonstrates remarkable integrity throughout his life despite facing numerous trials and tribulations. Here is an exploration of Joseph's integrity with biblical support:

♦ **Faithfulness in Adversity**:

Joseph's integrity is first highlighted when he is sold into slavery by his jealous brothers. Despite being betrayed and taken far from his family, he remains faithful to God and maintains his integrity. (Genesis 37:23-28)

♦ **Resisting Temptation**:

While serving in Potiphar's house, Joseph encounters temptation when Potiphar's wife tries to seduce him. Despite her advances and the potential consequences, Joseph remains steadfast in his integrity and refuses to sin against God. He responds, "How then can I do this great wickedness and sin against God?" (Genesis 39:7-12)

♦ Excellence in Service:

Even in slavery, Joseph demonstrates integrity by faithfully serving Potiphar. His diligence and integrity lead to him being entrusted with the management of Potiphar's household. (Genesis 39:4-6)

♦ Enduring False Accusations:

Joseph's integrity is tested again when he is falsely accused of attempting to seduce Potiphar's wife. Despite being innocent, he is thrown into prison. Yet, even in prison, he maintains his integrity and finds favor with the prison warden. (Genesis 39:19-23)

♦ Interpreting Dreams Truthfully:

While in prison, Joseph interprets the dreams of Pharaoh's cupbearer and baker with integrity, accurately predicting their outcomes. He credits God with the ability to interpret dreams, acknowledging God's sovereignty. (Genesis 40:8, 41:15-16)

♦ Forgiveness and Reconciliation:

Joseph's integrity is fully revealed when he forgives his brothers who had betrayed him and orchestrates a reconciliation with his family. Despite the pain they caused him, Joseph harbors no bitterness but instead extends forgiveness and reconciliation, recognizing God's greater purpose in their actions. (Genesis 45:1-15)

♦ Providing for His Family:

Even after reconciling with his family, Joseph continues to demonstrate integrity by providing for them during the famine and ensuring their well-being in Egypt. He remains committed to his family despite their past actions against him. (Genesis 45:16-24, 47:12)

♦ Honoring God's Plan:

Throughout Joseph's story, his integrity is deeply rooted in his faith in God's plan for his life. Despite facing adversity and uncertainty, he trusts in God's sovereignty and remains obedient to Him, fulfilling God's purpose for him to save many lives. (Genesis 50:20)

Joseph's life exemplifies integrity in every aspect – from his faithfulness in adversity to his forgiveness and reconciliation with his family. His unwavering commitment to righteousness, even in the face of temptation and injustice, serves as a timeless example of integrity for believers to emulate.

Moses

Moses, a central figure in Judaism, Christianity, and Islam, is revered not only for his role in leading the Israelites out of bondage in Egypt but also for his embodiment of integrity throughout his leadership journey.

The story of Moses begins in the book of Exodus, where he is born during a time when the Israelites are enslaved in Egypt. His early life is marked by extraordinary events, including being rescued from the Nile River by Pharaoh's daughter and raised as an Egyptian prince, unaware of his true heritage. However, upon learning of his Israelite identity and witnessing the oppression of his people, Moses' sense of justice is ignited, setting him on a path that defines his legacy.

One of the defining moments of Moses' life is his encounter with the burning bush, where God commissions him to lead the Israelites out of Egypt. This pivotal moment not only marks the beginning of Moses' leadership journey but also sets the stage for his unwavering commitment to integrity. Despite his initial reluctance and self-doubt, Moses accepts the daunting task with humility and faith, trusting in God's guidance every step of the way.

Throughout the Exodus narrative, Moses demonstrates several key attributes of integrity that serve as timeless lessons for leaders:

♦ **Courage:**

Moses displays immense courage in confronting Pharaoh, the most powerful ruler of his time, demanding the release of the Israelites. Despite facing resistance and hardship, he remains steadfast in his conviction, refusing to back down until justice is served.

♦ **Humility:**

Despite his elevated position as a leader, Moses remains humble before both God and his people. He does not seek glory or recognition for himself but instead defers to God's authority and prioritizes the well-being of the Israelites more than anything else.

♦ **Honesty:**

Moses consistently speaks the truth, even when it is difficult or unpopular. He does not shy away from delivering God's message, even when it incites anger or opposition. His integrity lies in his commitment to transparency and sincerity in all his dealings.

♦ **Compassion:**

Moses shows compassion and empathy towards his fellow Israelites, advocating for their rights and welfare. He is deeply attuned to their suffering and actively works to alleviate their plight, exemplifying the true essence of servant leadership.

♦ **Faithfulness:**

Moses remains faithful to his calling and to the divine purpose entrusted to him. Despite facing numerous challenges and setbacks, he never wavers in his belief that God will deliver his people to the promised land. His unwavering faith serves as a source of inspiration and strength for those under his leadership.

The story of Moses serves as a timeless example of leadership guided by integrity, moral courage, and unwavering faith. His legacy continues to resonate across cultures and generations, reminding us of the transformative power of leaders who lead with integrity and righteousness. As contemporary leaders navigate complex challenges and uncertainties, the timeless lessons from Moses' leadership journey offer invaluable insights into the enduring principles of ethical leadership.

Job

Job is often celebrated for his unwavering faith and steadfastness in the face of immense suffering, making him a symbol of endurance and integrity.

The Book of Job begins with an introduction to Job, described as a man of great wealth and piety who lived in the land of Uz. He was known for his righteousness, feared God, and shunned evil. However, Job's faith is severely tested when Satan challenges God, suggesting that Job's devotion is only because he has been blessed with prosperity and protection.

God permits Satan to test Job's faith, but with the condition that he cannot harm Job physically. Consequently, Job's life is beset by a series of tragedies: he loses his livestock, servants, and all ten of his children in quick succession. Despite these calamities, Job remains steadfast in his faith, declaring, **"Naked I came from my mother's womb, and naked I will depart. The Lord gave and the Lord has taken away; may the name of the Lord be praised" (Job 1:21).**

As Job's suffering intensifies, he is afflicted with painful boils from head to toe. His wife urges him to curse God and die, but Job refuses, maintaining his integrity. He is then visited by three friends, Eliphaz, Bildad, and Zophar, who come to comfort him. However, they end up engaging in lengthy theological debates, with Job defending his innocence and questioning why he is suffering despite his righteousness.

Job's Integrity

Job's integrity is evident throughout the story in several keyways:

♦ Faithfulness in Adversity:

Despite losing everything dear to him and experiencing excruciating physical pain, Job refuses to renounce his faith or curse God. He remains resolute in his belief in God's justice and goodness.

♦ Refusal to Sin

Job maintains his moral integrity even under extreme duress. He rejects his wife's suggestion to curse God and remains blameless in his conduct, refusing to give in to despair or bitterness.

♦ Honesty and Self-Reflection

Throughout the narrative, Job engages in honest introspection and self-examination. He acknowledges his own mortality and imperfection but asserts his innocence of any grave sin that would warrant such suffering.

♦ Trust in God's Justice

Despite his confusion and anguish, Job trusts in God's wisdom and justice. He longs for an audience with God to plead his case directly, confident that God will vindicate him in the end.

The story of Job in the Bible serves as a profound meditation on the nature of suffering, faith, and divine providence. Job's unwavering integrity in the face of unimaginable hardship continues to inspire readers across generations. His example reminds believers of the importance of remaining steadfast in faith, maintaining moral integrity, and trusting in God's ultimate sovereignty, even during life's greatest trials.

King David

Leading with integrity is a timeless principle that transcends cultures, epochs, and contexts. In the Bible, King David stands out as a quintessential example of leadership guided by integrity. His life, as depicted in the Old Testament, offers profound insights into the essence of leadership characterized by honesty, moral uprightness, and accountability.

David's journey to kingship is marked by various trials and tribulations, which tested his character and integrity. From his humble beginnings as a shepherd boy, chosen by God to become the king of Israel, to his eventual reign over the nation, David faced numerous challenges that displayed his commitment to leading with integrity.

One of the defining moments in David's life is his confrontation with Goliath, the Philistine giant. While the entire Israelite army trembled in fear, David, armed with nothing but a sling and stones, fearlessly stepped forward to face the enemy. His unwavering faith in God and his courage in the face of adversity demonstrated his integrity and conviction in doing what was right, regardless of the odds.

As king, David's integrity was further tested in his interactions with his subjects and his handling of power. Despite his status as the most powerful man in the kingdom, David remained humble and just, always seeking the welfare of his people above his own interests. He prioritized righteousness and justice, even when it meant acknowledging his own mistakes and facing the consequences.

One of the most famous incidents illustrating David's integrity is his affair with Bathsheba and the subsequent murder of her husband, Uriah. When confronted by the prophet Nathan about his wrongdoing, David did not resort to denial or evasion but instead acknowledged his sins and repented sincerely before God. This episode highlights David's willingness to take responsibility for his actions and his commitment to living a life guided by moral principles.

Despite his flaws and failures, David's legacy as a leader of integrity endures. He is remembered not only for his military prowess or political achievements but also for his unwavering devotion to God and his commitment to righteousness. Through his example, David teaches us that true leadership is not merely about wielding power or authority but about serving others with humility, honesty, and integrity.

In contemporary leadership discourse, the story of King David serves as a powerful reminder of the importance of ethical leadership. Leaders across various domains can draw inspiration from David's life and strive to emulate his commitment to integrity, transparency, and accountability in their own leadership practices. By leading with integrity, like David, leaders can earn the trust and respect of their followers and leave a legacy of positive impact and influence.

Daniel

Daniel is a prominent figure in the Bible, known for his unwavering integrity and leadership qualities. His story, found in the Book of Daniel in the Old Testament, offers many insights into leading with integrity, even in adversity.

Background

Daniel was a young Israelite who was taken captive to Babylon when Nebuchadnezzar, the king of Babylon, besieged Jerusalem. Despite being uprooted from his homeland, Daniel remained faithful to his beliefs and committed to serving God.

Integrity in the Face of Temptation

One of the earliest displays of Daniel's integrity is seen in his refusal to defile himself with the royal food and wine provided by the Babylonian king. Instead, he requested to be given only vegetables and water, demonstrating his commitment to following God's dietary laws (Daniel 1:8-16).

Wisdom and Interpretation

Daniel's ability to interpret dreams and visions granted him favor with Babylonian kings and displayed his wisdom. When King Nebuchadnezzar had troubling dreams, Daniel not only interpreted them accurately but also demonstrated humility in acknowledging that his wisdom came from God (Daniel 2).

Courageous Stand for Truth

Daniel's integrity is further highlighted in his refusal to bow down and worship King Darius's decree, which forbade praying to any god or man except the king himself. Despite the threat of being thrown into a den of lions, Daniel continued to pray openly to his God, displaying unwavering faith and commitment (Daniel 6).

Humility in Leadership

Throughout his service in Babylon, Daniel never sought power or glory for himself. Even when interpreting dreams that foretold the downfall of kings and kingdoms, he did so with humility and reverence for God's sovereignty.

Trustworthiness and Reliability

Daniel's reputation for honesty and reliability earned him positions of authority and trust within the Babylonian and Persian empires. He served various kings faithfully, always prioritizing the interests of the kingdom over personal gain.

Resilience in Adversity

Despite facing numerous trials and challenges, including political intrigue, persecution, and exile, Daniel remained steadfast in his faith and commitment to God. His resilience in adversity serves as an inspiring example of perseverance and endurance.

Legacy of Faithful Leadership

Daniel's legacy as a leader of integrity transcends generations, inspiring countless individuals to uphold moral principles and stand firm in their beliefs, even when faced with opposition. His life exemplifies the timeless truth that true leadership is rooted in character, honesty, and devotion to God.

In summary, Daniel's story in the Bible provides a compelling blueprint for leading with integrity. His unwavering commitment to faith, humility, courage, and honesty serves as a timeless example for leaders in any context, emphasizing the importance of moral principles and steadfast devotion to one's beliefs, even in the most challenging circumstances.

Jesus Christ

Leading with integrity is a concept deeply rooted in various religious and philosophical traditions, and Jesus Christ's teachings in the Bible offer profound insights into this principle. Throughout the New Testament, Jesus exemplifies integrity in his actions, teachings, and interactions with others. Here, we will delve into some key aspects of how Jesus Christ embodies leading with integrity:

♦ Consistency between words and actions

One of the fundamental aspects of integrity is the alignment between what one professes and how one behaves. Jesus consistently practiced what he preached, emphasizing the importance of sincerity and truthfulness. In **Matthew 5:37, he teaches, "Let your 'Yes' be 'Yes,'** and **your 'No,' 'No."** This underscores the importance of honesty and reliability in communication, which are essential traits of integrity in leadership.

♦ Service-oriented leadership

Jesus' leadership style was characterized by humility and a focus on serving others rather than seeking power or status. In **Mark 10:45, he states, "For even the Son of Man did not come to be served, but to serve, and to give his life as a ransom for many."** This selfless attitude demonstrates that true leadership involves sacrificial service for the greater good, reflecting integrity in prioritizing the needs of others over personal gain.

♦ Compassion and empathy

Jesus consistently showed compassion and empathy towards those marginalized or suffering. He associated with sinners, healed the sick, and reached out to the outcasts of society, demonstrating inclusivity, and understanding. Integrity in leadership involves genuine concern for the well-being of all individuals, irrespective of their status or background.

♦ Ethical decision-making:

Jesus consistently upheld ethical principles in his teachings and actions, even when faced with difficult choices or opposition. He emphasized love, justice, and forgiveness, challenging societal norms and standing up against injustice. Integrity in leadership requires a commitment to moral courage and doing what is right, even in the face of adversity.

♦ **Transparency and accountability:**

Jesus promoted transparency and accountability in relationships and leadership. He encouraged honesty and openness, condemning hypocrisy and deceit. In Luke 8:17, he declares, "For there is nothing hidden that will not be disclosed, and nothing concealed that will not be known or brought out into the open." This underscores the importance of integrity in maintaining transparency and being accountable for one's actions.

♦ **Forgiveness and reconciliation:**

Jesus emphasized the importance of forgiveness and reconciliation in interpersonal relationships. He taught his followers to forgive others as they themselves are forgiven by God. This emphasis on reconciliation fosters trust and strengthens relationships, reflecting integrity in leadership through a commitment to healing and restoration.

♦ **Faithfulness and perseverance:**

Throughout his ministry, Jesus remained steadfast in his mission despite facing numerous challenges and obstacles. He endured suffering and sacrificed his life for the sake of humanity. Integrity in leadership involves a similar commitment to perseverance and faithfulness to one's values and principles, even in challenging times.

In conclusion, the example of Jesus Christ in the Bible provides a compelling model of leading with integrity. His teachings and actions emphasize the importance of consistency, service, compassion, ethical decision-making, transparency, forgiveness, reconciliation, and perseverance. Leaders who aspire to lead with integrity can draw inspiration from Jesus' example and strive to embody these principles in their own lives and leadership roles.

Apostle Paul

Leading with integrity is a fundamental aspect of effective leadership, and one of the most notable examples of this principle can be found in the biblical figure of the Apostle Paul. Paul, originally known as Saul of Tarsus, underwent a profound transformation from a persecutor of early Christians to one of the most influential leaders of the early Christian church. His leadership style, characterized by integrity, courage, and unwavering commitment to his principles, serves as a timeless model for leaders across various domains.

◆ Personal Transformation:

Paul's journey exemplifies the power of personal transformation. Prior to his conversion, he zealously persecuted Christians, believing them to be heretics. However, his encounter with the risen Christ on the road to Damascus led to a radical change in his beliefs and priorities. This transformation demonstrates the importance of humility and openness to new perspectives in leadership. A leader who can acknowledge and learn from past mistakes is better equipped to lead with integrity.

◆ Commitment to Truth and Justice:

Throughout his ministry, Paul demonstrated an unwavering commitment to truth and justice. He fearlessly spoke out against injustice and corruption, even when it meant facing persecution and imprisonment. His letters to various early Christian communities, preserved in the New Testament, are filled with exhortations to uphold moral principles and live lives of integrity. Leaders can learn from Paul's example by prioritizing honesty, transparency, and ethical conduct in their decision-making processes.

♦ **Servant Leadership:**

Paul's leadership style was characterized by humility and a willingness to serve others. Despite his status as an apostle, he often referred to himself as a servant or bondservant of Christ. He prioritized the needs of others above his own, tirelessly working to spread the message of Jesus Christ and build up the early Christian communities. This servant-leadership model emphasizes the importance of empathy, compassion, and selflessness in leadership.

♦ **Courage in the Face of Adversity:**

Paul faced numerous challenges and hardships throughout his ministry, including persecution, imprisonment, and physical suffering. Despite these obstacles, he remained steadfast in his faith and continued to boldly proclaim the gospel message. His courage serves as an inspiration for leaders facing adversity, reminding them to persevere in the pursuit of their goals and values, even in the face of opposition.

♦ **Consistency and Authenticity:**

Paul's leadership was marked by consistency and authenticity. He practiced what he preached, living in accordance with the principles he espoused. His letters reveal a deep sincerity and genuine concern for the well-being of others. Leaders can emulate Paul's example by aligning their words with their actions and fostering trust and credibility among their followers.

In conclusion, the Apostle Paul stands as a timeless example of leadership with integrity. His transformational journey, commitment to truth and justice, servant-leadership ethos, courage in adversity, and authenticity serve as guiding principles for leaders seeking to make a positive impact in their communities and organizations. By following in his footsteps, leaders can cultivate cultures of integrity, resilience, and ethical leadership.

Incorporating Integrity into your Leadership Style

Incorporating integrity into your leadership style is essential for fostering trust, respect, and credibility within your team or organization. Integrity in leadership involves aligning your actions, decisions, and behaviors with ethical principles and values, and consistently demonstrating honesty, transparency, and accountability in all aspects of your leadership role.

♦ Lead by Example:

As a leader, your actions speak louder than words. Demonstrate integrity in your everyday behavior by consistently following through on your commitments, being honest and transparent in your communication, and upholding ethical standards even when faced with tough decisions or challenges. When you lead by example, you set a clear standard for integrity that others will follow.

♦ Communicate Openly and Honestly:

Foster a culture of transparency and open communication within your team or organization.

Encourage honest feedback, listen actively to concerns or opinions, and communicate openly about decisions, changes, and challenges. Being transparent builds trust and demonstrates your commitment to integrity in leadership.

◆ **Set Clear Expectations:**

Clearly define expectations and standards of behavior for yourself and your team. Articulate core values and ethical guidelines that guide decision-making and behavior and hold yourself and others accountable for upholding these standards. By setting clear expectations, you create a framework for integrity to thrive.

◆ **Make Ethical Decisions:**

When faced with ethical dilemmas or tough decisions, prioritize integrity over expediency or personal gain. Consider the impact of your decisions on stakeholders, adhere to ethical principles and legal standards, and seek advice or input from others when necessary. Making ethical decisions reinforces your commitment to integrity and earns the respect of those you lead.

◆ **Act with Consistency:**

Consistency is key to building trust and credibility as a leader. Ensure that your actions, decisions, and behaviors align with your values and principles consistently over time. Avoid sending mixed messages or behaving inconsistently, as this can undermine trust and damage your reputation as a leader of integrity.

◆ **Hold Yourself Accountable:**

Take responsibility for your actions and decisions and hold yourself to the same standards of integrity that you expect from others. Acknowledge and learn from mistakes, take corrective action when necessary, and demonstrate humility and self-awareness in your leadership approach. By holding yourself accountable, you set a positive example for others to follow.

♦ **Empower Others:**

Encourage and empower others to act with integrity in their roles. Provide opportunities for professional development, foster a supportive and inclusive environment, and recognize and reward ethical behavior and contributions. By empowering others to uphold integrity, you create a culture where integrity is valued and practiced at all levels of the organization.

♦ **Seek Feedback and Continuously Improve:**

Solicit feedback from peers, colleagues, and team members on your leadership style and approach to integrity. Actively listen to constructive criticism, reflect on areas for improvement, and strive to continuously grow and develop as a leader. By seeking feedback and being open to learning, you demonstrate a commitment to personal and professional growth, which is integral to effective leadership with integrity.

Incorporating integrity into your leadership style requires self-awareness, commitment, and ongoing effort. By leading with integrity, you not only inspire trust and confidence in those you lead but also contribute to a positive and ethical organizational culture that fosters growth, innovation, and success.

30 Days Integrity Meditation

1. Proverbs 11:3 - "The integrity of the upright guides them, but the crookedness of the treacherous destroys them."

2. Psalm 78:72 - "And David shepherded them with integrity of heart; with skillful hands he led them."

3. Proverbs 20:7 - "The righteous lead blameless lives; blessed are their children after them."

4. 1 Kings 9:4 - "As for you, if you walk before me faithfully with integrity of heart and uprightness, as David your father did, and do all I command and observe my decrees and laws..."

5. Proverbs 10:9 - "Whoever walks in integrity walks securely, but whoever takes crooked paths will be found out."

6. Titus 2:7-8 - "In everything set them an example by doing what is good. In your teaching show integrity, seriousness and soundness of speech that cannot be condemned, so that those who oppose you may be ashamed because they have nothing bad to say about us."

7. Psalm 25:21 - "May integrity and uprightness protect me, because my hope, Lord, is in you."

8. Proverbs 28:6 - "Better the poor whose walk is blameless than the rich whose ways are perverse."

9. Ephesians 4:29 - "Do not let any unwholesome talk come out of your mouths, but only what is

helpful for building others up according to their needs, that it may benefit those who listen."

10. Proverbs 21:3 - "To do what is right and just is more acceptable to the Lord than sacrifice."

11. Proverbs 12:22 - "The Lord detests lying lips, but he delights in people who are trustworthy."

12. Ephesians 6:6 - "Obey them not only to win their favor when their eye is on you, but as slaves of Christ, doing the will of God from your heart."

13. Colossians 3:17 - "And whatever you do, whether in word or deed, do it all in the name of the Lord Jesus, giving thanks to God the Father through him."

14. Proverbs 28:18 - "The one whose walk is blameless is kept safe, but the one whose ways are perverse will fall into the pit."

15. Micah 6:8 - "He has shown you, O mortal, what is good. And what does the Lord require of you? To act justly and to love mercy and to walk humbly with your God."

16. Psalm 101:2-3 - "I will be careful to lead a blameless life—when will you come to me? I will conduct the affairs of my house with a blameless heart. I will not look with approval on anything that is vile. I hate what faithless people do; I will have no part in it."

17. 2 Corinthians 8:21 - "For we are taking pains to do what is right, not only in the eyes of the Lord but also in the eyes of man."

18. Proverbs 16:11 - "Honest scales and balances belong to the Lord; all the weights in the bag are of his making."

19. Ephesians 4:25 - "Therefore each of you must put off falsehood and speak truthfully to your neighbor, for we are all members of one body."

20. Romans 12:17 - "Do not repay anyone evil for evil. Be careful to do what is right in the eyes of everyone."

21. Colossians 3:9 - "Do not lie to each other, since you have taken off your old self with its practices."

22. Psalm 41:12 - "Because of my integrity you uphold me and set me in your presence forever."

23. Proverbs 2:7 - "He holds success in store for the upright, he is a shield to those whose walk is blameless."

24. Ephesians 4:15 - "Instead, speaking the truth in love, we will grow to become in every respect the mature body of him who is the head, that is, Christ."

25. Proverbs 15:21 - "Folly brings joy to one who has no sense, but whoever has understanding keeps a straight course."

26. James 3:17 - "But the wisdom from heaven is first pure; then peace-loving, considerate, submissive, full of mercy and good fruit, impartial and sincere."

27. Proverbs 10:29 - "The way of the Lord is a refuge for the blameless, but it is the ruin of those who do evil."

28. Ephesians 4:31-32 - "Get rid of all bitterness, rage and anger, brawling and slander, along with every form of malice. Be kind and compassionate to one another, forgiving each other, just as in Christ God forgave you."

29. Proverbs 14:2 - "Whoever fears the Lord walks uprightly, but those who despise him are devious in their ways."

30. Philippians 4:8 - "Finally, brothers and sisters, whatever is true, whatever is noble, whatever is right, whatever is pure, whatever is lovely, whatever is admirable—if anything is excellent or praiseworthy—think about such things."

LEGACY AND SUCCESSION

Legacy and succession are fundamental concepts in various aspects of human life, including business, leadership, family, and culture. These concepts revolve around the passing of influence, authority, assets, values, traditions, and responsibilities from one generation to the next. They carry significant implications for individuals, organizations, and societies as they shape continuity, growth, and the preservation of identity over time.

Legacy

Legacy refers to the impact, contributions, and imprint left behind by an individual, group, organization, or civilization. It encompasses both tangible and intangible elements, such as wealth, knowledge, values, achievements, reputation, and cultural heritage.

Types of Legacy

◆ **Personal Legacy:** This includes an individual's actions, values, beliefs, and relationships that shape their impact on others and the world.

◆ **Professional Legacy:** In the context of careers and professions, this pertains to the contributions, innovations, and influence an individual leaves within their field.

◆ **Organizational Legacy:** Organizations build legacies through their culture, achievements, products, services, and impact on stakeholders.

◆ **Cultural Legacy:** Refers to the traditions, arts, literature, customs, and historical landmarks passed down through generations within a society or community.

Building a Legacy

◆ **Purpose and Values:** A clear sense of purpose and adherence to core values guides individuals and organizations in creating a meaningful legacy aligned with their beliefs and goals.

◆ **Impactful Actions:** Taking deliberate actions and making choices that have a positive and lasting influence on others and the world.

◆ **Leadership and Mentorship:** Effective leadership and mentorship empower others to succeed and carry forward the legacy.

♦ **Innovation and Creativity:** Innovation drives progress and ensures that legacies remain relevant and adaptive to changing environments.

♦ **Social Responsibility:** Contributing to the well-being of society and addressing social challenges adds depth and significance to a legacy.

Importance of Legacy

♦ **Identity and Continuity:** Legacies preserve identity and ensure continuity across generations, strengthening bonds and fostering a sense of belonging.

♦ **Inspiration and Motivation:** Inspiring stories of past achievements and contributions motivate individuals and organizations to strive for greatness.

♦ **Learning and Growth:** Studying legacies provides valuable lessons and insights for personal, professional, and societal development.

♦ **Impact and Influence:** Legacies shape perceptions, influence behavior, and leave a mark on history, contributing to the collective progress of humanity.

Succession

Succession refers to the process of transferring authority, leadership, ownership, or responsibilities from one entity to another, typically from one generation to the next or from one leader to a successor within an organization.

Types of Succession

♦ **Family Succession:** Involves the passing of leadership and ownership of a family business or estate from one generation to the next.

♦ **Corporate Succession:** Occurs within companies when leadership positions, such as CEO or board members, transition to new individuals.

♦ **Political Succession:** Involves the transfer of political power from one administration or ruler to another through elections, appointments, or inheritance.

♦ **Cultural Succession:** Refers to the transmission of cultural traditions, values, and practices from older to younger generations.

Process of Succession

♦ **Identification of Successors:** Identifying and grooming suitable candidates with the necessary skills, knowledge, and qualities to assume leadership roles.

♦ **Preparation and Training:** Providing training, mentorship, and developmental opportunities to prepare successors for their future responsibilities.

♦ **Transition Planning:** Developing a comprehensive plan for the smooth transfer of authority, ensuring minimal disruption to operations and continuity of vision.

♦ **Communication and Stakeholder Engagement:** Transparent communication with stakeholders, including employees, shareholders, and family members, is essential to garner support and manage expectations during the succession process.

♦ **Evaluation and Feedback:** Regular evaluation and feedback help assess the progress of successors and identify areas for improvement.

Importance of Succession

♦ **Continuity and Stability:** Succession ensures the continuity and stability of organizations, institutions, and traditions across generations.

♦ **Renewal and Innovation:** New leadership brings fresh perspectives, ideas, and energy, driving innovation and adaptation to changing circumstances.

♦ **Talent Development:** Succession planning fosters talent development and retention by providing growth opportunities for high-potential individuals.

♦ **Risk Mitigation:** Proactive succession planning mitigates risks associated with unexpected leadership departures, ensuring a seamless transition, and avoiding disruptions.

♦ **Legacy Preservation:** Effective succession ensures the preservation and advancement of the legacy built by predecessors, honoring their contributions and achievements.

In conclusion, legacy and succession are intertwined concepts that play pivotal roles in shaping individuals, organizations, and societies. By understanding their significance and embracing best practices in building legacies and planning for succession, individuals and institutions can leave a lasting impact, inspire future generations, and ensure continuity and prosperity for years to come.

Biblical Foundation for Legacy and Succession

Legacy and succession are significant themes in the Bible, particularly in the Old Testament where family lineage, inheritance, and the passing of leadership roles are frequently discussed. Here are some key examples:

♦ **Abraham and Isaac:** The story of Abraham and his son Isaac is a prominent example of legacy and succession. Abraham, considered the father of the Israelites, passes on his covenant with God to Isaac, who becomes the next patriarch.

♦ **Jacob and his sons:** Jacob, also known as Israel, passes on his blessing and inheritance to his twelve sons, who become the twelve tribes of Israel. This passing of the blessing and the subsequent roles within the family demonstrate the importance of succession in biblical narratives.

♦ **Davidic Dynasty:** King David is promised by God that his descendants will rule over Israel forever (2 Samuel 7:12-16). This promise establishes the Davidic dynasty, where the kingship is passed down through David's lineage, culminating in Jesus Christ, who is often referred to as the "Son of David."

♦ **Moses and Joshua:** Moses, the great leader who led the Israelites out of Egypt, passes on leadership to Joshua before his death. Joshua then leads the Israelites into the Promised Land, continuing the legacy of Moses.

♦ **Elisha and Elijah:** Elisha is chosen as the successor to the prophet Elijah. Before Elijah is taken up to heaven, Elisha asks for a double portion of his spirit, indicating his desire to continue Elijah's work and legacy.

♦ **Jesus and his disciples:** Jesus, throughout his ministry, is preparing his disciples to carry on his teachings and spread the message of the Gospel after his crucifixion and resurrection. This passing of the torch from Jesus to his disciples is a central aspect of Christian theology.

These examples demonstrate how legacy, and succession are woven into the fabric of biblical narratives, highlighting the importance of passing on blessings, responsibilities, and leadership roles from one generation to the next.

Abraham to Isaac

The story of Abraham and Isaac in the Bible is one of the most profound narratives depicting the passing of leadership from one generation to the next. It is a tale rich in symbolism and meaning, illustrating themes of faith, obedience, sacrifice, and the continuity of divine promises. Let us delve into the details:

Abraham's Leadership

Abraham, initially known as Abram, is introduced in the book of Genesis as the patriarch chosen by God to lead a new nation. He is depicted as a man of great faith, who, despite his old age, believed in God's promise to make him the father of many nations. His leadership was characterized by his unwavering faith in God and his willingness to follow divine commands, even when they seemed incomprehensible.

Abraham's journey begins when God calls him to leave his homeland and embark on a journey to a land that God will show him. This act of leaving his familiar surroundings symbolizes Abraham's willingness to step into the unknown, trusting in God's guidance—a fundamental trait of effective leadership.

Throughout his life, Abraham encounters numerous trials that test his faith. One of the most significant tests comes when God commands him to sacrifice his son Isaac as a burnt offering. This command challenges not only Abraham's faith but also his understanding of God's character. Despite the immense emotional turmoil, Abraham demonstrates obedience and prepares to carry out the sacrifice, showing his commitment to God more than anything else.

Isaac's Role

Isaac, Abraham's son, plays a crucial role in the narrative as the one chosen to carry on his father's legacy. Born to Abraham and Sarah in their old age, Isaac is regarded as the child of promise, through whom God's covenant with Abraham will be fulfilled. As such, Isaac represents the continuity of God's plan and the future of the nation that Abraham is called to lead.

In the story of the binding of Isaac (also known as the Akedah), Isaac willingly accompanies his father to the place of sacrifice, unaware of the true purpose of their journey. His obedience and submission to his father's will mirror Abraham's obedience to God—a parallel that highlights the intergenerational transfer of faith and commitment.

Passing the Baton

The pivotal moment in the narrative occurs when Abraham is about to sacrifice Isaac, and God intervenes, providing a ram caught in a thicket as a substitute sacrifice. This intervention not only demonstrates God's faithfulness and provision but also marks a profound transition in leadership.

Through this ordeal, Abraham proves his unwavering devotion to God, solidifying his legacy as a faithful servant and leader. At the same time, Isaac emerges from the experience as a symbol of resilience and continuity, poised to inherit the mantle of leadership from his father.

The story of Abraham and Isaac, therefore, serves as a powerful allegory for the passing of the leadership baton from one generation to the next. It underscores the importance of faith, obedience, and trust in God's providence, while also highlighting the interconnectedness of past, present, and future in the fulfillment of divine promises.

Lessons for Leadership

♦ **Faith and Trust:** Effective leadership requires unwavering faith and trust in a higher purpose or guiding principles.

♦ **Obedience and Sacrifice:** Leaders must be willing to make sacrifices and demonstrate obedience to principles greater than themselves.

♦ **Continuity and Legacy:** A leader's legacy is not only about personal achievements but also about preparing the next generation to carry forward the mission and vision.

♦ **Divine Providence:** Leaders should recognize and acknowledge the role of divine providence or external forces beyond their control in shaping their leadership journey.

The story of Abraham and Isaac provides timeless lessons on leadership succession, emphasizing the importance of faith, obedience, and continuity in fulfilling a greater purpose.

Jacob and His Sons

The passing of the leadership baton from Jacob to his sons is a pivotal moment in the biblical narrative, particularly in the book of Genesis. Jacob, also known as Israel, plays a vital role in the story of the patriarchs, and his passing of leadership signifies the transition of power and responsibility to the next generation. This event is significant not only in terms of familial succession but also in terms of the fulfillment of divine promises and the continuation of the covenant established with Abraham.

Jacob, the son of Isaac and Rebekah, inherits the covenant promises made to his grandfather Abraham. Throughout his life, Jacob faces numerous trials and struggles, including conflicts with his brother Esau, deception by his uncle Laban, and the loss of his beloved wife Rachel. Despite these challenges, Jacob emerges as a key figure in the history of the Israelite people.

As Jacob nears the end of his life, he gathers his twelve sons to impart his final blessings upon them. This event, recorded in Genesis 49, serves as Jacob's last act of leadership and authority over his family. Each son receives a unique blessing tailored to his character and future role within the nation of Israel.

The blessings bestowed by Jacob carry profound significance, as they not only foretell the future of each son but also establish the tribal identities that will shape the Israelite nation. For example, Judah receives a blessing that foreshadows the eventual rise of the Davidic monarchy, while Joseph is granted blessings of fertility, strength, and prosperity, reflecting his future prominence in Egypt.

The passing of the leadership baton from Jacob to his sons symbolizes the continuity of God's plan for His chosen people. Despite Jacob's personal flaws and shortcomings, his faithfulness to God ensures that the covenant promises will be fulfilled through his descendants. By entrusting leadership to his sons, Jacob ensures that the legacy of faith and obedience will endure for generations to come.

Furthermore, the narrative of Jacob and his sons highlights themes of family dynamics, sibling rivalry, and the complexities of human relationships. The struggles and conflicts within Jacob's family serve as a reminder that even the chosen people of God are not immune to human frailty and sin. However, through divine providence and grace, God works through imperfect individuals to accomplish His purposes in the world.

In summary, the passing of the leadership baton from Jacob to his sons represents a crucial moment in the biblical narrative, marking the transition of authority and responsibility to the next generation. Through Jacob's blessings, the future of the Israelite nation is foretold, setting the stage for the fulfillment of God's promises and the establishment of His kingdom on earth.

Passing the Leadership Baton: David Dynasty

The transition of leadership from one generation to another is a crucial phase in the lifecycle of any organization or dynasty. In the case of the David Dynasty, this transition was marked by significant historical and biblical importance. The David Dynasty, which traces its origins to King David of Israel, experienced several pivotal moments of leadership succession, each carrying its own set of challenges, triumphs, and legacies.

♦ Founding of the Dynasty

The David Dynasty began with King David, who is revered in both biblical and historical accounts as one of the greatest rulers of ancient Israel. David's rise to power, his conquests, and his establishment of Jerusalem as the capital laid the foundation for a dynasty that would shape the course of Israelite history for generations to come.

♦ David's Succession Planning

Despite his accomplishments, David faced numerous trials during his reign, including conflicts within his own family. One of the most well-known episodes involves the struggle for succession between his sons, particularly Absalom and Solomon. David's handling of these challenges, his efforts to groom Solomon for leadership, and his eventual designation of Solomon as his successor exemplify the importance of effective succession planning in ensuring the continuity and stability of a dynasty.

♦ Solomon's Reign and Legacy

Solomon ascended to the throne following David's death, inheriting not only the crown but also the responsibility of governing a kingdom that was at its zenith of power and influence. Solomon's reign is renowned for its prosperity, wisdom, and architectural achievements, most notably the construction of the First Temple in Jerusalem. However, his later years were marred by excesses, oppression, and the seeds of division that would eventually lead to the fragmentation of the kingdom after his death.

♦ Challenges of Succession

The transition of leadership from Solomon to his successors marked a period of turbulence and instability for the David Dynasty. The division of the kingdom into the northern kingdom of Israel and the southern kingdom of Judah, as well as the succession of various monarchs, including both righteous and corrupt rulers, underscored the complexities and pitfalls inherent in passing the leadership baton from one generation to the next.

♦ Lessons Learned

The history of the David Dynasty offers several valuable lessons on leadership succession. Firstly, effective succession planning is essential for ensuring continuity and preventing power struggles within a dynasty or organization. Secondly, the character, competence, and integrity of the successor are crucial factors that can determine the fate of the dynasty. Lastly, the ability to adapt to changing circumstances, navigate conflicts, and uphold the values and vision of the founder are vital for sustaining the legacy of the dynasty across generations.

In conclusion, the story of the David Dynasty serves as a timeless narrative that resonates with the challenges and complexities of leadership succession. By studying the successes and failures of past leaders, we can glean valuable insights into the principles and practices that underpin effective succession planning and ensure the enduring legacy of dynasties, organizations, and civilizations.

Passing the leadership baton: Moses to Joshua

The transition of leadership from Moses to Joshua is a significant event in the biblical narrative, specifically within the context of the Israelites' journey from slavery in Egypt to the Promised Land. This transition represents a pivotal moment in the history of the Israelites and offers profound insights into leadership, succession planning, and the fulfillment of divine promises. Let us delve into the details of this transition:

Background:

♦ **Moses' Leadership:** Moses was the central figure in leading the Israelites out of Egypt. He served as the mediator between God and the people, receiving the Ten Commandments and guiding the Israelites through their wilderness journey.

♦ **Joshua's Role:** Joshua was Moses' protégé, a courageous warrior, and a faithful servant of God. He distinguished himself in battle against the Amalekites and was appointed by Moses to lead the Israelite army.

Moses' Recognition of Joshua:
♦ **Divine Appointment:** Moses recognized Joshua as his successor through divine guidance. It was God who instructed Moses to commission Joshua as the new leader (Deuteronomy 31:7-8).

♦ **Qualities of Joshua:** Moses observed Joshua's faithfulness, courage, and unwavering commitment to God. These qualities made Joshua the ideal candidate to lead the Israelites into the Promised Land.

Passing the Baton

♦ **Public Acknowledgment:** Moses publicly declared Joshua as his successor before the entire assembly of Israel (Deuteronomy 31:7). This declaration ensured a smooth transition and established Joshua's authority in the eyes of the people.

♦ **Impartation of Authority:** Moses laid his hands on Joshua, symbolizing the transfer of leadership authority and responsibility (Numbers 27:18-23). This act signified continuity and legitimacy in leadership succession.

Joshua's Acceptance and Commission

♦ **Acceptance of Responsibility:** Joshua accepted the mantle of leadership with humility and reverence. He recognized the enormity of the task before him but remained steadfast in his trust in God's guidance.

♦ **Divine Commission:** God reaffirmed Joshua's leadership role and promised to be with him as He was with Moses (Joshua 1:5). This divine commission provided Joshua with the assurance and confidence needed to lead the Israelites across the Jordan River.

Lessons on Leadership Succession

♦ **Preparation and Mentoring:** Moses invested time and effort in mentoring Joshua, preparing him for the challenges of leadership. Effective succession planning requires identifying and nurturing future leaders within the organization.

♦ **Divine Guidance:** The transition from Moses to Joshua underscores the importance of seeking divine guidance in leadership succession. Leaders should rely on God's wisdom and direction when appointing successors.

♦ **Continuity and Vision:** While leadership transitions bring change, they should also ensure continuity in vision and purpose. Joshua continued the mission initiated by Moses, leading the Israelites towards the fulfillment of God's promises.

♦ **Humility and Trust:** Both Moses and Joshua exemplified humility and trust in God throughout the transition process. Leaders must humbly acknowledge their successors and trust in God's providence for the future.

In summary, the passing of the leadership baton from Moses to Joshua serves as a timeless example of effective leadership succession guided by divine wisdom, mentorship, humility, and trust. It highlights the importance of preparing future leaders, seeking divine guidance, and maintaining continuity in vision and purpose for the advancement of God's kingdom.

Elijah to Elisha

The transfer of leadership from Elijah to Elisha in the biblical narrative is a profound and symbolic event that carries significant implications for leadership succession, mentorship, and spiritual inheritance. The story is found in the Old Testament, primarily in the books of 1 Kings and 2 Kings, and it offers valuable insights into the dynamics of passing on leadership responsibilities.

Elijah, a prominent prophet in Israel during the reign of King Ahab, was instrumental in confronting the idolatry and apostasy that plagued the nation. He performed miracles, confronted false prophets, and fearlessly stood for the worship of the one true God. However, as he neared the end of his ministry, he was instructed by God to anoint Elisha as his successor.

The account of Elijah passing the leadership baton to Elisha unfolds in several stages, each carrying its own significance:

♦ The Call of Elisha

In 1 Kings 19:19-21, Elijah encounters Elisha while he is plowing with a team of oxen. Elijah throws his cloak over Elisha, symbolizing the call to discipleship and succession. Elisha immediately recognizes the significance of this act and, after seeking permission from his family, follows Elijah, leaving behind his former way of life.

♦ The Mentorship Relationship

For several years, Elisha serves as Elijah's attendant and apprentice. He learns from Elijah's teachings, witnesses his miracles, and accompanies him on his journeys. This period of mentorship is crucial for Elisha's development as a leader, as he absorbs Elijah's wisdom, courage, and faithfulness.

♦ The Request for a Double Portion of Elijah's Spirit

As Elijah's ministry ends, he and Elisha embark on a journey to various places, symbolizing the passing of the mantle of leadership. Along the way, Elijah offers Elisha the opportunity to stay behind, but Elisha remains steadfast in his commitment to accompany his mentor to the end. When they finally reach the Jordan River, Elijah asks Elisha what he can do for him before he is taken away. Elisha responds by requesting a double portion of Elijah's spirit (2 Kings 2:9). This request reflects Elisha's desire not only to continue Elijah's prophetic ministry but also to surpass it, signifying his readiness to assume leadership with greater power and authority.

♦ The Ascension of Elijah and the Inheritance of Elisha

As Elijah is taken up to heaven in a whirlwind, Elisha witnesses this miraculous event. He cries out, **"My father, my father! The chariots of Israel and its horsemen!"** (2 Kings 2:12), acknowledging Elijah's significance as a spiritual father and leader of the nation. Elisha then picks up Elijah's cloak, which had fallen from him, and uses it to part the waters of the Jordan, demonstrating that the spirit and power of his mentor now rest upon him. This symbolic act marks the official transition of leadership from Elijah to Elisha.

♦ Elisha's Ministry:

Following Elijah's departure, Elisha steps into his role as the primary prophet in Israel. He performs miracles, confronts kings, and continues to speak on behalf of God to the nation. Elisha's ministry reflects the continuation of Elijah's legacy and his unique calling and anointing.

In summary, the passing of the leadership baton from Elijah to Elisha is a profound example of mentorship, discipleship, and succession in the biblical narrative. It underscores the importance of investing in the next generation of leaders, imparting wisdom, and spiritual authority, and trusting God's guidance in the transition of leadership. Elisha's willingness to learn, his bold request for a double portion of his mentor's spirit, and his subsequent faithfulness in carrying out his calling serve as timeless lessons for leaders in all spheres of life.

Jesus and His Disciples

Passing the leadership baton from Jesus to his disciples is a pivotal aspect of Christian theology and history, encapsulating themes of mentorship, empowerment, and the continuation of a divine mission. The narrative is deeply rooted in the Gospels of the New Testament, particularly in the accounts of Jesus' ministry and his interactions with his chosen followers.

♦ Selection of the Disciples

Jesus' ministry began with the selection of his disciples, ordinary men whom he called to follow him. Among them were fishermen, a tax collector, and other individuals from various social classes. This act of selection symbolizes Jesus' intentional choice of individuals to become the leaders of his movement after his departure.

♦ Training and Mentorship

Throughout his ministry, Jesus served as a teacher and mentor to his disciples. He imparted spiritual wisdom through his teachings, parables, and personal interactions. Jesus not only taught them about the principles of his kingdom but also demonstrated servant leadership through his actions, emphasizing humility, compassion, and self-sacrifice.

♦ Empowerment and Commissioning

As Jesus' earthly ministry approached its climax, he began to prepare his disciples for their future roles as leaders. One of the most significant moments illustrating this transition is the "Great Commission" found in the Gospel of Matthew (Matthew 28:16-20). In this passage, Jesus instructs his disciples to make disciples of all nations, baptizing them and teaching them to obey everything he has commanded. This commissioning empowers the disciples to carry on Jesus' mission of spreading the gospel and building the kingdom of God.

♦ The Role of Peter:

Among the disciples, Peter holds a prominent position as a leader. Jesus specifically entrusted him with the keys to the kingdom of heaven (Matthew 16:19), symbolizing authority and responsibility. Despite Peter's shortcomings and moments of weakness, Jesus reaffirmed his leadership role, instructing him to "feed my sheep" (John 21:15-17), thereby charging him with the care and guidance of the early Christian community.

♦ Pentecost and the Gift of the Holy Spirit

Following Jesus' ascension, the disciples gathered in Jerusalem, where they experienced the outpouring of the Holy Spirit on the day of Pentecost (Acts 2:1-4). This event marked a significant turning point, as the disciples were filled with boldness and empowered to proclaim the gospel with power and conviction. The presence of the Holy Spirit enabled them to continue Jesus' ministry and carry out their leadership roles effectively.

♦ Expansion of the Early Church:

Guided by the Holy Spirit, the disciples played pivotal roles in the expansion of the early Christian church. They preached the gospel, performed miracles, established new communities of believers, and provided leadership and pastoral care to the growing Christian movement.

♦ **Legacy and Continuation:**

The passing of the leadership baton from Jesus to his disciples illustrates a model of succession and continuity within Christian leadership. The disciples, empowered by Jesus and filled with the Holy Spirit, carried forward his mission, laying the foundation for the spread of Christianity throughout the world.

In summary, the relationship between Jesus and his disciples embodies the principles of mentorship, empowerment, and continuity within Christian leadership. Through his teachings, example, and commissioning, Jesus prepared his followers to carry on his mission, ensuring that his legacy would endure beyond his earthly ministry.

Planning for a successful legacy and succession

Planning for a successful legacy and succession involves carefully strategizing and implementing a plan to ensure the smooth transition of leadership, wealth, and values from one generation to the next. Whether in the context of a family business, a charitable foundation, or personal wealth management, effective legacy and succession planning requires foresight, communication, and attention to detail. Here is a detailed breakdown of the key components involved:

♦ **Clarify Your Objectives:**

Begin by defining your goals and objectives for the future. This could include preserving family wealth, maintaining the continuity of a business, passing on values and traditions, or supporting charitable causes. Consider the needs and aspirations of current and future generations, considering their skills, interests, and values.

♦ **Assess Your Current Situation:**

Conduct a thorough assessment of your current assets, including financial resources, investments, real estate, intellectual property, and any other relevant holdings. Evaluate the legal and tax implications of transferring ownership or control of these assets to future generations.

♦ **Develop a Succession Plan:**

Identify potential successors within the family or organization and assess their readiness and capabilities for assuming leadership roles. Establish clear criteria and processes for selecting and grooming successors, including training, mentorship, and leadership development programs. Consider appointing non-family members or external advisors to key positions to bring in fresh perspectives and expertise.

♦ **Create a Governance Structure:**

Establish a robust governance structure to oversee the implementation of your legacy and succession plan. Define the roles and responsibilities of family members, trustees, advisors, and other stakeholders involved in decision-making and management. Develop policies and procedures for resolving conflicts, making strategic decisions, and ensuring accountability and transparency.

♦ **Address Legal and Tax Considerations:**

Work with legal and financial advisors to draft and review legal documents such as wills, trusts, partnership agreements, and shareholder agreements. Minimize tax liabilities through estate planning strategies such as gifting, charitable giving, and the use of trusts and other tax-efficient vehicles. Stay informed about changes in tax laws and regulations that may affect your legacy and succession plan and update your strategy accordingly.

♦ **Communicate Effectively:**

Foster open and honest communication among family members and stakeholders about the purpose, values, and goals of the legacy and succession plan. Share information about financial matters, business operations, and other relevant topics to build trust and alignment. Encourage active participation and collaboration in decision-making processes to ensure buy-in and commitment from all parties involved.

♦ **Monitor and Adjust:**

Regularly review and evaluate the effectiveness of your legacy and succession plan, adjusting as needed in response to changing circumstances or goals. Keep abreast of market trends, industry developments, and family dynamics that may impact the implementation of your plan. Continuously invest in the development of future leaders and the sustainability of your legacy over the long term.

♦ **Document Your Plan:**

Document your legacy and succession plan in writing, including key objectives, strategies, roles, responsibilities, and contingency plans. Make sure all relevant parties have access to this documentation and understand their roles and obligations. Update the plan regularly to reflect changes in your circumstances, preferences, or external factors.

By following these steps and integrating them into a comprehensive and well-executed plan, you can ensure a smooth and successful transition of your legacy to future generations while preserving your values, wealth, and vision for the future.

30 Days Meditation on Legacy and Succession

1. Proverbs 11:3 - "The integrity of the upright guides them, but the crookedness of the treacherous destroys them."

2. Psalm 78:72 - "And David shepherded them with integrity of heart; with skillful hands he led them."

3. Proverbs 20:7 - "The righteous lead blameless lives; blessed are their children after them."

4. 1 Kings 9:4 - "As for you, if you walk before me faithfully with integrity of heart and uprightness, as David your father did, and do all I command and observe my decrees and laws..."

5. Proverbs 10:9 - "Whoever walks in integrity walks securely, but whoever takes crooked paths will be found out."

6. Titus 2:7-8 - "In everything set them an example by doing what is good. In your teaching show integrity, seriousness and soundness of speech that cannot be condemned, so that those who oppose you may be ashamed because they have nothing bad to say about us."

7. Psalm 25:21 - "May integrity and uprightness protect me, because my hope, Lord, is in you."

8. Proverbs 28:6 - "Better the poor whose walk is blameless than the rich whose ways are perverse."

9. Ephesians 4:29 - "Do not let any unwholesome talk come out of your mouths, but only what is helpful for building others up according to their needs, that it may benefit those who listen."

10. Proverbs 21:3 - "To do what is right and just is more acceptable to the Lord than sacrifice."

11. Proverbs 12:22 - "The Lord detests lying lips, but he delights in people who are trustworthy."

12. Ephesians 6:6 - "Obey them not only to win their favor when their eye is on you, but as slaves of Christ, doing the will of God from your heart."

13. Colossians 3:17 - "And whatever you do, whether in word or deed, do it all in the name of the Lord Jesus, giving thanks to God the Father through him."

14. Proverbs 28:18 - "The one whose walk is blameless is kept safe, but the one whose ways are perverse will fall into the pit."

15. Micah 6:8 - "He has shown you, O mortal, what is good. And what does the Lord require of you? To act justly and to love mercy and to walk humbly with your God."

16. Psalm 101:2-3 - "I will be careful to lead a blameless life—when will you come to me? I will conduct the affairs of my house with a blameless heart. I will not look with approval on anything

that is vile. I hate what faithless people do; I will have no part in it."

17. 2 Corinthians 8:21 - "For we are taking pains to do what is right, not only in the eyes of the Lord but also in the eyes of man."

18. Proverbs 16:11 - "Honest scales and balances belong to the Lord; all the weights in the bag are of his making."

19. Ephesians 4:25 - "Therefore each of you must put off falsehood and speak truthfully to your neighbor, for we are all members of one body."

20. Romans 12:17 - "Do not repay anyone evil for evil. Be careful to do what is right in the eyes of everyone."

21. Colossians 3:9 - "Do not lie to each other, since you have taken off your old self with its practices."

22. Psalm 41:12 - "Because of my integrity you uphold me and set me in your presence forever."

23. Proverbs 2:7 - "He holds success in store for the upright, he is a shield to those whose walk is blameless."

24. Ephesians 4:15 - "Instead, speaking the truth in love, we will grow to become in every respect the mature body of him who is the head, that is, Christ."

25. Proverbs 15:21 - "Folly brings joy to one who has no sense, but whoever has understanding keeps a straight course."

26. James 3:17 - "But the wisdom from heaven is first pure; then peace-loving, considerate, submissive, full of mercy and good fruit, impartial and sincere."

27. Proverbs 10:29 - "The way of the Lord is a refuge for the blameless, but it is the ruin of those who do evil."

28. Ephesians 4:31-32 - "Get rid of all bitterness, rage and anger, brawling and slander, along with every form of malice. Be kind and compassionate to one another, forgiving each other, just as in Christ God forgave you."

29. Proverbs 14:2 - "Whoever fears the Lord walks uprightly, but those who despise him are devious in their ways."

30. Philippians 4:8 - "Finally, brothers and sisters, whatever is true, whatever is noble, whatever is right, whatever is pure, whatever is lovely, whatever is admirable—if anything is excellent or praiseworthy—think about such things."

MORDEN DAY LEADERS

There are several modern leaders known for leading with compassion. Here are a few examples:

♦ **Jacinda Ardern**

The Prime Minister of New Zealand gained global recognition for her compassionate leadership style, particularly in the wake of the Christchurch mosque shootings in 2019. Ardern's response was characterized by empathy, unity, and swift action.

♦ **Justin Trudeau**

As the Prime Minister of Canada, Trudeau has been praised for his empathetic approach to governance. He has championed progressive policies on diversity, inclusion, and social justice issues, often emphasizing the importance of empathy and understanding.

♦ **Angela Merkel:**

During her tenure as Chancellor of Germany, Merkel has demonstrated compassionate leadership, particularly in her response to the European migrant crisis. She has advocated for a humanitarian approach to migration and has emphasized the importance of empathy and solidarity.

♦ **Pope Francis**

As the leader of the Catholic Church, Pope Francis is known for his compassionate stance on various social issues, including poverty, inequality, and environmental sustainability. He has emphasized the importance of empathy, mercy, and compassion in addressing the world's most pressing challenges.

♦ **Tsai Ing-wen**

Serving as the President of Taiwan, Tsai Ing-wen has been praised for her compassionate leadership, particularly in her response to the COVID-19 pandemic. She implemented effective public health measures while also prioritizing support for vulnerable populations and frontline workers.

♦ **Tim Cook - CEO of Apple Inc.**

Cook has emphasized values such as empathy, inclusion, and environmental sustainability in his leadership of Apple. Under his leadership, Apple has taken strides in promoting diversity and inclusion and has prioritized environmental responsibility.

♦ **Satya Nadella - CEO of Microsoft**

Nadella has transformed Microsoft's culture by emphasizing empathy and a growth mindset. He promotes a leadership philosophy focused on empowering employees, fostering inclusion, and driving innovation through empathy and understanding.

♦ **Melinda Gates - Co-chair of the Bill & Melinda Gates Foundation:**

Gates is a philanthropist and leader who advocates for issues such as women's empowerment, global health, and education. Her leadership is characterized by empathy, compassion, and a commitment to social change.

♦ **Indra Nooyi - Former CEO of PepsiCo**

Nooyi is known for her compassionate leadership style, prioritizing the well-being of employees and communities. She emphasized diversity, sustainability, and corporate responsibility during her tenure at PepsiCo.

These leaders demonstrate that leading with love is not just a philosophical concept but a practical and effective approach to leadership in the modern world. These leaders demonstrate that compassion can be a powerful guiding principle in governance, leading to more inclusive and empathetic policies and decision-making processes.

CONCLUSION

In "Biblical Principles of Leadership: Timeless Wisdom for Modern Leaders," we embarked on a profound journey through the annals of history, exploring the rich tapestry of leadership principles embedded within the pages of the sacred text. As we delved into the lives of biblical figures, from Moses to Esther, from David to Deborah, we unearthed invaluable insights that transcend time and culture, offering a beacon of guidance for leaders navigating the complexities of the modern world.

Throughout this enlightening exploration, one resounding theme emerged: the essence of servant leadership. From the selflessness of Jesus washing his disciples' feet to the humility of King Solomon seeking wisdom more than anything else, the Bible illuminates the transformative power of leading with integrity, compassion, and a steadfast commitment to serving others.

Furthermore, we discovered the importance of resilience in the face of adversity, drawing inspiration from the unwavering faith of figures like Job and Joseph, who endured trials and tribulations with unwavering trust in a higher purpose. Their stories remind us that true leadership is not immune to challenges but rather fortified by them, emerging stronger and more resilient with each test of character.

Moreover, the Bible imparts timeless wisdom on the art of decision-making, emphasizing the significance of seeking divine guidance, consulting wise counsel, and exercising discernment rooted in ethical principles. Whether faced with monumental choices like Joshua leading the Israelites into the Promised Land or everyday decisions encountered in the boardroom or classroom, the scriptures offer a blueprint for making sound judgments with eternal significance.

As we conclude our exploration of "Leadership Lessons from the Bible," it becomes evident that the wisdom contained within its pages transcends the boundaries of time and space, offering a timeless roadmap for leaders in every sphere of life. Whether you are a CEO guiding a multinational corporation, a community organizer rallying for change, or a parent shaping the next generation, the principles gleaned from biblical leadership are as relevant today as they were millennia ago.

May this book serve as a catalyst for transformation, inspiring leaders to emulate the exemplary virtues of those who came before us and to lead with humility, courage, and unwavering faith. For in the enduring words of Proverbs 11:14, "Where there is no guidance, a people fall, but in an abundance of counselors, there is safety." Let us heed the counsel of the ages and embark on a journey of leadership guided by timeless wisdom and eternal truth.

GLOSSARY

Biblical Leadership: Leadership principles and practices derived from the teachings and examples found in the Bible, primarily focusing on figures like Moses, David, Jesus Christ, and others.

Timeless Lessons: Universal principles and insights from biblical narratives that are relevant and applicable across different historical periods and cultural contexts.

Modern Leaders: Individuals in contemporary society who seek to apply biblical wisdom to their leadership roles, regardless of their religious affiliation.

Servant Leadership: A leadership approach emphasizing humility, empathy, and a focus on serving others rather than wielding authority for personal gain. Derived from Jesus Christ's teachings and servant leadership examples in the Bible.

Visionary Leadership: Leadership characterized by a clear vision for the future, inspired by biblical figures like Nehemiah, who led the rebuilding of Jerusalem's walls.

Integrity: Upholding moral and ethical principles in leadership, drawing from biblical teachings on honesty, transparency, and accountability.

Wisdom: Making sound decisions based on biblical wisdom, which involves seeking divine guidance, discernment, and understanding.

Courage: Demonstrating bravery and resilience in the face of adversity, drawing inspiration from biblical figures like Joshua and Esther.

Team Building: Fostering collaboration, unity, and mutual support among team members, as exemplified by biblical narratives such as the apostles' teamwork in spreading Christianity.

Communication: Effective communication skills, including active listening, clear articulation of ideas, and persuasive speech, as demonstrated by biblical leaders like Moses and Paul.

Adaptability: Being flexible and open to change, guided by biblical examples such as Joseph's ability to adapt to various circumstances and thrive in adversity.

Empowerment: Encouraging and equipping others to fulfill their potential, echoing the leadership style of Jesus Christ in empowering his disciples.

Humility: Modesty and a willingness to learn from others, exemplified by biblical figures like King David, who acknowledged his shortcomings and sought divine guidance.

Resilience: Perseverance in the face of challenges and setbacks, drawing strength from biblical stories of resilience, such as Job's enduring faith in God during trials.

Stewardship: Responsible management and utilization of resources entrusted to leaders, reflecting biblical teachings on stewardship and accountability before God.

Influence: Impacting others positively through leadership, recognizing the influence of biblical leaders like Deborah and Gideon in inspiring and mobilizing communities.

Compassion: Demonstrating empathy and care for others, following the example of Jesus Christ's compassion towards the marginalized and oppressed.

Justice: Upholding fairness and righteousness in leadership, rooted in biblical principles of justice and concern for the marginalized and vulnerable.

Prayer: Seeking divine guidance and strength through prayer, as modeled by biblical leaders such as Daniel and Solomon.

Legacy: Leaving a lasting impact through leadership that aligns with biblical values, aiming to build a legacy of faith, service, and righteousness.

BIBLIOGRAPHY

Abell, D. F. (2006). The future of strategy is leadership. *Journal of Business Research*, *59*(3), 310–314. https://doi.org/10.1016/J.JBUSRES.2005.09.003

Ahn, M. J., Biosciences, H., South, I., Francisco, S., Adamson, J. S. A., & Dornbusch, D. (2004). From Leaders to Leadership: Managing Change. *Http://Dx.Doi.Org/10.1177/107179190401000409*, *10*(4), 112–123. https://doi.org/10.1177/107179190401000409

Ahn, M. J., & Ettner, L. W. (2014). Are leadership values different across generations?: A comparative leadership analysis of CEOs v. MBAs. *Journal of Management Development*, *33*(10), 977–990. https://doi.org/10.1108/JMD-10-2012-0131

Ali, M., Li, Z., Haider, M., Khan, S., & Mohi Ud Din, Q. (2020). Does humility of project manager affect project success? Confirmation of moderated mediation mechanism. *Management Research Review*, *44*(9), 1320–1341. https://doi.org/10.1108/MRR-10-2020-0640/FULL/HTML

Ali, M., Li, Z., Khan, S., Shah, S. J., & Ullah, R. (2021). Linking humble leadership and project success: the moderating role of top management support with mediation of team-building. *International Journal of Managing Projects in Business*, *14*(3), 545–562. https://doi.org/10.1108/IJMPB-01-2020-0032/FULL/HTML

Alisic, E. (2012). Teachers' perspectives on providing support to children after trauma: A qualitative study. *School Psychology Quarterly*, *27*(1), 51–59. https://doi.org/10.1037/A0028590

Asag-Gau, L., & Dierendonck, D. Van. (2011). The impact of servant leadership on organisational commitment among the highly talented: The role of challenging work conditions and psychological empowerment. *European Journal of International Management*, *5*(5), 463–483. https://doi.org/10.1504/ejim.2011.042174

Bible, K. J. (n.d.). *Vinnys Edition of the*. Retrieved March 10, 2024, from www.CutePDF.com

Boyatzis, R. E., Smith, M. L., & Blaize, N. (2017). Developing Sustainable Leaders Through Coaching and Compassion. *Https://Doi.Org/10.5465/Amle.2006.20388381*, *5*(1), 8–24. https://doi.org/10.5465/AMLE.2006.20388381

Bryant, J. H. (2010). Leading with love in a fear-based world. *Leader to Leader*, *2010*(56), 32–38. https://doi.org/10.1002/LTL.412

Byrne-Jiménez, M. C., & Yoon, I. H. (2019). Leadership as an Act of Love: Leading in Dangerous Times. *Frontiers in Education*, *3*, 418412. https://doi.org/10.3389/FEDUC.2018.00117/BIBTEX

Calvó-Armengol, A., Martí, J. de, & Prat, A. (2015). Communication and influence. *Theoretical Economics*, *10*(2), 649–690. https://doi.org/10.3982/TE1468

Changing roles: Leadership in the 21st century - ScienceDirect. (n.d.). Retrieved March 10, 2024, from https://www.sciencedirect.com/science/article/pii/S0090261600884 478

Chen, C. Y., Chen, C. H. V., & Li, C. I. (2013). The Influence of Leader's Spiritual Values of Servant Leadership on Employee Motivational Autonomy and Eudaemonic Well-Being. *Journal of Religion and Health*, *52*(2), 418–438. https://doi.org/10.1007/S10943-011-9479-3

Chinomona, R., Mashiloane, M., & Pooe, D. (2013). The influence of servant leadership on employee trust in a leader and commitment to the organization. *Mediterranean Journal of Social Sciences*, *4*(14), 405–414. https://doi.org/10.5901/MJSS.2013.V4N14P405

Choudhary, A. I., Akhtar, S. A., & Zaheer, A. (2013). Impact of Transformational and Servant Leadership on Organizational Performance: A Comparative Analysis. *Journal of Business Ethics*, *116*(2), 433–440. https://doi.org/10.1007/S10551-012-1470-8

Church Leadership: Vision, Team, Culture, Integrity, Revised Edition - Lovett H. Weems JR. - Google Books. (n.d.). Retrieved March 10, 2024, from https://books.google.com/books?hl=en&lr=&id=-LwdnvIqv90C&oi=fnd&pg=PT13&dq=church+leadership&ots=hVr bUmTcDO&sig=g8yKhbzT8M2KR1SK9uIFr63PA18#v=onepage& q=church%20leadership&f=false

Coetzer, M. F., Bussin, M., Geldenhuys, M., Van Dierendonck, D., Gunnarsdóttir, S., & Patterson, K. A. (2017). The Functions of a Servant Leader. *Administrative Sciences 2017, Vol. 7, Page 5*, *7*(1), 5. https://doi.org/10.3390/ADMSCI7010005

Crippen, C. (2004). Servant-Leadership as an Effective Model for Educational Leadership and Management: First to serve, then to lead. *Management in Education*, *18*(5), 11–16. https://doi.org/10.1177/089202060501800503

de Waal, A., & Sivro, M. (2012). The Relation Between Servant Leadership, Organizational Performance, and the High-Performance Organization Framework. *Journal of Leadership and Organizational Studies*, *19*(2), 173–190. https://doi.org/10.1177/1548051812439892

Dess, G. G., & Picken, J. C. (2000). Changing roles: Leadership in the 21st century. *Organizational Dynamics*, *28*(3), 18–34. https://doi.org/10.1016/S0090-2616(00)88447-8

Dubrin, A. J. (2011). *Principles of Leadership Sixth Edition.* www.cengage.com/global

Dumas, C., & Beinecke, R. H. (2018). Change leadership in the 21st century. *Journal of Organizational Change Management, 31*(4), 867–876. https://doi.org/10.1108/JOCM-02-2017-0042

Dutta, S., & Khatri, P. (2017). Servant leadership and positive organizational behaviour: the road ahead to reduce employees' turnover intentions. *On the Horizon, 25*(1), 60–82. https://doi.org/10.1108/OTH-06-2016-0029

Eliot, J. L. (2020). Resilient Leadership: The Impact of a Servant Leader on the Resilience of their Followers. *Https://Doi.Org/10.1177/1523422320945237, 22*(4), 404–418. https://doi.org/10.1177/1523422320945237

Eva, N., Robin, M., Sendjaya, S., van Dierendonck, D., & Liden, R. C. (2019). Servant Leadership: A systematic review and call for future research. *The Leadership Quarterly, 30*(1), 111–132. https://doi.org/10.1016/J.LEAQUA.2018.07.004

From Leaders to Leadership: Managing Change - Mark J. Ahn, John S.A. Adamson, Daniel Dornbusch, 2004. (n.d.). Retrieved March 10, 2024, from https://journals.sagepub.com/doi/abs/10.1177/107179190401000409

Hale, J. R., & Fields, D. L. (2007). Exploring servant leadership across cultures: A study of followers in Ghana and the USA. *Leadership, 3*(4), 397–417. https://doi.org/10.1177/1742715007082964

Haslam, S. A., Reicher, S. D., & Platow, M. J. (2020). The New Psychology of Leadership : Identity, Influence and Power. *The New Psychology of Leadership.* https://doi.org/10.4324/9781351108232

Hogan, R., & Kaiser, R. B. (2005). What we know about leadership. *Review of General Psychology, 9*(2), 169–180. https://doi.org/10.1037/1089-2680.9.2.169/ASSET/IMAGES/LARGE/10.1037_1089-2680.9.2.169-FIG1.JPEG

Hogan, R., & Warrenfeltz, R. (2003). Educating the Modern Manager. *Academy of Management Learning & Education, 2*(1), 74 84. https://doi.org/10.5465/AMLE.2003.9324043

Jaramillo, F., Grisaffe, D. B., Chonko, L. B., & Roberts, J. A. (2009). Examining the impact of servant leadership on sales force performance. *Journal of Personal Selling and Sales Management, 29*(3), 257–275. https://doi.org/10.2753/PSS0885-3134290304

Krumrei-Mancuso, E. J. (2018). Humility in Servant Leadership among Christian Student Leaders: A Longitudinal Pilot Study. *Journal of Psychology and Theology, 46*(4), 253–267. https://doi.org/10.1177/0091647118807177/ASSET/IMAGES/LARGE/10.1177_0091647118807177-FIG1.JPEG

LEADING WITH COMPASSION: THE KEY TO CHANGING THE ORGANIZATIONAL CULTURE AND ACHIEVING SUCCESS. (2017). *Psychosociological Issues in Human Resource Management, 5*(1), 160–175.

Leading with love in a fear-based world - Bryant - 2010 - Leader to Leader - Wiley Online Library. (n.d.). Retrieved February 8, 2024, from https://onlinelibrary.wiley.com/doi/abs/10.1002/ltl.412

Lunenburg, F. C. (2012). *Power and Leadership: An Influence Process. 15*(1).

Manning, T. (2012). Managing change in hard times. *Industrial and Commercial Training, 44*(5), 259–267. https://doi.org/10.1108/00197851211244997/FULL/HTML

Mertel, T., & Brill, C. (2015). What every leader ought to know about becoming a servant leader. *Industrial and Commercial Training, 47*(5), 228–235. https://doi.org/10.1108/ICT-02-2015-0013

Mittal, R., & Dorfman, P. W. (2012). Servant leadership across cultures. *Journal of World Business, 47*(4), 555–570. https://doi.org/10.1016/J.JWB.2012.01.009

Morden, T. (1997). Leadership as vision. *Management Decision, 35*(9), 668–676. https://doi.org/10.1108/00251749710186504/FULL/PDF

Morris, J. A., Brotheridge, C. M., & Urbanski, J. C. (2005). Bringing humility to leadership: Antecedents and consequences of leader humility. *Human Relations, 58*(10), 1323–1350. https://doi.org/10.1177/0018726705059929

Nauman, S., Musawir, A. U., Munir, H., & Rasheed, I. (2022). Enhancing the impact of transformational leadership and team-building on project success: the moderating role of empowerment climate. *International Journal of Managing Projects in Business, 15*(2), 423–447. https://doi.org/10.1108/IJMPB-02-2021-0031/FULL/PDF

Nielsen, R., Marrone, J. A., & Slay, H. S. (2010). A new look at humility: Exploring the humility concept and its role in socialized charismatic leadership. *Journal of Leadership and Organizational Studies, 17*(1), 33–43. https://doi.org/10.1177/1548051809350892

NIV Study Bible, Fully Revised Edition - Zondervan, - Google Books. (n.d.). Retrieved March 10, 2024, from https://books.google.com/books?hl=en&lr=&id=_7C-DwAAQBAJ&oi=fnd&pg=PR1&dq=NIV+Bible&ots=gEVz22p9zC&sig=YWmZ0bt1HVjPyfdK-ekkww_HyyM#v=onepage&q=NIV%20Bible&f=false

Peterson, S. J., Galvin, B. M., & Lange, D. (2012). Ceo servant leadership: Exploring executive characteristics and firm performance. *Personnel Psychology, 65*(3), 565–596. https://doi.org/10.1111/J.1744-6570.2012.01253.X

Pontefract, D. (2024). BLOOM: A NEW LEADERSHIP DUTY OF CARE. *Leader to Leader,* *2024*(111), 47–52. https://doi.org/10.1002/LTL.20780

Poorkavoos, M. (2016). *COMPASSIONATE LEADERSHIP: WHAT IS IT AND WHY DO ORGANISATIONS NEED MORE OF IT? COMPASSIONATE LEADERSHIP.* www.roffeypark.com

Reimagining Faith and Management: The Impact of Faith in the Workplace - Google Books. (n.d.). Retrieved February 8, 2024, from https://books.google.com/books?hl=en&lr=&id=sAAaEAAAQBAJ&oi=fnd&pg=PA32&dq=Leading+with+faith&ots=CPT9OcPGEh&sig=Ab-Md3VSLG-D2LyA1gRVXFuvt4Y#v=onepage&q=Leading%20with%20faith&f=false

Resilient Leadership: The Impact of a Servant Leader on the Resilience of their Followers - Jason L. Eliot, 2020. (n.d.). Retrieved March 10, 2024, from https://journals.sagepub.com/doi/full/10.1177/1523422320945237

Russell, R. F. (2001). The role of values in servant leadership. *Leadership & Organization Development Journal,* *22*(2), 76–84. https://doi.org/10.1108/01437730110382631

Saqib, S. (n.d.). *The Role of Leadership in Strategy Formulation and Implementation.* Retrieved February 8, 2024, from https://www.researchgate.net/publication/284601403

Silverberg, N. B. (2011). Leadership by example. *Leader to Leader, 2011*(59), 4–7. https://doi.org/10.1002/LTL.447

Sousa, M., & van Dierendonck, D. (2017a). Servant Leadership and the Effect of the Interaction Between Humility, Action, and Hierarchical Power on Follower Engagement. *Journal of Business Ethics, 141*(1), 13–25. https://doi.org/10.1007/S10551-015-2725-Y

Sousa, M., & van Dierendonck, D. (2017b). Servant Leadership and the Effect of the Interaction Between Humility, Action, and Hierarchical Power on Follower Engagement. *Journal of Business Ethics, 141*(1), 13–25. https://doi.org/10.1007/S10551-015-2725-Y/TABLES/3

The Disciple-Making Pastor: Leading Others on the Journey of Faith - Bill Hull - Google Books. (n.d.). Retrieved February 8, 2024, from https://books.google.com/books?hl=en&lr=&id=kL6_9Rtq17cC&oi=fnd&pg=PA9&dq=Leading+with+faith&ots=QVj_Hqbfwh&sig=hgPLnsV-ZcYikrpQVyPaz8P4RZE#v=onepage&q=Leading%20with%20faith&f=false

The leader relationship: building teamwork with and among employees | Emerald Insight. (n.d.). Retrieved March 10, 2024, from https://www.emerald.com/insight/content/doi/10.1108/01437730010377890/full/html

Tjosvold, D., & Wong, A. S. h. (2000). The leader relationship: building teamwork with and among employees. *Leadership & Organization Development Journal, 21*(7), 350–354. https://doi.org/10.1108/01437730010377890/FULL/PDF

van Dierendonck, D., & Patterson, K. (2015). Compassionate Love as a Cornerstone of Servant Leadership: An Integration of Previous Theorizing and Research. *Journal of Business Ethics, 128*(1), 119–131. https://doi.org/10.1007/S10551-014-2085-Z

Walters, K. N., & Diab, D. L. (2016). Humble Leadership: Implications for Psychological Safety and Follower Engagement. *Journal of Leadership Studies, 10*(2), 7–18. https://doi.org/10.1002/JLS.21434

Waterman, H. (2011). Principles of "servant leadership" and how they can enhance practice. *Nursing Management (Harrow, London, England : 1994), 17*(9), 24–26. https://doi.org/10.7748/NM2011.02.17.9.24.C8299

Zimmermann, M. G., Eguíluz, V. M., & Miguel, M. S. (2001). *Cooperation, Adaptation and the Emergence of Leadership.* 73–86. https://doi.org/10.1007/978-3-642-56472-7_6/COVER

ABOUT THE AUTHOR

Caleb Ochimana, a distinguished author, Teacher, pharmacist, Entrepreneur and public health specialist with an impressive academic background, holding two master's degrees, including a Master of Public Health (MPH), a Master of Business Administration (MBA), and a Postgraduate Diploma in Theology. A graduate of the prestigious Harvard University, Hult International Business School, Ahmadu Bello University and The Redeemed Christian Bible College.

Beyond his academic achievements, Caleb is a compassionate advocate for the marginalized and underserved. Through his foundation and healthcare organizations, he has been a voice for the voiceless, working tirelessly to improve healthcare access and awareness.

In his personal life, Caleb is married to Helen and is blessed with two children, Joshua, and Jessica. This rich tapestry of experience, expertise, and personal connection infuses Caleb's book on Biblical Principles of Leadership with a unique and compassionate perspective that promises to make a significant impact in the field of leadership around the world.

www.ingramcontent.com/pod-product-compliance
Lightning Source LLC
Chambersburg PA
CBHW070409290526
45791CB00005B/1694